T0323820

LITERARY THEORY

THE BASICS

Now in its fourth edition, *Literary Theory: The Basics* is an essential guide to the complicated and often confusing world of literary theory. Readers will encounter a broad range of topics from Marxist and feminist criticism to postmodernism, queer studies, and ecocriticism.

Literary Theory: The Basics shows, in an always lucid and accessible style, how literary theory and practice are connected, and considers key theories and approaches including:

- humanist criticism;
- structuralist and poststructuralist theory;
- postcolonial theory;
- posthumanism, ecocriticism, and animal studies;
- digital humanities and print culture studies.

Literary theory has much to say about the wider world of humanities and beyond, and this guide helps readers to approach the many theories and debates with confidence. Expanded with updates throughout, this is the go-to guide for understanding literary theory today.

Hans Bertens is Professor Emeritus of Comparative Literature at Utrecht University, the Netherlands, and Past President of the International Comparative Literature Association. He has published in English and Dutch on postmodernism, American literature, and literary theory.

The Basics

The Basics is a highly successful series of accessible guidebooks which provide an overview of the fundamental principles of a subject area in a jargon-free and undaunting format.

Intended for students approaching a subject for the first time, the books both introduce the essentials of a subject and provide an ideal springboard for further study. With over 50 titles spanning subjects from Artificial Intelligence to Women's Studies, *The Basics* are an ideal starting point for students seeking to understand a subject area.

Each text comes with recommendations for further study and gradually introduces the complexities and nuances within a subject.

TRANSNATIONAL LITERATURE
PAUL JAY

ENGLISH GRAMMAR
MICHAEL MCCARTHY

PRAGMATICS
BILLY CLARK

SEMIOTICS (FOURTH EDITION)
DANIEL CHANDLER

ENGLISH VOCABULARY
MICHAEL MCCARTHY

TRANSLATION (SECOND EDITION)
JULIANE HOUSE

MEDIEVAL LITERATURE
ANGELA JANE WEISL AND ANTHONY JOSEPH CUNDER

ELT
MICHAEL MCCARTHY AND STEVE WALSH

For a full list of titles in this series, please visit www.routledge.com/The-Basics/book-series/B

LITERARY THEORY

THE BASICS

FOURTH EDITION

Hans Bertens

Routledge
Taylor & Francis Group

LONDON AND NEW YORK

Designed cover image: redtea, Getty

Fourth edition published 2024
by Routledge
4 Park Square, Milton Park, Abingdon, Oxon OX14 4RN

and by Routledge
605 Third Avenue, New York, NY 10158

Routledge is an imprint of the Taylor & Francis Group, an informa business

© 2024 Hans Bertens

First edition published by Routledge 2001

Third edition published by Routledge 2014

Every effort has been made to contact copyright-holders. Please advise the publisher
of any errors or omissions, and these will be corrected in subsequent editions.

British Library Cataloguing-in-Publication Data
A catalogue record for this book is available from the British Library

Library of Congress Cataloging-in-Publication Data
Names: Bertens, Johannes Willem, author. Title: Literary theory : the basics / Hans
Bertens. Description: Fourth edition. | New York : Routledge, 2024. |
Series: The basics | Includes bibliographical references and index. |
Identifiers: LCCN 2023059082 (print) | LCCN 2023059083 (ebook) |
Subjects: LCSH: Criticism--History--20th century. | Literature--History and criticism--
Theory, etc. Classification: LCC PN94 .B47 2024 (print) | LCC PN94 (ebook) |
DDC 801/.950904--dc23/eng/20231226 LC record available at https://lccn.loc.gov/
2023059082LC ebook record available at https://lccn.loc.gov/2023059083

ISBN: 978-1-032-44691-2 (hbk)
ISBN: 978-1-032-44692-9 (pbk)
ISBN: 978-1-003-37343-8 (ebk)

DOI: 10.4324/9781003373438

Typeset in Bembo
by Taylor & Francis Books

CONTENTS

INTRODUCTION

There was a time when the interpretation of literary texts and literary theory seemed two different and almost unrelated things. Interpretation was about the actual meaning of a poem, a novel, or a play, while theory seemed alien to what the study of literature was really about and even presented a threat to the reading of individual poems, novels, and other literary texts because of its reductive generalizations. Over the years, however, interpretation and theory have moved closer and closer to each other. In fact, for many people involved in literary studies interpretation and theory cannot be separated at all. They would argue that when we interpret a text we always do so from a theoretical perspective, whether we are aware of it or not, and they would also argue that theory cannot do without interpretation.

The premise of *Literary Theory: The Basics* is that literary theory and literary practice – the practice of interpretation – can indeed not very well be separated and certainly not at the more advanced level of academic literary studies. One of its aims, then, is to show how theory and practice are inevitably connected and *have* always been connected. Although the emphasis is on the 1970s and after, the first three chapters focus on the most important views of literature and of the individual literary work of the earlier part of the twentieth century. This is not a merely historical exercise. A good understanding of for instance the New Criticism that dominated literary criticism in the United States from the mid-1930s until 1970 is indispensable for students of literature. Knowing about the New Criticism will make it a lot easier to understand other, later modes of reading. More importantly, the New Criticism has by no

DOI: 10.4324/9781003373438-1

means disappeared. In many places, and especially in secondary education, it is still very much alive. Likewise, an understanding of what is called structuralism makes the complexities of so-called poststructuralist theory a good deal less daunting and has the added value of offering an instrument that is helpful in thinking about culture in general.

This book, then, is both an introduction to literary theory and an admittedly somewhat sketchy history of theory. But it is a history in which what has become historical is simultaneously still actual: in the field of literary studies a whole range of approaches and theoretical perspectives – those focused on meaning and those focused on form, those that are political and those are (seemingly) apolitical, the old and the new – operate next to each other in relatively peaceful coexistence. In its survey of that range of positions *Literary Theory: The Basics* will try to do equal justice to a still actual tradition and to the radical character of the new departures of the last four decades. We still ask 'what does it mean?' when we read a poem or novel or see a play. But we have additional questions. We ask 'has it always had this meaning?' Or, 'what does it mean to whom?' And, 'why does it mean what it means?' Or, perhaps surprisingly, 'who wants it to have this meaning and for what reasons?' As we will see, such questions do not diminish literature. On the contrary, they make it more relevant and interesting.

In the last decade, a number of critics have expressed a growing impatience with what is now simply called 'theory' – and which has, as we will see, ventured far beyond strictly literary territory. There is no denying that theory in its eagerness to uncover hidden patterns of exclusion and bring to light hidden assumptions has sometimes pushed things to rather implausible extremes or that theory's desire to be radical has occasionally seemed a goal in itself. Especially after 9/11 and subsequent events, theory's more extravagant claims seemed to some commentators armchair exercises that had little or no relation to what happened in the real world.

But a return to modes of critical interpretation that are not, in one way or another, informed by some form of theory is impossible. We can't go home again. Or, to be more precise, we can perhaps go home again, but not with the illusion that our home is theory-free. As I have already noted, almost all literary critics would claim that every interpretation is governed by certain assumptions and that interpretation can only seem theory-free if we are unaware of them – if we are blind to what we are doing. Theory is here to stay, and the great majority of literary academics would not want it otherwise. They believe that theory has dramatically sharpened and widened our understanding of a great many fundamental issues and expect that theory, in its restless grappling with ever new issues, will continue to enhance our understanding (even if it may in the process also come up with things that severely test our intellectual patience).

This new edition of *Literary Theory: The Basics* is revised, brought up to date, and expanded with sections on digital humanities and print culture studies. And like the earlier editions it casts its net rather wide. Since the theories that have emerged within literary studies have been so thoroughly assimilated by various other disciplines, a book on literary theory has much to say about the wider world of the humanities and beyond. It is with that assimilation in mind that this new edition ventures into territory that, although not literary, is practically next of kin, and adds a section on media studies.

READING FOR MEANING
PRACTICAL CRITICISM AND NEW CRITICISM

ENGLISH MEANING

If we want to understand English and American thinking about literature in the twentieth century a good starting point is the nineteenth-century figure of Matthew Arnold (1822–1888), English educator, poet (once famous for his rather depressing but much anthologized 'Dover Beach'), and professor of poetry at Oxford University. As Chris Baldick put it in his overview of English and American criticism: 'Most of the twentieth century … could safely be said to belong to the "Arnoldian age" in English-language criticism' (Baldick 1996: 15). Arnold's views, which assigned a very special role to literature, and further enhanced its prestige, were not wholly new. In fact, his central idea that, apart from its aesthetic and pleasing qualities, literature also had important things to teach us was already familiar in antiquity, and we see it repeated time and again over the ages. So we find Thomas Jefferson, future president of the future United States of America, observing that 'a lively and lasting sense of filial duty is more effectually impressed on the mind of a son or daughter by reading "King Lear" than by all the dry volumes of ethics and divinity that were ever written' (letter to Robert Skipwith, 3 August 1771). However, Arnold is not interested in the more practical aspects of the idea that literature is a source of instruction – moral or otherwise – but places it in a spiritual context.

Writing in the second half of the nineteenth century, Arnold saw English culture as seriously threatened by the negative effects

DOI: 10.4324/9781003373438-2

of industrialization, by a persuasive utilitarianism, by the secularization that had its origins in the growing influence of scientific thinking, and by a 'Philistinism' that was loosened upon the world by the social rise of a self-important, money-oriented, and utterly conventional middle class, which was characterized by 'vulgarity', 'coarseness', and 'unintelligence'. The modern world had become 'mechanical' and 'external', and with the spiritual comforts of religion increasingly questionable now that the sciences – in particular Darwin's theory of evolution – seemed set on undermining the authority of Bible and Church, Arnold foresaw a crucial, semi-religious role for in particular poetry:

> More and more mankind will discover that we have to turn to poetry to interpret life for us, to console us, to sustain us. Without poetry, our science will appear incomplete; and most of what now passes with us for religion and philosophy will be replaced by poetry.
>
> (Arnold 1970 [1880]: 340)

'The future of poetry', Arnold tells his readers, 'is immense, because in poetry ... our race, as time goes on, will find an ever surer and surer stay'. This radical claim for poetry – made in an 1880 essay called 'The Study of Poetry' – is in fact the culmination of claims that Arnold had for decades been making on behalf of what he called 'culture' and which in a book called *Culture and Anarchy* (1869) he had defined as 'the best that has been thought and said in the world' (Arnold 1971 [1869]: 6). As this makes clear, that 'best' is not necessarily confined to poems, but there is no doubt that he saw poetry as its major repository. The special importance that he accords to poetry is not as surprising as it may now seem. It accurately reflects the status of preeminent literary genre that poetry, especially in its lyrical form, enjoyed in Arnold's time. Moreover, in giving poetry this illustrious, almost sacred, function Arnold builds on ideas that earlier in the nineteenth century had been formulated by Romantic poets like Percy Bysshe Shelley (1792–1822), who had attributed a special, visionary status to poetry, and on a long tradition, going back to the classics, that likewise gives literature, and especially poetry, special powers. It was only natural, then, for Arnold to put forward poetry as the major embodiment of 'culture'.

What does Arnold have in mind with 'the best that has been thought and said in the world'? Strangely enough, *Culture and Anarchy*, although very outspoken, is not very clear on this point. Arnold has no trouble making clear by what forces and in which ways that 'best' is threatened: the evil is summarized by the 'anarchy' of his title, which includes the self-centred unruliness of the working-class and 'the hideous and grotesque illusions of middle-class Protestantism' (Arnold 1971 [1869]: 63). He is, however, not very precise in his definitions of 'the best'. This is partly because he assumes that his readers already know: he does not have to tell them because they share his educational background and his beliefs. But it is also due to its elusiveness. Arnold can tell us where to find it, for instance in Hellenism – the Greek culture of antiquity, with its 'aerial ease, clearness, and radiancy' (134) – but can only describe what it expresses: an attitude towards life, a way of being in the world. Included in this attitude we find 'freedom from fanaticism', 'delicacy of perception', the 'disinterested play of consciousness', and an 'inward spiritual activity' that has 'for its characters increased sweetness, increased light, increased life, increased sympathy' (60–64). What culture would seem to amount to is a deeply sympathetic and self-effacing interest in, and contemplation of, the endless variety that the world presents. For Arnold, poetry probes life more deeply, is more sympathetic towards its immensely various manifestations, and is less self-serving than anything else, and so we must turn to poetry 'to interpret life for us'. Because poetry has the power to interpret life, we can also turn to it if we want to be consoled or to seek sustenance. With the persuasiveness of religious explanations seriously damaged, poetry has the now unique power of making sense of life, a sense from which we can draw comfort and strength. Moreover – and here we see the idea of 'instruction' – culture allows us to 'grow', to become more complete and better human beings. As Arnold puts it in *Culture and Anarchy*: 'Religion says, *The kingdom of God is within you*; and culture, in like manner, places human perfection in an *internal* condition, in the growth and predominance of our humanity proper, as distinguished from our animality' (47).

AN UNCHANGING HUMAN CONDITION?

Let me for a moment turn to one of Arnold's major examples of the culture he extols: 'Hellenism', the complex of intellectual and emotional attitudes expressed in the civilization of ancient Greece. Like all university-educated people of his time, Arnold was thoroughly familiar with classical history and literature. So familiar, in fact, that in some ways he sees Greek epics and plays that are more than 2,000 years old as contemporary texts. The classics and the ideal of culture that they embody are timeless for Arnold. This is a vitally important point: 'the best that has been thought and said in the world', whether to be found in the classics or in later writers, is the best for every age and every place.

From Arnold's perspective, this makes perfect sense. After all, culture and its major means of expression, poetry, must take the place of a religion that equally was for every age and every place. If we allow ourselves to come under the influence of 'culture', we can all transcend the limitations imposed on us by class, place, and character, and acquire the cultured sensitivity and respectful, even reverent, attitude towards the world that 'culture' holds up for us. In fact, this is what Arnold would like all of us to do: to escape from the place and the time we live in and to transform ourselves into citizens of an ideal world in which time does, in a sense, not pass and in which we are in some ways – the ways that count – all the same. After all, in Arnold's view 'culture' is of all time: it exists in an autonomous sphere where time- and place-bound personal, political, or economic considerations have been left behind. We can only fully enter the realm of culture if we choose, at least temporarily, to disregard the here and now of personal ambition, political manoeuvring, and economic gain. It is important to note that this does not exclude anyone on principle. But it is even more important to note that the complex of values that underlies, and is expressed in, Arnold's culture is not necessarily as universally valid as Arnold believed it was.

LIBERAL HUMANISM

Although that may not be immediately clear, this view of culture has important implications. Arnold is of course aware that culture will always to some extent reflect its time and place of origin – in the sense that for instance medieval and early modern literature will assume that the Sun revolves around a static planet Earth – but with regard to what it *really* has to tell us it stands apart from time and place, that is, from history. With regard to its essence, culture *transcends* history. We must assume, then, that its creators – the poet supreme among them – also transcend time and place – at least as long as the act of creation lasts. A timeless culture must be the creation of timeless minds, that is, of minds that can at least temporarily disregard the world around them. This brings us to an important question: where does a creative mind that has temporarily soared free of its mundane environment find the insights that will allow it to contribute to 'the best that has been thought and said'? The answer must be that the source of that wisdom can only be the individual creator. Poets find what is valuable and has real meaning in *themselves*; they just *know*.

Arnold was by no means unique in his view of the creative individual. It was shared by the large majority of his contemporaries and by the countless writers and critics who in the course of the twentieth century would more or less consciously follow his lead. More importantly, it is still the prevailing view of the individual – not just the creative ones – in the Western world. This view of the individual – or *subject*, to use a term derived from philosophy – is central to what is called *liberalism* or *liberal humanism*, a philosophical/political cluster of ideas in which the ultimate autonomy and self-sufficiency of the subject are taken for granted. Liberal humanism assumes that all of us are essentially free and that we have largely – or at least to an important extent – created ourselves on the basis of our individual experiences. It is easy to see that this view of the subject is pervasively present in our culture and in our social institutions. The legal system, for instance, starts from the assumption that we have a certain autonomy. If your lawyer succeeds in convincing the court that the murder you thought you could get away with was not a deliberate act that you could have decided against, but was ordered by those voices in your head, you will be declared insane. Likewise, democracies do not set up elections with the expectation that people will wander mindlessly into a voting booth and make a completely arbitrary choice between the candidates. Our social institutions expect us to be reasonable and to be reasonably free. Because of that freedom, we ourselves are supposedly the source of the value and the meaning we attach to things. As liberal subjects we are not the sum of our experiences but can somehow stand outside experience: we are not defined by our circumstances but are what we are because our 'self' has been there all along and has, moreover, remained remarkably inviolate and stable. Not surprisingly, in much of Western literature, and especially in lyric poetry and realistic fiction, individuals present themselves, or are portrayed, along these lines. In the realistic novels of the mid-nineteenth century, characters again and again escape being defined by their social and economic situation because they are essentially free. Since what they are – their 'self' – is largely independent from their situation, the circumstances in which they find themselves can be transcended. Realism suggests that the characters that it presents find the reasons for their actions and decisions inside themselves. Because this liberal humanist view of the individual is as pervasively present in our world as it was in the nineteenth century, it also characterizes much of our contemporary literature.

For many present-day critics and theorists this is a deeply problematic view. In the later chapters of this book we will encounter various objections to this liberal humanist perspective. Let me here point at one possible problem. What if we cannot remake ourselves at will and if access to Arnold's 'the best' depends on, for instance, education? If that is the case, Arnold's campaign for a 'culture' that supposedly has universal validity begins to look like self-righteousness. In fact, a sceptic might easily see that campaign as a move in a struggle for power and status: for the power to define culture, to decide what the 'best' is, and for membership of the cultural elite. Even if we grant Arnold's claim and accept that his idea of culture does indeed represent the most humane, most tolerant, most morally sensitive perspectives that human civilization has come up with, we would still have a problem. If we are not free to create ourselves and to choose our own destiny access would be restricted to the privileged who happen to be born with the right disposition.

In short, there are serious problems with Arnold's humanist conception of culture and poetry. I should, in all fairness to Arnold, say that it has taken almost a hundred years for these problems really to register and that even now his views are still seductive. Isn't it true that many of us, at least at some point in our

life, want to see literature as a high-minded enterprise by and for
sensitive and fine-tuned intellectuals that is somehow several steps
removed from the trivial push-and-pull of ordinary life? It is an
alluring prospect: to have a place to go where in a hushed silence,
the sort of silence that we very appropriately find in a library, we
meet with the kindred, equally sensitive people who have written
the works we read. It is a place where time does not pass and
where in some ways – the ways that count – we are all the same.
'[T]he best books', the American philosopher Ralph Waldo
Emerson (1803–1882) tells us in his famous essay 'The American
Scholar' (1837), 'impress us ever with the conviction that one
nature wrote and the same reads'. We, the readers, are of course
only the passive consumers of what they, the writers, have actively
produced, but doesn't that difference tend to fall away? Especially
so since the texts we read are in the act of reading lifted out of
their historical context and so to a certain extent cut loose from
their creators?

It is too good to be true. How can we, apart from everything
else, possibly know whether the seemingly kindred spirits that we
meet in that timeless place do indeed share our perspectives and
concerns? What guarantee is there that we do not only see our
concerns in such sharp relief because we ignore what we do not
want to see? Perhaps Arnold is right about Hellenism's 'aerial
ease, clearness, and radiancy', but where in that phrase are the
murder and mayhem of so many of the Greek classics? Can the
Greeks, or can Chaucer, or Dante, or even Shakespeare, who all
lived in worlds dramatically different from our own, really have
been in some important way similar to ourselves? Perhaps 'delicacy of perception', the 'disinterested play of consciousness', and
the other qualities that Arnold attributes to his ideal culture are
indeed of all times, even if in different periods and places they
will have been framed by different historical circumstances. But
since we cannot travel back in time we will never know. 'The
past is another country; they do things differently there', the
narrator of L.P. Hartley's novel *The Go-Between* tells us (Hartley
1953: 9), and he may well be right. In the final analysis, Arnold's
historical continuum between Hellenism and the high culture of
his own time – the poetry that must interpret life for us – is an
act of faith.

LITERATURE AS CIVILIZATION'S LAST STANCE

When Matthew Arnold died, in 1888, English literature was fairly well established as an academic subject in both England and America. Interestingly, in British India English had already since the 1830s served to familiarize the 'native' elite with 'Englishness' and to anglicize them to the extent that they were prepared to have themselves anglicized. However, English literature as it was studied in the late nineteenth and early twentieth century could not very well be regarded as a serious intellectual discipline. Academic English was largely devoted to the history of the English language and to its older forms, such as Middle and Old English (the absolutely unintelligible language of *Beowulf*). The study of literature was largely the province of well-educated men of letters who preferred high-minded evaluations and discussions of an author's sensibility to critical analysis and attention to the structure – the actual workings – of literary texts.

What really changed things and moved them in a direction we can more readily recognize is the intervention of a young American poet, T.S. Eliot (1888–1965), who had moved to England before the outbreak of the First World War, and the British government's desire to find a place for the study of English literature somewhere in its educational schemes. While Eliot, whose views I will deal with in a moment, was primarily influential in the universities, the government-controlled Board of Education gave English literature a solid place in secondary education. It is worth noting how closely the so-called 'Newbolt Report' of 1921 that the Board had commissioned follows in Arnold's footsteps: 'Great literature', it tells us, is 'a timeless thing'. It is 'an embodiment of the best thoughts of the best minds, the most direct and lasting communication of experience by man to man' (Newbolt Report 1921: 15). What is more, great literature may serve as 'a new element of national unity' and help to overcome class differences. As the report's authors tell us, 'An education fundamentally English would, we believe, at any rate bridge, if not close, this chasm of separation' (22). Great literature, with its focus on a spiritual realm where all our petty quarrels are forgotten or have become irrelevant, could overcome social conflict and anti-patriotic sentiment. What the report in fact suggests, although it never says so in so many words, is that social and economic inequality pales next to the equality we can find in the study – or perhaps the mere reading – of great texts.

It is always easy to criticize the ideals of the past and we should perhaps not come down too hard on these English educators or on their American counterparts, who somewhat earlier had put forward the study of English and in particular American literature as an important binding principle in a nation trying to assimilate large numbers of immigrants. Apart from everything else, they may also have had the spiritual well-being of British and American students at heart. Still, the idea that literature might be instrumental in forging national unity has some consequences we must look at because it introduces a criterion that is absent from Arnold's view of poetry as the interpreter of life. If literature is supposed to promote national unity it makes good sense to throw out those texts that emphasize disunity – tension between social classes, between religious denominations, between regions – or that are openly unpatriotic. For Arnold such texts, if they were sensitive and intelligent enough, were perfectly admissible. In fact, Arnold's 'disinterested play of consciousness' will inevitably – although of course not exclusively – lead to critical assessments of the outside world. But if literature is used to foster national unity – in other words, if it is used to create or keep alive a national identity – critical assessments of the nation's mercenary politics or its cultural vulgarity will no longer be very welcome.

ARNOLD'S ACADEMIC HERITAGE: THE ENGLISH SCENE

As I have just noted, in the more academic sphere the most influential spokesman for Arnold's vision was the young expatriate American poet T.S. Eliot. In the early 1920s Eliot did what Arnold had largely avoided: he set out to define the criteria that 'the best that had been thought and said in the world' would have to meet and he undertook the mission to actually identify that 'best' in so far as it had been expressed in literary form. In other words, after drawing up the admission requirements he used them to establish which texts met those criteria and which failed to do so. The canon – the list of good and even great literary works – that he set out to construe in the

1920s would dominate virtually all English and American discussions of literature until the 1970s and is still a powerful influence.

For Eliot, poetry – the genre in which he was most interested – was profoundly impersonal. This is not to say that he denied poets the right to express themselves in their poetry, although it would not be too difficult to extract that position from his writings. In 'Tradition and the Individual Talent', for instance, we find him claiming that the poet has 'not "a personality" to express, but a particular medium' (Eliot 1972 [1919]: 75). Eliot's main aim, however, is to deflect his readers' attention from everything he considers of at best secondary importance – the poet's personal or social circumstances – and to get poetry itself on centre stage. Eliot, then, objects to highly emotional outpourings and personal confidences because they tend to focus our attention on the poet rather than the poetry. What is more, from Eliot's perspective they also make for bad and superficial poems. This does not mean that he is against the expression of deep feelings in poetry. However, expressions of profound emotion should not have an autobiographical dimension. Even if the emotion is unquestionably the poet's, it should be conveyed in such a way that the poet's private life plays no role in its presentation. What the poet needs to look for, Eliot tells us in 'Hamlet', another essay from 1919, is an 'objective correlative': 'a set of objects, a situation, a chain of events which shall be the formula of that particular emotion' (Eliot 1969 [1919]: 145). Emotion must be conveyed indirectly. The poet's emotion should be invested in a carefully selected and appropriate 'objective correlative', which will then evoke the proper response in the reader. Moreover, emotion must always be kept in check by what Eliot called 'wit', a quality that he required of all poetry and by which he means an ironic perception of things, a – sometimes playful – awareness of paradoxes and incongruities that poses an intellectual challenge to the reader. It follows from this that Eliot had little use for, for instance, the low-keyed soft-focus emotionality of Alfred Tennyson (1809–1892):

> Tears, idle tears, I know not what they mean,
> Tears from the depth of some divine despair
> Rise in the heart, and gather to the eyes,
> In looking on the happy autumn-fields,
> And thinking of the days that are no more.
>
> ('Tears, Idle Tears', 1847)

In contrast with this sort of poetry, Eliot's own poetry presents what might – somewhat unkindly – be described as a terse, tight-lipped, ironic melancholy that makes a striking use of images, juxtapositions, inversions, and other poetic strategies. It is a poetry that fully demands the reader's close attention. '[P]oets in our civilization, as it exists at present, must be difficult', Eliot told his readers in 'The Metaphysical Poets' (Eliot 1969 [1921]: 289). The corresponding complexity of its language and form forces us to take poetry seriously in its own right. It effectively rules out sentimentality and it makes it difficult to see it in, for instance, autobiographical terms.

The integration of intellect and emotion and, less insistently, of profundity and playfulness, that Eliot sees as an absolute condition for good poetry drastically limits his list of worthwhile poets. In fact, for Eliot, writing in the 1920s, literature had taken a wrong turn more than two centuries before. In 'The Metaphysical Poets' he argues that the so-called 'Metaphysical poets' of the seventeenth century still knew how to fuse thought and feeling, and seriousness and lightness, in their poetry. After their heyday, however, a 'dissociation of sensibility' had set in, whereby intellect, emotion, and other formerly integrated qualities had gone their separate ways (Eliot 1969 [1921]: 288). For Eliot this had led to poetry that errs either on the one side – sterile rationality, for instance – or on the other – excessive emotion or a levity that turns into irresponsibility – and that, because of such failures, is always condemned to mediocrity.

With hindsight, we can see that Eliot proclaims his own poetic practice and that of his fellow modernist poets of the early twentieth century as the general norm. With hindsight we can also see that Eliot's nostalgia for a past when people were supposedly still whole in the sense that they knew how to combine thought and feeling – reason and emotion – harmoniously was fed by a deep dissatisfaction with the contemporary world.

It may at first sight not be clear what this has to do with Eliot's views of literature. However, like the large majority of his contemporaries, Eliot, following Arnold, consciously places poetry – and by implication all literature that meets his criteria – in opposition to the modern world. He seeks in poetry the sort of profound experience that the modern world, in which materialistic values, individualism, and the notion of 'progress' have come to dominate, cannot offer. For Eliot, the natural, organic unity that is missing from the world and that we ourselves have also lost with the advent of scientific rationalism and the utilitarian thinking of industrialization – the 'dissociation of sensibility' – is embodied in aesthetic form in poetry. So even if poetry has no answers to any questions we might ask, it is still of vital importance and it allows us to recapture temporarily a lost ideal of wholeness in the experience of reading. As Eliot's fellow American Robert Frost (1874–1963) phrased it from a slightly different perspective, poetry provides 'a momentary stay against confusion'. Because of its integration of thought and feeling and of opposing attitudes in a coherent aesthetic form poetry, rather paradoxically, could even serve that function if the confusion itself was its major theme (as, for instance, in Eliot's 'The Waste Land' of 1922) and if its formal disjunctions helped to convey that theme. The poem's fragmentary form very effectively signalled the fragmentation of the modern world.

Although Eliot is obviously very much interested in poetic technique and in the *form* of specific poems – an interest that would be worked out by a group of American poets and critics, the so-called New Critics – he is ultimately even more interested in a poem's *meaning*. Poetry should convey complex meanings that allow us to see things in a new light. Our job, then, is to interpret poems, after which we can pass judgment on them, that is, establish how well they succeed in creating and conveying the complexity of meaning that we expect from them. 'Here lies Fred, / He is dead' does not pass muster. The idea that we read poems, and literature in general, because they contain deep *meanings* is now a commonplace. However, as will become clear in the course of this book, the meaning of a specific literary work cannot have a monopoly on our interest. An interest in the *form* of the poem, novel, or play in question – and, by extension, in the form of literature as a whole – is equally legitimate, as is an interest in a literary work's *politics*. But those complications will have to wait.

CAMBRIDGE, ENGLAND

Eliot, although trained as a philosopher, was not affiliated with a university. But he was one of the most exciting poets of his generation and also one whose philosophical interests made him think long and hard about the nature and function of literature. Inevitably, his views of literature were immediately picked up by young university teachers. Eliot's most influential following emerged at Cambridge University with the literary academic I.A. Richards (1893–1979) and the group that would somewhat later be led by the critic F.R. Leavis (1895–1978). Although each of them in his own way disagreed with some of Eliot's claims, they were excited by the intellectual rigour and the demanding standards that characterized his critical writings. Richards and Leavis initiated two intimately related 'schools' that would give shape to English and American thinking about literature for almost fifty years.

In the hands of Richards – and, a bit later, of his fellow academic William Empson – Eliot's emphasis on the poem itself became what we call *practical criticism*. In a famous experiment Richards withheld all extra-textual information – title of the poem, author's name, year of publication, explanatory commentary – and asked undergraduate students (and some tutors) to interpret poems that were thus completely stripped of context. It would be difficult to think up a more text-oriented approach. Shocked by the result of his experiments, which demonstrated that his students were utterly incapable of reading poetry and kept making the most basic mistakes, Richards advocated 'practical criticism', a mode of reading in which the closest attention was paid to all textual detail. Now usually called 'close reading', it has survived everything that happened in English-language literary studies since Richards and is still with us.

'Practical criticism' served two purposes. The first purpose is by now familiar. Like so many young intellectuals of the period, Richards had deep misgivings about the contemporary world and, like Arnold, saw in poetry an antidote to a spiritual malaise that seemed to pave the way for chaos. If the moral order would indeed fall apart because of the loss of traditional values that he saw around him, we would, Richards suggested, 'be thrown back, as Matthew Arnold foresaw, upon poetry. It is capable of saving us; it is a perfectly possible means of overcoming chaos' (Richards 1926: 83). Poetry, because it 'is the completest mode of utterance' (Richards 1934: 163), and the arts in general, could save us because it is there that we find what is truly, and lastingly valuable – what gives meaning to our lives:

The arts are our storehouse of recorded values. They spring from and perpetuate hours in the lives of exceptional people, when their control and command of experience is at its highest, hours when the varying possibilities of existence are most clearly seen and the different activities which may arise are most exquisitely reconciled, hours when habitual narrowness of interests or confused bewilderment are replaced by an intricately wrought composure.

(Richards 1938: 66–67)

This statement is not in the last place interesting because it so clearly illustrates Richards's humanist view of the creative subject. The keywords are 'control', 'command', 'reconciled', and 'composure'. But those qualities and that process of reconciliation are not exclusively the prerogatives of 'exceptional people'. They create a mental experience for whoever takes a genuine interest in a work of art and may therefore affect and transform them. The arts, then, help us to evaluate our own experience, to assess our personal life. As the 'storehouse of recorded values', the arts 'supply the best data for deciding what experiences are more valuable than others' (Richards 1938: 111). For Richards art also has an important educational, almost therapeutic function: 'It is less important to like "good" poetry and dislike "bad", than to be able to use them both as a means of ordering our minds' (Richards 1929: 349). Poetry is all the better equipped for this because its language is not *scientific* but *emotive*. Scientific language is for Richards language that refers to the real world and makes statements that are either true or false. The emotive language of literature, however, conveys a certain type of knowledge which is not scientific and factual but allows us to connect with superior feelings and attitudes.

'Practical criticism', with its exclusively textual orientation, was an ideal programme for identifying all the conflicting forces that for Richards (following Eliot) were reconciled with each other and transcended in good poetry. Named after the book – *Practical Criticism* (1929) – in which Richards had reported his Cambridge experiments, it became a major instrument in spreading the idea that the best poems created a precarious coherence out of conflicting perspectives and emotions. As we will see, in the United States this view would develop into the New Criticism that in the 1930s and 1940s became the major mode of criticism there.

THE NOVEL AS GREAT ART

So far, we have been almost exclusively concerned with poetry. F.R. Leavis, the other Cambridge academic who would put a – highly personal – stamp on especially English literary studies, was, at least initially, no exception. Leavis, too, started out with poetry and also took Eliot's views as his guiding light. In the course of the 1930s he accordingly subjected the history of English poetry to an icy scrutiny in order to separate the wheat from the chaff, in the process relegating a good many English poets of up till then fine repute (including John Milton) to minor status. In particular nineteenth-century poets, standing collectively accused of a 'divorce between thought and feeling, intelligence and sensibility' – a condemnation in which we clearly hear Eliot's 'dissociation of sensibility' – did not fare well (see, for instance, '"Thought" and Emotional Quality', in Leavis 1975: 71–93).

However, his work of the later 1940s, in which he sets out to revalue the English novel, is more pertinent here. Until Leavis changed the picture, fiction had gone largely unnoticed. Novels cannot very well be subjected to the same sort of analysis that we use with poems, especially not the substantial, if not actually sprawling, novels that until the end of the nineteenth century were more or less the rule. But Leavis's discussions of fiction would in any case have departed from the course set out by Eliot and Richards. By the 1940s Leavis had already in his discussions of poetry begun to include a moralistic dimension that is almost completely absent from the work of his American contemporaries, the New Critics. Leavis increasingly comes to judge poems in terms of the 'life' and the 'concreteness' they succeed in conveying. In other words, he begins to discuss content as relatively independent of form while for the New Critics, as we will see below, form and content were inextricably interwoven. While for the New Critics and an ever greater number of affiliated academics a text's form created the ironic maturity of its content, for Leavis form became increasingly of secondary importance. What the literary work should provide was a mature apprehension of authentic life, and certainly not one that was too ironic and therefore emotionally sterile (he was not charmed by the ironies of James Joyce's *Ulysses* [1922], which Eliot had thought a great work of art). Like so many others, Leavis was dismayed by what he saw as the superficiality and commodification of the contemporary world, and, much like Eliot, looked back to Elizabethan England when people had still led authentic lives as members of an organic community. Literature represented and expressed a world of interrelated values and ideals shaped over the centuries and rooted in communal life.

For Leavis, authentic representations of life depended on a writer's personal authenticity and moral integrity. As he said in his 1948 *The Great Tradition* of the novelists he considered great: 'they are all distinguished by a vital capacity for experience, a kind of reverent openness before life, and a marked moral intensity' (Leavis 1962 [1948]: 17). One of Leavis's 'great' novelists, the English writer D.H. Lawrence (1885–1930), had already offered a characteristically provoking illustration of such openness:

> If the bank clerk feels really piquant about his hat, if he establishes a lively relation with it, and goes out of the shop with the new straw hat on his head, a changed man, be-aureoled, then that is life.
> The same with the prostitute. If a man establishes a living relation to her, if only for a moment, then that is life. But if it *doesn't*: if it is just for the money and function, then it is not life, but sordidness, and a betrayal of living.
> If a novel reveals true and vivid relationships, it is a moral work, no matter what the relationships may consist in.
>
> (Lawrence 1972a [1925]: 129)

Because they believe that because of its scope and its attention to authentic detail the novel can represent life in all its fullness, it is for Leavis and Lawrence superior to whatever the other arts or the human sciences (such as psychology or sociology) may have to offer. It can, moreover, make us participate in that fullness. As Lawrence said: 'To be alive, to be man alive, to be whole man alive: that is the point. And at its best, the novel, and the novel supremely, can help you' (Lawrence 1972b [1936]: 135). What Leavis calls 'great literature' shows us 'life' and it allows us to judge ourselves and the world, not by propounding moral dogma, but through 'representative experience'.

This is an attractive programme for the novel – and for us. Who would not want to live authentically and to defend the forces of life against whatever may happen to threaten it? However, like so many attractive programmes it falls apart upon closer scrutiny. Who is to define a mature apprehension of life, a vital capacity for experience, or a reverent openness before life? And what about the morals that are felt so intensely? Do we know what exactly constitutes the right set of morals? In any case, given his interest in full representations of life in its totality, Leavis almost inevitably came to focus on the novel. If you want scope, the novel has more to offer than lyrical poetry. So, somewhat belatedly, Leavis brought the novel into the amazing professionalization of the study of English as it had started in the 1920s (drama, and in particular Shakespeare, many of whose plays lent themselves to an approach in poetic terms, had already been embraced in the 1930s). This is not to say that novels had been completely ignored. But Leavis elevated this interest into a programme. Moreover, he significantly expanded its scope, arguing that literary criticism, and in particular criticism of the novel, provided the best imaginable basis for criticizing contemporary culture, anticipating the social critique and the critique of ideology that much later would come to characterize literary studies. As we will see in the later chapters of this book, literary studies – although broader defined than Leavis ever imagined – is still very strongly involved in social and cultural critique, albeit in ways that Leavis would quite probably have abhorred.

MEANING IN THE UNITED STATES

In the 1930s, the work of Eliot, Richards, and Leavis found a warm welcome on the other side of the Atlantic among a group of poets, including John Crowe Ransom (1888–1974), Allen Tate (1899–1979), Robert Penn Warren (1905–89), and Cleanth Brooks (1906–1994), who in the mid-1930s initiated a professionalization of American literary studies comparable to the developments in England.

These New Critics, as they came to be called (the label derives from the title of Ransom's 1941 book *The New Criticism*), shared the misgivings of their English colleagues about the contemporary world. They, too, saw around them a world driven by a desire for profit in which the so-called triumphs of modern science, in combination with capitalistic greed, threatened to destroy tradition and everything that was not immediately useful – including poetry. Like their English mentors, they turned to an idealized past, initially that of the agrarian American South, in which organic unity was not yet threatened by the utilitarian industrialization and commercialization of Western modernity.

The New Critics, then, saw poetry as a means of resisting the negative effects of the ever increasing commodification of their world. Because of its internal organization – its formal structure – a poem created unity out of apparent opposites and out of its internal tensions and thereby presented a vital alternative. As Brooks said, 'The poet ... must return to us the unity of experience itself' (Brooks 1942: 212). In creating coherent wholes out of the full variety and contradictory complexity of life, poetry halted and transcended the chaotic flux of actual experience. As John Crowe Ransom put in a 1937 essay called 'Criticism, Inc.': 'The poet perpetuates in his poem an order of existence which in actual life is constantly crumbling beneath his touch' (Ransom 1972 [1937]: 238). In perpetuating such fleeting orders, one of the poet's main strategies was the use of paradox with, as Brooks put it, 'its twin concomitants of irony and wonder'. By means of paradoxes 'the creative imagination' achieves 'union'. That 'fusion is not logical', Brooks continues, 'it apparently violates science and common sense; it welds together the discordant and the contradictory' (Brooks 1972 [1942]: 300–01).

In this emphasis on paradox and irony the New Critics clearly follow Eliot and Richards. They, too, see poems as storehouses of authentic values and as expressing important truths about the complexities of life that no other medium can convey nearly as effectively. This is so, Brooks suggests, because 'apparently the truth which the poet utters can be approached only in terms of paradox' (Brooks 1972 [1942]: 292), while for Ransom the 'imagination' is an 'organ of knowledge [that] presents to the reflective mind the particularity of nature; whereas there is quite another organ, working by a technique of universals, which gives us science' (Ransom 1938: 156). In some ways, however, they follow their own course. Richards had been seriously interested in the effects of poetry upon its readers. The New Critics exclude both the poet – as Richards had done in *Practical Criticism* – and the reader from their approach to poetry. We do not have to know about the poet's intentions because only those intentions are relevant which have actually been realized in the poem itself and to let intentions that are not in some way present in the poem influence our reading leads to skewed interpretations. This 'intentional fallacy', as it was called by W.K. Wimsatt (1907–1975) and Monroe Beardsley (1915–1985), had its counterpart in what they termed the 'affective fallacy', which led to interpretations unduly influenced by the reader's emotional response to a poem. As a result, the New Critics focus more on the actual *form* of literary works than their English counterparts. In fact, within the context of English and American criticism their approach to literature might well be considered *formalist* and it does indeed often go by that label. However, compared to the European formalists that I will discuss in the next chapters, their interest in form is relatively limited. They are not interested in form for its own sake, but in form as contributing to a text's meaning. Indeed, as Wimsatt put it, the aim of literary criticism is 'to give a valid account of the relation between poetic form and poetic meaning' (Wimsatt 1965: 244).

The New Critics' lack of interest in how the poem affects its readers does not mean that they denied the special character of poetic language. As Brooks tells us, 'the poet's language … is a language in which the connotations play as great a part as the denotations' (Brooks 1972 [1942]: 295). Moreover, for the New Critics, too, a poem had to be fully experienced in order to be effective. 'A poem should not mean, but be', as they said, echoing Richards's 'It is never what a poem *says* which matters, but what it *is*' (Richards 1926: 3). Reading a poem should be a complete experience that engages all our faculties and that far exceeds merely extracting its 'message'. Anything but the entirety of its paradoxes, opposites, and reconciling ironies is reductive and damaging. 'Close reading', that is, the focus on the text that Richards and Leavis had promoted so vigorously in England, in the hands of the New Critics became closer than ever. With the author's intentions and the reader's response removed from the scene, the study of literature restricted itself to analysing the poetic text's techniques and strategies: the system of checks and balances that creates the diversity in unity that we experience. Although it probably seems counterintuitive, from this perspective it is not the poet – about whose intentions we usually know next to nothing – but indeed the poem itself that delivers unity. What organizes the poem – brings its diverse elements together – is not so much authorial intention as an abstract principle, the principle of *coherence*, which the New Critics assumed present and active in any 'good' poem. In good poetry, and, by extension, all good literature, the principle of coherence keeps the text's paradoxes and possible contradictions in check. Some may object that this does not make much sense because literary texts do not spring up overnight and all by themselves in remote and mysterious areas, so that it might seem a bit perverse to exclude the author from the discussion of a text. But it makes a good deal of practical sense. In some cases we do not even know who the author is and in many cases we can only guess at the author's intentions because we have no information. Moreover, when we have that information it does not necessarily illuminate the poem, at least not from the perspective that I am discussing here. As we have seen, these critics assume that good literature is not bound by time and place. It transcends the limitations of its place of origin (and of the author) and addresses the complexities of an essentially unchanging human condition. The concrete intentions of the author, or the circumstances that triggered the poem, are therefore mostly or even wholly irrelevant. What does it matter if we know that Poet X wrote this particular poem because he was hopelessly in love with the undeserving Lady Y? The poem in question will be worthwhile only if it does *not* give us all the details but focuses on scorned love in general. In this sense, information about authorial intention or the direct occasion for a work of literature may be damaging rather than helpful. For humanist critics such as Eliot, Richards, Leavis, and the New Critics, human nature and the human condition have not changed over time and are essentially the same the world all over. The human condition is not black, or white, or brown; it does not speak English or Tagalog; it is not prehistoric, medieval, or postmodern; it does not lean towards deep-sea fishing, pig farming, or business administration. Such details will inevitably feature in a literary work, but they are secondary to what a good poem, novel, or play has to offer.

THE REIGN OF THE CRITICS AND ITS LIMITATIONS

In his 1937 essay 'Criticism, Inc.' John Crowe Ransom tells us that criticism 'might be seriously taken in hand by professionals' (Ransom 1972 [1937]: 229). Aware that he is perhaps using 'a distasteful figure', he nonetheless has 'the idea that what we need is Criticism, Inc., or Criticism, Ltd.' The essay catches the new professionalism that literary academics on both sides of the Atlantic were not unreasonably proud of and invites us to look at the role that Ransom had in mind for himself and his fellow professionals. One part of their self-appointed task stands out. As we have seen, for the New Critics and their English colleagues, literature, and in particular poetry, constituted a line of defence against the world of vulgar commerce and amoral capitalist entrepreneurialism that they held responsible for the moral decline of the Western world. But who was to decide which works of literature among the plenitude that the past has left us (and to which the present keeps on adding) actually contain 'the best that has been thought and said in the world', to use Arnold's words again? Who was to expose the at first sight attractive poems that because of their limited view and superficial emotions ultimately, even if unintentionally, undermined Arnold's 'culture'?

If literature takes the place of religion, as Arnold had prophesied, then critics are the defenders of the faith. For a period of fifty years the large majority of literary academics on both sides of the Atlantic saw themselves as the elect, as an intellectual and moral elite that had as its central task to safeguard 'life', the fullness of human experience. In the minds of the Leavisites especially, but also the others who partly or wholly shared their views, criticism and social critique were so intimately interwoven that they could not be separated from each other. As I have already suggested, the interrelatedness of literary criticism and social critique is still a hallmark of English and American literary studies, as is the role of the literary academic as social critic, even if that social critique is no longer offered from a politically and culturally conservative angle but as often as not from a leftist one.

But let me return to the specific view of literature that we find among the first generations of literary academics. With hindsight, we can easily see the intimate relationship between their discussions of structure, irony, and other textual features, and a good many indisputably important literary works of the period: Eliot's 'The Waste Land' (1922), Ezra Pound's *Cantos* (1925–1960), Virginia Woolf's *To the Lighthouse* (1927), James Joyce's *Ulysses* (1922), William Faulkner's *The Sound and the Fury* (1929), and countless other poems, novels, and plays. What was essentially an early twentieth century view of literature, formed under the influence of specific historical circumstances, became a prescription for all ages. Predictably, the large number of writers who for one reason or another had operated in a different mode (Walt Whitman, for instance, with his long descriptive passages) fell from grace. Literary history was reshaped in the image of the early twentieth century. Whereas we can see the 'irony' that the writers and the critics of the period valued so highly as a defensive strategy in a confusing world of rapid social and technological change, they themselves genuinely believed it to be an infallible sign of 'maturity' and proceeded to demote all texts (and writers) that did not meet the required standard.

We can also see now that the required standard is heavily *gendered*. (This anticipates a much fuller discussion of 'gender' in a later chapter, but it must be mentioned here.) Eliot's 'wit', the 'irony' of Richards and the New Critics, and the 'maturity' of Leavis all serve to underline a shared masculinist perspective. This is not to say that they have no place for female writers – in its first instalment Leavis's 'great tradition' of English novelists includes two male and two female writers. But in a period in which self-discipline (the self-discipline of the poet who refuses to personalize the poem), wit, a controlling irony, and related qualities were all seen as typically male, whereas overt emotions and a refusal to intellectualize experience were seen as typically female, the female writers elected for inclusion in the literary pantheon were admitted because they met a male standard.

Practical criticism and New Criticism have had a lasting influence. Their preoccupation with the text and nothing but the text would live on after their demise, which is perhaps less surprising if we realize that in particular the New Critical view of the text falls well within the range of the enormously influential theorization of the work of art – the aesthetic object – proposed by the German philosopher Immanuel Kant (1724–1802), who had argued that the true work of art is characterized by a 'disinterested' autonomy, that it is not instrumental and has no purpose except being itself. Even now the textual orientation of the New Criticism in particular is still a force to be reckoned with, although always tempered by other considerations and mostly – but not necessarily – stripped of its conservative prejudices. It is of course only natural that their focus on texts, and not for instance landscaping, should still play a central role in literary studies. It is less obvious, however – counterintuitive as it may seem – that *meaning* should be so prominent. In the next two chapters we will look at approaches to literature in which the meaning of individual texts, which in England and America provided the major drive for literary studies, is of at best secondary importance.

SUGGESTIONS FOR FURTHER READING

There is no shortage of books on the English and American literary-critical heritage. Two very accessible and even-handed studies are Chris Baldick's *The Social Mission of English Criticism, 1848–1932* (1983), which has chapters on Arnold, Eliot, Richards, and Leavis, and his more recent *Criticism and Literary Theory 1890 to the Present* (1996), which covers some of the same ground, but also discusses the New Criticism and later developments. Mark Jancovich's *The Cultural Politics of the New Criticism* (1993) is especially interested in what the New Critics saw as their social mission.

Gerald Graff's *Professing Literature: An Institutional History* (1987) maps the institutionalization of literary studies in the United States while *Masks of Conquest: Literary Study and British Rule in India* (1989) by Gauri Viswanathan offers a fascinating account of 'English' in colonial India.

Eliot's early essays – 'Tradition and the Individual Talent', 'Hamlet', 'The Metaphysical Poets' – are still worth reading. Those who would like to see the New Criticism in action, can also still go directly to the source. Cleanth Brooks's *The Well-Wrought Urn: Studies in the Structure of Poetry* (1942) contains a number of now classic essays while Brooks's collaboration with Robert Penn Warren in *Understanding Poetry* (1939) led to an enormously influential textbook that illustrates the New Critical mode of interpretation in exemplary fashion. Leavis's approach to poetry and the poetic tradition comes through vividly in his *New Bearings in English Poetry* (1932) and *Revaluation* (1936); *The Great Tradition* (1948) is a good example of his equally uncompromising criticism of the novel. Richard Storer's *F.R. Leavis* (2009) offers a brief but comprehensive overview of Leavis's work while Zhang Dandan's *Literary Criticism, Culture and the Subject of English: F.R. Leavis and T.S. Eliot* (2021) compares and contrasts his criticism and cultural critique with those of Eliot. *Praising It New: The Best of the New Criticism*, edited by Garrick Davis (2008) collects essays by Eliot, Ransom, Brooks, Tate and a number of lesser-known critics such as Yvor Winters and J.V. Cunningham. For those who want to know more about 'close reading', David Greenham's *Close Reading: The Basics* (2018) offers a good discussion and practical illustrations.

READING FOR FORM AND FUNCTION
FORMALISM AND EARLY STRUCTURALISM, 1914–1960

INTRODUCTION

In spite of the enormous influence of Eliot, Leavis, and the New Critics, our current perspectives on the study of literature perhaps owe more to Continental Europe than to England and America. The continental European tradition of literary studies that is responsible for this begins in Russia, in the second decade of the twentieth century, in Moscow and St. Petersburg. It finds a new home in Prague in the 1920s, when the political climate in Russia has become too repressive, and travels to France (by way of New York City) after the Second World War, where it comes to full bloom in the 1960s and begins to draw widespread international attention. It is in France, too, that it provokes a countermovement that achieved its full force in the 1970s and 1980s and that is still a dominant presence in literary – and in cultural – studies.

Like its Anglo-American counterpart, this originally Russian approach to literature initially concentrated on poetry. But that is about all the two had in common. The English (later Anglo-American) line of development and the Russian one had nothing whatsoever to do with each other. The Russians who developed what they called the *formal method* – which gave them the name *formalists* – were totally unaware of what happened in England, while the English and the Americans were completely ignorant of the debates that took place in Russia (and later in Prague). It was only when a prominent

DOI: 10.4324/9781003373438-3

formalist, the Russian linguist Roman Jakobson (1896–1982) and his fellow formalists began to be translated into English in the late 1950s and 1960s that the English-speaking world began to take notice of their wholly different approach to literary art. But even then the response was slow, no doubt because the formalist approach was so foreign to what Eliot, Leavis, the New Critics, and their ubiquitous heirs saw as the mission of literature and of writing about literature. Significantly, the formalist perspective had to be picked up, assimilated, and further developed by the French before it really made an impact on English and American literary thought. In what follows I will concentrate on the work of the Russians and only look briefly at some later developments. What is relevant here is not historical comprehensiveness but a certain *way* of looking at literature that would much later have great impact in the English-speaking world.

EARLY FORMALISM

As the phrase 'formal method' will have suggested, the formalists were primarily oriented towards the *form* of literature. That focus on formal aspects does not mean that they could not imagine a possible moral or social mission for literature. As one of them, Viktor Shklovsky (1893–1984), put it in 1917 in an essay called 'Art as Technique', literature has the ability to make us see the world anew – to make that which has become familiar, because we have been overexposed to it, strange again. Instead of merely registering things in an almost subconscious process of recognition because we think we know them, we once again look at them: 'art exists that one may recover the sensation of life ... The purpose of art is to impart the sensation of things as they are perceived and not as they are known' (Shklovsky 1998 [1917]: 18). This process of de-familiarization causes us to see things in a fresh new light. What the formalists wanted to know is how literature works, how it achieves its de-familiarizing effects. For the New Critics the formal aspects of literary works were not unimportant. However, they were first of all interested in the form in which a poem presented itself because a close scrutiny of its formal aspects would lead us to the poem's real meaning. But the formalists were after what they considered bigger game and in order to do so ignored literature's role as a reflection of the world we live in, and gave it, even more than the New Criticism had done, an autonomous status – or gave at least the *aesthetic dimension* of literature an autonomous status, as Jakobson qualified their position in 1933.

From their earliest meetings, around 1914, the formalists are focused on what Jakobson in 1921 started to call 'literariness' – that which makes a text literary and intrinsically different from, say, a piece in *The Economist* or *Time*. In other words, although they always work with individual texts, what they are interested in is what all literary texts have in common, in a literary common denominator. Seeing the study of literature as a science, they concentrated like true scientists on general rules. 'What characterizes us', said Boris Eichenbaum (1885–1959), a prominent formalist, is 'the striving to establish on the basis of specific properties of the literary material, an independent literary science' (Steiner 1995: 13). Whereas practical criticism and the New Criticism focused on the individual meaning of individual texts, formalism wants to discover general laws – the more general the better.

The secret of 'literariness', the formalists decided, was that in poetry – the initial focus of their interest – ordinary language becomes 'defamiliarized'. While an article in *Time* aims for clarity and will therefore use plain language, poetry subjects language to a process of defamiliarization. It is this linguistic defamiliarization that then leads to a perceptual defamiliarization on the part of the reader, to a renewed and fresh way of looking at the world. How does poetry defamiliarize what I have just called 'plain' language? It employs an impressive range of so-called 'devices'. It uses, for instance, forms of repetition that one does not find in ordinary language such as alliteration, rhyme, a regular meter, or the subdivision in stanzas that we find in many poems. But poetry also uses 'devices' that one may come across in non-poetic language (although not with the same frequency) like metaphors and symbols. In so doing, it often also exploits the potential for ambiguity that language always has. Whereas a *Time* article tries to avoid ambiguities because it wants to be as transparent as possible, poetry makes use of all the second (and third) meanings that words and phrases tend to have, plus all the associations they evoke. What all these devices have in common is that they have a universal and timeless character – like the laws of science – and they always draw attention to *themselves*: they remind us that we first of all are dealing with language and not with the real world because they signal their own difference from the non-literary language that we ordinarily use (and which we take to represent the world). Advertising agencies are well aware of this. Not too long ago the Dollar Shave Club tried to boost its sales of razors with the slogan 'Shave Time, Shave Money', a phrase that inevitably draws our attention to its own language. Because its ingenious play with language catches the eye and makes it stand out among other ads it probably also effectively served its purpose: to sell more razors. (Harley Davidson's 1977 'All for Freedom, Freedom for All' was not bad either.) For the formalists, then, poetry is not poetry because it employs time-honoured and profound themes to explore the human condition but rather because in the process of defamiliarizing the language it draws attention to its own artificiality, to the *way* it says what it has to say. As Roman Jakobson said in 1921, poetry is a mode of language characterized by an orientation towards its own form. Or as he put it in 'What Is Poetry?' of 1934:

> Poeticity is present when the word is felt as a word and not a mere representation of the object being named or an outburst of emotion, when words and their compositions, their meaning, their external and inner form acquire a weight and value of their own instead of referring indifferently to reality.

> (Jakobson 1987 [1934]: 378)

What poetry's orientation upon its own form first of all allows us to see in a fresh manner is language itself. What that language refers to – what it communicates – is of secondary importance. In fact, if a work of art draws attention to its own form, then that form becomes part of its content: its form is part of what it communicates. (This is obvious in paintings that are completely abstract: since such paintings do not refer us to the outside world they can only 'be' about themselves. They force us to pay attention to their form – dots, lines, colours – because that is all they have to offer.)

Now the idea of defamiliarization works well enough in the case of poetry, and the difficult, wilfully innovative and defamiliarizing modernist poetry of the period perfectly confirms the validity of defamiliarization as the ultimate criterion in establishing 'literariness'. But it is not so easy to make the defamiliarizing 'devices' of poetry work for fiction: the most obvious ones – rhyme, for instance – simply do not occur in fiction and the less obvious ones, like imagery, can also be found, even if not to the same degree, in ordinary usage. It is true that there are novels that in spite of this achieve an impressive degree of defamiliarization. This, for instance, is how Russell Hoban's *Riddley Walker* of 1980 takes off: 'On my naming day when I come 12 I gone front spear and kilt a wyld boar he parbly ben the las wyld pig on the Bundel Downs' (Hoban 1982 [1980]: 1). But novels like this are rare. Usually we have to look pretty closely to find real deviations from ordinary language.

FABULA AND SYUZHET

Viktor Shklovsky and Boris Tomashevski (1890–1957) argued that fiction did not achieve its effects through the defamiliarization of language but through the defamiliarization of *presentation* and even through the defamiliarization of the events that it presented. In order to clarify the defamiliarization of presentation they juxtaposed two concepts, introduced by Shklovsky in 1921: *fabula* and *syuzhet* (or *suzhet*, depending on how one transcribes the Russian alphabet). The *fabula* is a straightforward account of something, it tells us what actually happened. It is what we usually call the 'plot'. For instance: John Doe kills his cousin Jack to become the sole heir of a fortune and sits back to wait for the demise of the aged and infirm uncle – old J.J. Doe, his cousin's father of which he now is the only remaining kin – who controls the money. The police work hard at solving the case but fail to do so. J.J. Doe hires a private eye who naturally succeeds where the police have failed. John Doe is arrested and duly sentenced.

These are the bare bones of the sort of story that one finds in countless private eye novels. But this is not how the standard private eye novel would tell it. The novel would begin with the private eye being invited by J.J. Doe to come to his mansion to talk about the case. The fact that the murder has been committed by John will not become clear until we have almost reached the end. As in all detective novels, the author manipulates the *fabula* to create maximum suspense. Such a manipulation of the *fabula* creates the *syuzhet* (the *story* as it is actually told) and it is the *syuzhet* that has the defamiliarizing effect that devices have in poetry: like rhyme, for instance, the *syuzhet* calls attention to itself. Moreover, it defamiliarizes the events of the story because it actively interferes with the story's chronology. (I will discuss in a moment why we usually do not experience that attention-calling effect when we read, say, a detective novel.) It will immediately be obvious that one and the same *fabula* or plot can give rise to a good many *syuzhets* or stories. That insight became the basis for a book that much later would enjoy widespread influence, Vladimir Propp's 1928 *The Morphology of the Folktale*, which I will briefly look at because it forms an important link between the formalists and the French so-called structuralists of the 1960s.

FOLK TALES

It had struck Propp (1895–1970) that if you looked closer at many Russian folk tales and fairy tales you actually found one and the same underlying story. In *Folktale* he tries to show how a hundred different tales are in fact variations upon – in other words, *syuzhets* of – what seemed to be one and the same underlying *fabula*. This is a rather free use of the *fabula/syuzhet* opposition, which the formalists saw as operating within one and the same text, and in many of Propp's tales there is no difference between *fabula* and *syuzhet* as understood in formalist terms. In a simple, chronologically told fairy tale without flashbacks and other narrative tricks the story is in fact identical with the plot. Still, Propp's at the time revolutionary idea that a hundred rather widely varying folk and fairy tales might actually tell one and the same underlying story is clearly inspired by the distinction between *fabula* and *syuzhet*.

How is one and the same *fabula* possible if in some fairy tales we have characters who play important roles – a prince, a forester, a hunter, a miller, a good fairy, an evil queen – and who are yet wholly absent from others? How could all these tales possibly be presentations of the same basic plot? Propp very ingeniously solves this problem by thinking in terms of *actors* and *functions*, by which he means acts or events that crucially help the story along. Let me try to give an idea how this works. One of the actors that Propp identifies – and which he sees returning in all his tales – is the 'helper'. Since that is not relevant to the function – all that he or she has to do is offer an act of help that keeps the story moving – Propp need not further specify who or what the 'helper' is. The 'helper' can be either male or female, can be a forester (as in 'Little Red Riding Hood') or hunter (as in 'Snow White'), can be old or young, rich or poor, and so on – the possibilities are infinite. In one of his examples Propp illustrates the act of helping with examples from four fairy tales. In the first one the hero is given an eagle who carries him to another kingdom, in the second one the hero is given a horse that gets him there. In the third tale he is presented with a boat, and in the fourth one he is given a ring that magically produces a number of young men who carry him where he wants to go. The people who help the hero are different, the hero himself has different names, and the means of conveyance (if we can call an eagle a means of conveyance) are different. But the actor – and the function of the event – is in each case exactly the same. We might say that various story elements correspond to one plot element (if we take the liberty of seeing all the fairy tales in terms of one single plot).

Propp distinguishes a limited number of actors (or, in his term, 'dramatis personae') – hero, villain, seeker (often the hero), helper, false hero, princess – and thirty-one functions that always appear in the same sequence. I should add that all thirty-one of them do not necessarily make an appearance in every single fairy tale. Propp's fairy tales get along very well with only a selection, even if the final functions – the punishment of the villain and the wedding that symbolizes the happy ending – are always the same. It is also possible for a fairy tale to interrupt itself and start a new, embedded, sequence (and another one) or to put one sequence after another. The individual qualities of the characters, however, are always irrelevant. At Propp's level of abstraction only their acts – which derive from the functions – really count. The villain and the helper are unimportant except for what they *do* and what they do always has the same function in the various tales. This approach in terms of actors – embodied by interchangeable characters – and functions allows Propp to collapse a hundred different stories into the skeleton of one single plot. In my example of the detective story, all the different ways in which the story may be told – it could for instance begin with a description of the murder without giving away the identity of the murderer – would still have John Doe as the murderer and his cousin Jack as the victim. At Propp's level of abstraction, however, we ignore the actual characters and concentrate on their function within the story. If we look at Propp's tales from this abstract vantage point we see similarities between them that otherwise would have escaped our notice.

By presenting things in this way, Propp makes us see his folk tales as systems in which the functions that he identifies have a specific place. In my discussion of the New Critics I have suggested that they – a decade after Propp – saw the literary work, and in particular the poetic text they were preoccupied with, as a system of checks and balances, with the checks and balances obviously interrelated. In Propp's book the interrelatedness of the various elements of a text gets more emphasis because his clearly defined functions are part of an equally clearly defined chain (there is, after all, only one underlying plot). The 'helper' is always there to offer help, even if what he or she actually does may vary widely from tale to tale. Each of Propp's folk tales, then, contains an underlying *structure* of which the unsuspecting reader will usually not be aware. But if folk tales contain such a structure, then maybe other narratives, too, can be made to reveal an underlying structure. That idea would conquer literary academia more than thirty years later.

FORMALISM REVISITED

The formalists, too, came to see literature in systemic terms so that Jakobson and his colleague Yuri Tynyanov (1879–1943) in the same year that Propp published his work could already speak of the study of literature as a 'systematic science'. In its early phase, formalism had seen a poem as the totality of its 'devices': as the footing of a column of devices that were not necessarily related in any way. Apart from that, it had assumed that 'literariness' was the product of the inherent qualities of those devices. Those qualities, and the resulting literariness, could be identified, pointed at. And this is where early formalism went wrong. I have said above that the formalists were primarily interested in generalities. One general rule seemed unassailable: the rule that literariness is created by defamiliarizing devices. But the defamiliarizing potential of certain techniques or ways of presenting things is not an inalienable property. It manifests itself only in the right context. The only rule that can be formulated is that defamiliarization works by way of contrast, of *difference*. Because the early formalists presupposed a too rigid connection between a fixed set of devices and the principle of literariness, they did not see the devices that they regarded as the defining features of literary texts in their proper light.

They gradually gave up this position when it became clear that to identify the various ways in which literature differed from ordinary language was only a first step towards explaining how literature works. Why is it, for instance, that we do not ordinarily realize how thoroughly we are being manipulated in a detective novel? Could it be that the suspense keeps us from noticing? Or is it that we have become so familiar with the genre that we no longer see what is happening right under our noses? Could the process of familiarization that is responsible for our relative blindness with regard to our environment, including language, be at work within literature itself? The formalists decided that that was indeed the case. What is more, familiarization worked at two levels: that of the single literary work and that of literature as a whole. Now where we find familiarization we may also expect defamiliarization, or at least attempts at defamiliarization, and so the formalists started to look for processes of defamiliarization *within* literature – and within the individual literary work – itself.

As was the case with Propp, the more abstract level that this way of looking at things brought into the discussion, led the formalists away from 'devices' in the direction of 'functions'. Let us first look at defamiliarization within one and the same literary text. Imagine a long poem consisting of heroic couplets (lines of ten syllables – with the rhyme scheme *aa, bb, cc,* and so on). Carried along by its rather monotonous cadence we suddenly come across two non-rhyming lines of fourteen syllables each. These two lines function to defamiliarize the reading process because they make us stop and think. But this works also the other way around. Imagine a long poem of unrhymed lines of fourteen syllables each in which you suddenly come across heroic couplets. Now the heroic couplets would have the function of making us stop and think. In other words, whether a certain poetic technique serves as a defamiliarizing device depends on the larger background. To take this a bit further: the ability to defamiliarize our perception is not a quality that certain techniques inherently possess, it is all a matter of how a certain technique *functions* within a given literary work, and that function can change from text to text. What counts is the way and the extent to which it *differs* from its environment. It is of course true that certain techniques, like the use of extreme hyperboles, would defamiliarize most literary texts, but it is equally true that in a text filled from the start with extreme hyperboles another hyperbole would not even be noticed. Every imaginable literary technique, then, can either have a familiarizing or a defamiliarizing effect. Everything depends on the way it functions within a given text. Differentiation is the crucial factor. This led to a view of the literary work as a system that establishes a textual environment that is then again and again made new with the help of defamiliarizing devices. From this perspective it is first of all the system that dictates the actual techniques that will have to be used (long, non-rhyming lines in an environment of heroic couplets; heroic couplets among long non-rhyming lines). The system will of course offer a wide range of choice, but it will always demand difference.

Extending this insight to literature as such, the formalists came up with an interesting explanation of literary change. We all know that literature has changed over time. But why? Why do new genres emerge – the novel, for instance – and old ones disappear over the cultural horizon? And why do we find such rather considerable changes within genres itself? The novel has gone from realism (mid- and late nineteenth century) to modernism (early twentieth century) and postmodernism (1960s and beyond). What is the driving mechanism behind such developments? As Boris Eichenbaum said in 1926 (bracketing the role of individual authors), 'For us, the central problem of the history of literature is the problem of evolution without personality – the study of literature as a *self-formed social phenomenon*' (Eichenbaum 1965: 136). The formalist solution to this problem will not come as a surprise: defamiliarization. Literature as a whole renews itself through the development of, for instance, new genres, while genres in their turn defamiliarize (and thereby change) themselves through for example parody – a defamiliarizing strategy because it invariably focuses on peculiarities – and through the incorporation of new materials and techniques taken from other genres or from popular culture.

Acts of defamiliarization will only have a temporary effect: even the most innovative devices will with the passage of time lose their capacity to catch our attention. The idea that an everlasting dynamic between an inevitable process of familiarization and acts of defamiliarization is the driving mechanism behind literary change, in other words, the driving force in literary history, is ingenious and interesting. It tries to give answers to question of historical change that the New Critics, with their focus on the words on the page, could not even begin to address. But the formalist answers can only be part of a much larger picture. As they themselves realized in the later 1920s, literature is not wholly autonomous; it is not completely divorced from the world it exists in. Far-reaching social changes must have had consequences for the course of literary history. This was most fully realized by Mikhail Bakhtin (1895–1975), whose status as a formalist is not uncontested because he saw the novel as embodying his rather idiosyncratic philosophy of history and who argued that 'In the novel formal markers of languages, manners and styles are symbols for social points of view' (Bakhtin 1981: 357). His view of the novel as a 'heteroglossia', a world in which all manner of discourse, from the carnivalesque to the soberly religious, exist side by side, would much later become highly influential and will come back in Chapter 4.

But to return to the formalists' central concern, defamiliarization. It became increasingly clear that defamiliarization by itself cannot say anything about the nature of the devices that will be deployed. All it tells us is that change is inevitable. It does not tell us which new course that change will initiate. The real world, either in the form of history or of the individual author, cannot be kept out of the picture.

FURTHER DEVELOPMENTS

In the later 1920s the cause of formalism was taken up in Prague by Jan Mukařovský (1891–1975) and others, not in the least because Jakobson had moved there to get away from the political turmoil – and violence – in what had become the Soviet Union. I will in this brief section focus on what from our vantage point are the most relevant aspects of the way the Prague (or Czech) structuralists – named after what Jakobson had started to call 'structuralism' – contributed to literary theory.

Most importantly they further developed the idea that a literary text is a structure in which all the elements are interrelated and interdependent. There is nothing in a literary work that can be seen and studied in isolation. Each single element has a function through which it is related to the work as a whole. The formalists tended to focus on the defamiliarizing elements within literary art and did not pay much attention to all the elements that did not directly contribute to the defamiliarizing process. For the structuralists, however, everything played a role in what a text was and did.

One reason for arriving at this position is that, drawing on new insights in contemporary linguistics, they expanded the formalists' notion of 'function'. In so doing they gave a better theoretical foundation to the idea that literature is concerned with itself while they simultaneously explained how it could also refer to the outside world. As we have seen, for the formalists 'function' has to do with the way textual elements achieve effects of defamiliarization because of their difference from their environment. For the structuralists, a text in its entirety – and not just a literary text – has a function too, and it is on the basis of the way a text functions as a whole that we can distinguish between various sorts of texts. If we start with the not unreasonable assumption that a text is form of communication than its specific function is determined by its orientation. These orientations, worked out exhaustively by Jakobson in his famous 'Linguistics and Poetics' essay of 1960, are basically those of a so-called 'speech act' – they derive from what we do with speech. Let me illustrate some of the possibilities, using speech examples. One of the shortest texts in the language is 'Damn!' Expressing a range of emotions – disappointment, anger, surprise, and so on – 'Damn!' quite often is oriented towards the speaker him- or herself. It has, in Jakobson's terms, an 'expressive' or 'emotive' function. 'Hey, you!', however, is oriented towards the person that is addressed (the addressee). If we tell a friend about the movie we have just seen, or the near-accident we have witnessed, then our 'text' is oriented towards things in the outside world, it refers to the reality we both live in and has a 'referential' function. From this perspective in terms of orientation, literary texts are oriented towards themselves, but not in the way that 'Damn!' is often oriented towards its 'sender'. Literature focuses on its own *form*, its focus is on the *message* rather than on the sender, the addressee, or any other possible target. It is in other words oriented towards the way it presents itself and has a 'poetic' function.

Of course these orientations almost never occur in a pure form. If I'm all by myself 'Damn!' will probably be wholly oriented towards me, but if there are other people around I may very well be trying to catch their attention – to address them obliquely. Literary texts are oriented towards themselves (they are very conscious of their form and the outside world they would seem to refer to usually is wholly or at least partly fictional), but there are few works of literature that we cannot in one way or another make relevant to the world we live in. In other words, in actual practice texts quite often have more than one orientation and more than one function simultaneously. What counted for the structuralists is which orientation and accompanying function is *dominant*. This concept of the 'dominant' allowed them a view of literary texts that was a good deal more flexible than that of the formalists: literature referred primarily to itself, but it could also be taken as referring to the outside world, although the referential element would of course always have to be subservient to its orientation on the literary code, to the poetic function. (A text would cease to be literature if its dominant orientation shifted from the text itself – its form – to the outside world.) Moreover, as I have just pointed out, from this point of view the whole text functions as a coherent whole, kept together by its 'dominant'. It is a structure in which all elements, whether they defamiliarize or not, work together to create a certain orientation.

In a second move, the Prague group further theorized the idea of defamiliarization and gave it a place in their view of the literary work as a structure. Borrowing from psychological studies of the way our mind processes the infinite number of data that our senses present to it and filters out what seems irrelevant, the structuralists replaced defamiliarization by *foregrounding* (taken from such perception studies by one of the Russian formalists who had already described its potential for literary studies). Unlike defamiliarization, which would not seem to affect its immediate textual environment, foregrounding has the effect that it 'automatizes' neighbouring textual elements. It draws the reader's attention to itself and obscures whatever else may be going on right beside it. While defamiliarization points to a contrastive, but static, relationship between the defamiliarizing element and the other elements, foregrounding emphasizes the dynamism of that relationship: what one element gains in terms of being foregrounded, is lost by the other elements that constitute its background. In other words, just like the idea of a 'dominant', foregrounding implies a perspective that sees a text as a structure of interrelated elements. Foregrounding, with its structuralist orientation, has in contemporary literary criticism effectively replaced defamiliarization.

THE AXIS OF COMBINATION

In the late 1950s Roman Jakobson formulated what is probably the ultimate attempt to define the aesthetic function in poetry, that is, the 'literariness' of poetry. I will briefly discuss Jakobson's definition because it is one of the prime examples of the formal, 'scientific', approach to literature that marks continental European thinking about literature from the 1910s until the 1970s. 'The poetic function' – that is, literariness – Jakobson said, 'projects the principle of equivalence from the axis of selection into the axis of combination' (Jakobson 1960: 358). This is not an inviting formula but it is less impenetrable than it might seem to be.

Jakobson's definition departs from the simple fact that all words can be classified and categorized. Every time we use language what we say or write is a combination of words selected from a large number of classes and categories. Take for instance a bare bones sentence like 'Ma feels cold'. In this sentence we might have used 'Pa' or 'Jane' or 'John' (and so on) instead of 'Ma' and we might have used 'good', 'bad', 'hot' (and so on) instead of 'cold' without disrupting the sentence's grammar. The alternatives that I have mentioned are grammatically equivalent to 'Ma' or 'cold'. The selection process that starts up whenever we are on the point of speaking or writing is governed by rules that make us select words from large classes of grammatically equivalent words: nouns, verbs, adjectives, and so on. However, we also constantly make selections in the field of *meaning*. Here we are on less abstract ground than in the previous example and the starting point is what we actually want to say. Usually there will more than one way of saying what is virtually the same thing. The most obvious case is that of a word for which there is a perfect or almost perfect synonym, say 'begin' and 'start'. We will have to choose between two equivalents. Or we can choose from a group of words that is closely related with regard to meaning, for instance: man, guy, fellow, dude, gent, and so on. Which word we will actually choose may depend on the degree of colloquiality (or dignity) that we want to project or on how precise we want to be. In any case, we make a selection from a number of words that at least in one not unimportant respect – male human being – are equivalent in meaning. Both with regard to its (grammatical) structure and with regard to meaning (its semantic dimension) language knows all sorts of equivalence. It is this principle of (linguistic) equivalence that poetry borrows from what Jakobson calls 'the axis of selection' and then employs in the 'axis of combination'.

What Jakobson claims is that poetry makes its selections in order to create equivalences *between* the words it chooses. It can do so by way of alliteration, for instance, which is basically an equivalence between the sounds with which two or more words begin: 'The Soul selects her own Society' – to quote an Emily Dickinson poem which uses an initial 's' in three of its six words (one of which also ends with an 's'). Or poetry can create equivalences by way of rhyme, in which almost whole words are equivalent to each other (like 'words' and 'nerds'). But it can also do so by way of meter – iambic pentameters, for instance – which creates metric equivalences unknown or rare in ordinary language, by way of grammatical parallelisms, inversions and juxtapositions (which in order to work presuppose equivalence between the two elements involved) and numerous other ways. This is how Charles Dickens's *Tale of Two Cities* (1859) opens:

> It was the best of times, it was the worst of times, it was the age of wisdom, it was the age of foolishness, it was the epoch of belief, it was the epoch of incredulity, it was the season of Light, it was the season of Darkness.

Parallelism and juxtaposition go hand in hand to create a 'poetic' effect in a prose text.

This brings us back to the formalists' hunt for 'literariness'. However, literariness is here not the result of a number of discrete 'devices' that defamiliarize ordinary language, but of the specific organization of literary language which organizes itself along lines different from the organization of other uses of language. Literariness is the result of a specific structural principle, that of equivalence on the axis of combination. It is that equivalence that contributes to a literary text's coherence. As with the formalists, the question of meaning hardly arises. And it is obvious that the principle of equivalence has even less to say about the relative *merit*, the *value* of individual works of literature. A text that is absolutely jampacked with equivalences is not necessarily great literature. Still, Jakobson's formula stands as one of the most serious – and, I should add, successful – attempts to capture that what makes the bulk of Western literature, and especially poetry, different from the language we use in a recipe for brownies or a letter of complaint to our insurance company.

SUGGESTIONS FOR FURTHER READING

Russian Formalism: History-Doctrine (3rd edition 1981) by Viktor Erlich is the standard survey of formalism. Peter Steiner's *Russian Formalism: A Metapoetics* (1984) is a very good introduction; somewhat controversially, but quite helpfully, Steiner includes Jakobson and Propp in his discussion. A bit more thorough is Jurij Striedter's *Literary Structure, Evolution and Value: Russian Formalism and Czech Structuralism Reconsidered* (1989). Tony Bennett's *Formalism and Marxism* (2003) looks at formalism from a Marxist perspective (see Chapter 4) while in *The Origins of Russian Literary Theory: Folklore, Philology, Form* (2022) Jessica Miller looks back on formalism and its intellectual history and discusses its relevance for contemporary criticism. *Central and Eastern European Literary Theory and the West*, edited by Michal Mugratski, Schamma Schahadat, and Irina Wutsdorff (2023) is a wide-ranging collection of essays that examine the vicissitudes of formalism, Czech structuralism and lesser-known theoretical developments in the groves of Western Academe and introduce the work of some neglected theorists. Boris Eichenbaum's 'Introduction to the Formal Method' and Viktor Shklovsky's 'Art as Technique', available in many anthologies, are excellent introductions to early formalist thinking. Roman Jakobson's 'Closing Statement: Linguistics and Poetics', the ultimate in attempting to establish 'literariness', appeared originally in Thomas Sebeok's *Style in Language* (1960) and has frequently been reprinted. The major texts of Czech or Prague structuralism are available in Paul L. Garvin's *A Prague School Reader on Esthetics, Literary Structure, and Style* (1964).

READING FOR FORM
FRENCH STRUCTURALISM, 1950–1975

THE INEVITABILITY OF FORM

Why were the formalists and the Prague structuralists, the French structuralists that I will discuss in this chapter, and, to a lesser extent, the New Critics so preoccupied with the *form* of literary works? Why not concentrate on the *meaning* of a given work of literature, on what it has to tell us? Why waste time on something that would seem to be of secondary importance?

For many readers educated in the Anglo-American tradition, form and structure are not only alien to their interests – they do not read literature to learn about form and structure – but actually threaten the experience of reading. Many readers do not want to hear about things like form and structure because they seem to undermine the uniqueness and the spirituality of the novel or poem that they are reading. We are dealing here with an underlying humanistic perspective that is uneasy with form and structure because they ultimately seem to diminish our own uniqueness and spirituality and represent a severely reductionist approach to human beings and their cultural achievements.

Readers who can identify with this may have a point, as will become clear later in this chapter. Form, however, is inevitable. Art cannot do without form. No matter how life-like a novel or a movie may seem, it is the end product of countless decisions involving form. That is even true if we are not talking about fiction or a Hollywood movie, but about their real-life cousins reportage and documentary film. Imagine that we set up a camera on New York's Times Square or in London's Oxford Street, and

DOI: 10.4324/9781003373438-4

let it run from dawn till nightfall. We might argue that here we really have a slice of life, the ultimate realism in movie-making: the camera has only registered what actually happened in that part of Times Square or Oxford Street covered by the lens. (We have of course not moved the camera because that would have introduced a new perspective and would have constituted formal interference, no matter how rudimentary.) But we would above all have the most boring film ever made. What we would have is thousands of cars, taxi cabs, buses, and pedestrians passing in front of the lens. In order to make things more interesting we might have picked out one of these people, a man with a promising grim expression, and followed him with our camera. But in so doing we would immediately have been forced to make decisions on form. We could film the man while following him, and we could occasionally overtake him to get in front of him. We could for a moment focus on his legs to show that he's in haste. We could rent a helicopter and film him from above. Whatever we do excludes all the other options that we have. Even documentaries, then, no matter how true to life they seem, are the end product of a long line of decisions on the way their material is presented.

LANGUAGE AS A SYSTEM OF SIGNS

Whatever we do with images (as in movies) or with language always has a formal dimension. But what about the structure that I have just discussed? After all, structure is not something that we can easily identify. It's all very well to say that all the elements of a text are interconnected and that the various functions of these elements and the relations between them constitute a structure but that does not really help. However, for the French structuralism that is the main subject of this chapter structure is even more fundamental than form. Form is inevitably bound up with meaning; structure, however, is what makes meaning possible. It is that which enables meaning to emerge. This is an enigmatic claim that clearly needs some explanation. After all, we are not even aware of the structures that supposedly play a role in the creation of meaning. It seems to us that we ourselves create meaning. We create meaning by saying something, or by making a gesture, or through a work of art, if we happen to have the talent – we create meaning because we want to express something by way of language, music, choreography, painting, film, and a good many other means. Meaning would seem to be produced by you and me, and not by an invisible and intangible structure.

Structuralism has its origin in the thinking of the Swiss linguist Ferdinand de Saussure (1857–1913) who in the early twentieth century revolutionized the study of language. Nineteenth-century linguistics is mainly interested in the history of language – for instance, in how French and Italian developed out of Latin, or how English, Dutch, and German developed out of the West-Germanic language that the ancestors of the English, the Dutch, and the Germans shared some fifteen hundred years ago. They studied the origin of individual words (modern English 'way', for instance, derives from Old English 'weg' – and is still 'weg' in Dutch) and tried to formulate the laws that apparently govern processes of linguistic change. Comparing new and old forms of a language, and using related languages to support their findings, historical linguists were able to discover the rules that governed specific linguistic transformations and to reconstruct how the various European languages had developed over historical time.

Saussure adopted a completely different angle. Instead of the usual historical, diachronic approach – following language through time – he opted for an ahistorical, and far more abstract approach. To Saussure questions concerning the way particular languages changed over particular periods were subordinate to a more fundamental question: how does language work? So instead of on actual instances of language use – spoken or written – Saussure focused on the question of how language actually works in order to formulate general insights that would be valid for all language use and all languages. I should perhaps point out that this is also different from what grammarians – the other type of linguist around in Saussure's time – used to do. Grammarians wanted to describe the underlying grammatical rules that we automatically follow when we talk or write. So they analysed instances of language use – our individual utterances, which Saussure called *paroles* (plural) – to get at those rules. But Saussure was interested in how language as such works – in what he called *langue* – and not in the grammatical matrix of this or that language.

This approach led Saussure, whose work found wider circulation only after his death, to the idea that language should first of all be seen as a system of signs (he himself did not use the term 'structure'). Secondly, those signs are in first instance arbitrary – before they become conventions – and have not taken their specific form because of what they mean, but to be different from other signs. Let me explain this. The 'signs' are simply the words that we use: 'way', 'yard', 'yarn'. 'Way' is 'Weg' in German and some of us will know that it is 'chemin' in French and 'camino' in Spanish. We need only a very superficial knowledge of a foreign language to know that the words we use to refer to the objects around us are different in other languages. From that knowledge it is only a small step to the realization that the link between a word and what it refers to must be arbitrary. Since other languages have different words for what we call a 'way' – and for all our other words – and in spite of that would seem to function perfectly well, we can only conclude that calling a way a 'way' is not a necessity. There is clearly nothing in what we call a 'way' that dictates the particular word 'way'. If real world objects dictated our language we would obviously all use the same words for them. As it is, the relation between the sign 'way' and what it refers to is indeed fundamentally arbitrary – in the sense that 'way' could have been quite different. In fact, since it once was 'weg', it already *has* been different. The arbitrariness, of course, applies only to the *fundamental* relationship between words and what they refer to. In actual practice, those relationships have become a matter of convention. If we want to refer to an object, a table for instance, we automatically use the word that everybody uses. When Dr Seuss in 1950 first used the word 'nerd' in *If I Ran the Zoo*, the relationship between 'nerd' and what it referred to was arbitrary. As a matter of fact, if he had not provided illustrations with his story, we would have had a hard time figuring out what to make of 'nerd'. Now it is still arbitrary but also a matter of convention: there is now a standard relationship between 'nerd' and a certain type of person.

If the form of words is not dictated by their relationship with what they refer to, then that form must have its origin elsewhere. Saussure traces the origin of the form of words – of linguistic signs – to the principle of differentiation. New words like 'nerd' take their places among existing words because they are *different*.

The whole system is based on often minimal differences: in ways, days, rays, bays, pays, maze, haze, only the opening consonant is different. Words, then, function in a system that uses difference to create its components. (A more practical way of saying this is that we automatically fall back on difference if we want to coin a word.) As Saussure himself says of all the elements that make up a linguistic system: 'Their most precise characteristic is being what the others are not' (Saussure 1959 [1915]: 117). This is fairly self-evident. But then Saussure introduces an argument that seems completely counter-intuitive. The principle of difference that gives rise to the signs (words) of which language is made up, he tells us, also gives rise to their *meaning*.

A strong point in favour of Saussure's argument is that form and meaning cannot be separated. If we change 'ways' to 'days' or 'rays' we have not only a new form but also a new meaning. In other words, the differential principle does not only work to distinguish words from each other, it simultaneously distinguishes *meanings* from each other. A linguistic sign − a word − is both form and meaning. Saussure calls the form − the word as it is spoken or written − the *signifier* and the meaning the *signified*. A change in the signifier, no matter how minimal, means a new signified. We must accept that meaning is indeed bound up with differentiation. But is it the full story? Not quite. Here I must introduce another counterintuitive complication. A sign's meaning, its signified, is *not* an object in the real world, as we tend to think. That is again the way it might easily seem to us, and I have so far spoken freely of that what words refer to, but what they refer to is not the real world − at least not directly. Take a seemingly uncomplicated word like 'tree', which my *American Heritage College Dictionary* (3rd edition) defines as 'A perennial woody plant having a main trunk and usu. a distinct crown'. What this definition makes clear is that 'tree' does not refer to any single object in the real world but to a category of objects which may or may not have 'distinct crowns'. The meaning of the sign 'tree' includes oaks, beeches, and chestnuts but also dwarf pines and Douglas firs. Its *signified* is a man-made category, a concept. A little reflection will tell us that this is also true of other signs: love, table, child, field. They all refer to concepts − not unrelated to the real world, but clearly the product of generalization and abstraction. It is those concepts that we then apply in our actual use of language to the real word, where they then (may) have concrete referents.

Our intuition that meaning is bound up with the real world is not completely wrong, even if the relation between meaning and the world is a matter of convention and much less straightforward than we tend to think. But 'bound up with' is a vague phrase. Which of the two is dominant in this relationship? Do the real world and everything that it contains indirectly determine the meanings of our language or does our language determine our world? To put it more concretely: has the fact that there are chestnuts somehow given rise to the admittedly arbitrary sign 'chestnut' or does the fact that the sign 'chestnut' has somehow come into being allow us to see chestnuts as a separate species among trees? If we had the word 'horse' but not the word 'pony' would we still see ponies as ponies or would we see them as horses, much like all other horses, because our language would not offer us an alternative? If the latter were true, then it might be argued that language precedes thought and constitutes the framework within which thought must necessarily operate. Some theorists, including Saussure, have thought so and have argued that our reality is in fact constituted by our language. If that is indeed the case, then the language we inherit at birth is for all practical purposes an autonomous system that carves up the world for us and governs the way we see it. (It is never quite autonomous because we can tamper with it and for instance expand it — witness Dr Seuss's nerd.) This position which claims that our reality is determined by language is called *linguistic determinism* and I will have occasion to return to it later in this book. To many people such a position appears unnecessarily radical and turns an interesting insight with a limited range of application into an iron law. We can perhaps agree on two principles, however. If we for a moment forget about the way we use language (or language uses us) and focus on language itself, we can agree that if we see language as a system of signs, then the meanings that arise — the signifieds — are first of all arbitrary in their relationship to the real world and secondly the product of difference in the sense that difference has a crucial, enabling function. Without difference there would be no language and meaning at all. The role that difference plays in its turn implies that meaning is impossible without the whole system of differences: the structure within which difference operates. After all, signs must differ from other signs and they need these other signs to be different. Although meaning is in first instance produced, or at least enabled, by difference, it is at a more fundamental level produced, or again at least enabled, by the structure: by the *relations* between the signs that make up a language, or, to give this a wider application, between the elements that together make up a given structure. Meaning, then, resides not so much in those individual elements, but rather in the relationships between them – an admittedly improbable claim that will be explained further below.

ANTHROPOLOGICAL STRUCTURALISM

These principles are indispensable for an understanding of the various approaches to literature that together constitute the French literary structuralism of the 1960s and 1970s. They are even more indispensable for a proper understanding of the so-called *poststructuralism* that developed after structuralism and that I will introduce in a later chapter. It is, in fact, mainly with an eye on poststructuralism that I have offered such a detailed discussion of basic matters. Poststructuralism is also the reason why I will begin this overview of French structuralism with a discussion of its first, exclusively anthropological, phase. The anthropological structuralism that was developed in the later 1940s by the French anthropologist Claude Lévi-Strauss (1908–2009) has never had much direct relevance for literary studies but its indirect influence is still very considerable. So we will first make a brief detour through mid-twentieth century-anthropology.

Like all structuralisms, anthropological structuralism is directly indebted to the Saussurean concept of language as a sign system governed by difference. However, anthropological structuralism gave the idea of a system of signs that function in the first instance because they are different from each other a much wider range – already foreseen, incidentally by Saussure himself – and transposed it from linguistics to anthropology, that is, from the study of language to the study of cultures that from a 1950s Western perspective seemed alien.

The first anthropologist to see the potential of Saussure's analysis of language as a way of approaching the most diverse cultural phenomena was Lévi-Strauss. In the early decades of the twentieth century anthropology was still largely descriptive and functionalist:

it sought to record the myths, taboos, rituals, customs, manners, in short, everything that was recordable, of the non-Western cultures that it studied and tried to establish their function. Lévi-Strauss broke with that tradition in two major ways. The first way is indebted to Vladimir Propp's study of Russian fairy tales. Transposing Propp's idea to the field of myths, Lévi-Strauss tried to show how the most diverse myths, recorded in cultures that seemingly have no connection with each other, can be seen as variations upon one and the same system of ideas.

More important for our purposes here is that Lévi-Strauss saw the possibilities of Saussure's notion that meaning is ultimately the product of difference for the study of discrete cultural phenomena. For the structuralism that Lévi-Strauss developed in a series of major anthropological publications, the almost countless discrete elements that together make up a culture constitute a sign system. Eating customs, taboos with regard to menstruation, initiation and hunting rites, the preparation of food, the rules underlying so-called kinship relations – in short, everything that has a cultural origin, and is not biologically determined, counts as a sign. The discrete bits of culture that we can distinguish are not meaningful in themselves, but draw their meaning from the sign system in which they function and, more in particular, from their difference from other signs. As Lévi-Strauss put it in his study of the way masks were used in certain Native American cultures: 'A mask does not exist in isolation; it supposes other real or potential masks always by its side, masks that might have been chosen in its stead and substituted for it' (Lévi-Strauss 1982: 144). What a given element signifies within a culture depends on the system, and not on an intrinsic meaning (which it does not have). Masks 'which no one would have dreamed of comparing, cannot be interpreted each for itself and considered in isolation. They are parts of a system within which they transform each other. As in the case with myths, masks (with their origin myths and the rites in which they appear) become intelligible only through the relationships which unite them' (93). Just like the relationship between the linguistic sign and its real world referent, the relationship between a specific cultural phenomenon and what it expresses – its meaning – is arbitrary in the sense that it is determined by convention.

BINARY OPPOSITIONS

However, the relationship between a cultural sign and what it expresses is not necessarily completely arbitrary. Anthropological structuralism is also interested in the question of how our ancestors once, sometime during the evolutionary process that gave us the sort of conscious awareness of ourselves and our environment that animals lack, started to make sense of the world they found themselves in. A very basic mental operation consists in the creation of opposites: some things are edible, others are not, some creatures are dangerous, others are not. Classification in terms of such oppositions, in which the opposites are related to each other because they express either the presence or the absence of one and the same thing (edibility, danger, and so on), seems a natural thing to do, the more so since it would seem to be reinforced by nature itself. Man and woman constitute a binary pair, intimately related yet in a crucial way each other's biological opposite; our right hand and left hand constitute another closely related pair of opposites. Lévi-Strauss's basic assumption is that our primitive ancestors deployed this simple model, or structure, to get a grip on a world that slowly began to appear to them as something separate and alien. For Lévi-Strauss, the structure of primitive thinking is binary. Having acquired the rudiments of language, our ancestors must have started to categorize their world in very basic terms that always involved a presence and an absence – light/darkness, man-made/natural, above/below, noise/silence, clothes/naked, sacred/profane, and so on. Prehistoric men and women must have organized their experience around such +/− (that is, binary) oppositions.

For Lévi-Strauss such binary oppositions, the most fundamental of which is that between what is man-made and that which is part of nature (between culture and nature), constitute the basis of what we call culture. The basic apprehensions of reality that we find in those oppositions get translated into cultural acts. Once they have found expression in certain rites, taboos, customs, manners, and so on, they are permutated over time until, as often as not, they have become completely unrecognizable. In fact, they may appear in completely different and even contradictory guises in different cultures. In some cases, the meanings that were attached to the original opposites and that found expression in their cultural

revelation. We are usually aware that narratives start somewhere, really get going because something happens, take what would seem to be a time-out, and then get going again. However, even though the model operates on a high level of abstraction, it allows us to see a pattern that otherwise might have escaped us.

NARRATOLOGY

In its earlier years structuralist literary studies, often called *narratology* after Todorov had coined the term in 1969, mostly focussed on two questions: *what* is narrated and *how* is it narrated. The structuralists who tackled the first question generally followed Vladimir Propp's approach. *Sémantique structurale* (*Structural Semantics*), published in 1966 by A.J. Greimas (1917–1992), is clearly indebted to Propp's study of Russian fairytales, but offers a number of highly relevant refinements. Replacing Propp's cast of seven actors with six so-called *actants*, Greimas opts for a higher level of abstraction so that his actants give him a more precise instrument of analysis than Propp's characters. In the process those actants become more like basic narrative roles. In Greimas's scheme an actant, for instance the Opponent of the Subject (the latter the equivalent of Propp's Hero), need not be one single character but may be represented by various characters who all in their own way try to keep the Subject from achieving her or his aim. In another rearrangement of Propp's model, Greimas argues that one and the same character may operate as two wholly different actants, that is, function in two different roles. He further broadens his actantial concepts – and the usefulness of his analysis – by seeing for instance inanimate objects and abstractions in actantial terms, that is, as playing, or contributing to, the role of an actant. From here it is only a short step to seeing any narrative as a structure created by the relations between its actants. Greimas and the other structuralists who focused on *what* a narrative presents built an intricate analytical instrument that could map any narrative in great detail.

Other narratologists focussed on the way stories are told, on *how* the *what* of a story is presented. The most influential was Gérard Genette (1930–2018), whose *Discours du récit* (1972, translated as *Narrative Discourse* in 1980) is representative in its analysis of the structure of narrative presentation. This aspect of literature has of course for a long time had the attention of writers, who after all must take any number of decisions involving the way they are going to tell their story and it has also drawn a good deal of attention on the part of literary critics (*The Rhetoric of Fiction* by the American critic Wayne Booth, published in 1961, is a brilliant exposé of technical strategies). What distinguishes the structuralist approach to the way stories are told is their systematicity and – inevitably – their focus on the underlying structures that make stories (and thus meaning) possible.

I will briefly sketch Genette's project to give an idea of the structuralist approach to how stories are told. Although he introduces a number of completely new categories, he more often redefines existing categories and insights in terms of *relations*. As he states early in *Narrative Discourse,* 'Analysis of narrative discourse will thus be for me essentially a study of the relationships between narrative and story, between narrative and narrating, and ... between story and narrating' (Genette 1980: 11). Let me give an idea of how this works by looking at some redefinitions of familiar literary-critical insights. The first concerns the way in which the chronological *order* of the events and actions of for instance a novel (the formalists' *fabula*) is presented in the actual story (the *syuzhet*). We can express the relationship between the chronological order and the narrative order in terms that express their relative positions at a given point. The narration may temporarily lag behind the chronological order of events (which is what we find in a *flashback* – although Genette does not use the term), it may be synchronic with events, or it may run ahead of them (when the narrator speculates about the future, for instance). It may even present unlikely combinations of these possibilities: 'It would happen later, as we have already seen', to quote one of Genette's examples (83). Genette offers a detailed analysis of all the possible relations between the order of events and the order of narration and does so in a technical vocabulary that always calls to our attention that we are dealing with a relationship between two givens ('analepis', 'prolepsis', 'achrony', 'proleptic analepsis', 'analeptic prolepsus').

The second relationship that Genette discusses – that of *duration* – concerns the relationship between the time an event has taken up in the reality of the narrated world and the time that it takes to narrate that event. In order to avoid disastrous consequences – like our day-long film – narration must speed things up. Equal duration of event and narration may occasionally create unexpected and arresting effects – 'John walked walked walked walked walked walked walked upstairs' – but this is not the way we can usefully describe a marathon. We usually find equal duration only in the unembellished presentation of dialogue. The question that then arises is how we can map the various possibilities of compression.

The third relationship is that of *frequency*, which in Genette's scheme of things covers the relation between the number of times that an event occurs in the world that we are told about and the number of times that it is narrated. It is quite common for events that occur repeatedly to be described only once (a technique for which Genette uses the term 'iterative'). Such a narration might start with, 'We went for a swim every day, that whole summer', and might then describe who went to the beach, what they talked about, who fell in love with whom, the thunderstorms that gathered on the horizon in the late afternoon, and so on. The reader will understand that this description probably stretches things a bit – not one single rainy day, that whole summer? – but essentially covers a whole series of very similar events. Far less common is the reverse situation: an event that occurred only once is narrated repeatedly. But this is also not as strange as it may seem. A single event may be told by different characters from different perspectives, or it may be told by one and the same character at different points in her or his life (in which case we will also expect different perspectives).

Genette's most difficult analyses concern what in traditional literary criticism is called point of view and which he complicates considerably. Let me give an example. We all know that when writers sit down to begin a novel they have a whole range of possibilities at their disposal. There are first-person narratives, in which the story is told by an 'I' who is inside the story, and there are third-person narratives in which the narrator would seem to absent from the story that is being told. However, as a structuralist, Genette does not take as his starting point the writer who sits behind a desk and considers the available options, but the variations that are offered by the relations between the various elements that play roles in the way stories are told. This structuralist perspective, in which there is no place for the author, leads him to suggest that, although we usually do not realize it, a narrative that does not seem to have a narrator still must have one and that this narrator is always present in the story. This seems an unnecessary manoeuvre – why not simply identify their authors as the narrators of such stories? – but it is not so strange as it may seem. Imagine a novel that is told by an invisible third-person narrator and that is set in seventeenth-century New England. That narrator obviously must know the seventeenth-century world that the novel describes. But the reader may not for a second get the impression that the narrator is also very much aware of mobile phones, hard disks, and the Dow Jones index. In other words, the narrator functions as a continuum of the world that is described rather than as a continuum of the author. Even if we have our doubts about Genette's suggestion, we might well have to accept that the invisible, implied, narrator of such a third-person narrative is not identical with the author.

In any case, positing an invisible narrator inside a third-person narrative enables Genette to see first- and third-person narration in terms of the relation between narrator and character and allows him to set up a neat binary opposition. In a first-person narrative the narrator is identical with a character, in a third-person narrative the narrator is not identical with one of the characters. In the first case the narrator tells us about him- or herself (a first person), in the second case the narrator tells us about third persons. Genette calls the first type of narration *homodiegetic* and the second type *heterodiegetic* ('self' versus 'other'). The relationship between narrator and character is intimately bound up with the relationship between narrator and the world that is narrated. A 'homodiegetic' narrator is always involved in the world that is narrated. However, that involvement can be rather marginal. If I am at a party and tell a story about a weird thing that happened to me six years ago, I am, somewhat paradoxically, not part of the world that I am narrating. The course of time has made me *external* to that world. First-person stories will often combine 'external' descriptions, in which the narrator presents a former self, with current events in which the narrator participates and in which the relationship between narrator and the world that is narrated is *internal*. Heterodiegetic (third-person) narrators are not part of the world they narrate, not even if their creator – the author – *is* part of it. In Norman Mailer's *The Armies of the Night* (1968) the main character is Norman Mailer, who is participating in a march on the Pentagon. But for Genette the third-person narrator who always refers to Mailer in the third person – as Norman Mailer – is *not* the author and is therefore external to the narrated world.

Any reasonably experienced reader knows that the relationship between narrator and narrated world is a complicated matter. Even if we are well aware of who the general narrator is of the story or novel that we are reading, we may still encounter passages in which the identity of the narrator is far from clear. This is especially the case with what is called free indirect discourse, in which the narrator's descriptive reportage can so gradually give way to the reflections of one of the characters that at a certain point we honestly can no longer say to whom we are supposed to attribute what is being thought or through whose eyes we see what is being described (with whose 'point of view' we are dealing, in traditional terms). Are we still directly dealing with the narrator or have we slipped into the perspective of one of the characters? ('He realized that they would have to part, but he would always love, adore her, and remember the dimple in her chin'.) One of Genette's contributions to the way we talk about literature is his introduction of the term *focalization* for dealing with this complication of the relation between narrator and the world that is being narrated (Genette derived the term from a New Critical source: Cleanth Brooks and Austin Warren's 1943 notion of 'focus of narration'). If the narrator has indeed given way to the perspective of one of the characters – even if that perspective is still described for us by the narrator – the narration takes place through a *focalizer*. 'Focalization' then allows Genette to draw broad distinctions between various types of narrative.

This is not more than an introduction to Genette's narratology. It will be obvious, however, that the relations that I have sketched here and the others that Genette identifies can be further broken down and refined into a highly sophisticated analytical apparatus. Genette's narratology focuses and directs the way we look at texts and it assists us in the interpretation of complex texts. In fact, we know that it can do so, because *Narrative Discourse* is not only a work of structuralist literary theory, it is also a brilliant dissection of the narrative strategies of Marcel Proust's *À la recherche du temps perdu* (*Remembrance of Things Past*; 1913–1927), which functions as Genette's main textual source. However, as the narratologists themselves also realized, there is more to a narrative text than an analysis of narrative strategies and techniques will reveal. In *The Narrative Act: Point of View in Prose Fiction* (1981) Susan Sniader Lanser called attention to narratology's 'complete disregard of gender' (46) and also brought ideology, value, and authorial intention into play. In his *Reading for the Plot* (1984) Peter Brooks, arguing that structuralist narratology was too 'static and limiting', focused on what makes the plot move forward and on the forces that keep the reader interested, such as 'the play of desire in time that makes us turn pages and strive towards narrative ends' (xiii). And continuing her work on gender and narratology, Lanser's *Fictions of Authority: Women Writers and the Narrative Voice* (1997) sought to show that fiction by female authors makes use of specific modes of narration. Other critics, finding other themes and issues that the first generation of narratologists had failed to take into account, joined them so that narratology was combined, as often as not very productively, with practically every mode of literary criticism.

READING THE READER – A BRIEF EXCURSION

Peter Brooks's interest in the reader was not accidental. In the 1970s and 1980s critics began to pay serious attention to the role of the reader. In Germany Hans-Robert Jauss and Wolfgang Iser, who both taught at the University of Konstanz, argued that the meaning of a literary text is not so much a property of that text, but the product of interaction between text and reader and that, moreover, that meaning cannot be carved in stone because all literary texts are shot through with sites of indeterminacy or undecidability (a notion developed in the 1930s by the Polish literary theorist Roman Ingarden). It is readers who, drawing on their individual experiences and guided by their expectations, fill in the text's gaps and create its meanings. That vital participation in the creative process does, however, not imply a license to produce wholly idiosyncratic readings. A text's meanings will be bounded by its overall structure so that the reader may be said to complete rather than to create the text.

In the US this focus on reception – on how readers 'receive' literary texts – took a more radical turn, with several critics arguing that a text's meaning was (almost) wholly the reader's creation. In *5 Readers Reading* (1975) Norman Holland, who approached reading from a psychoanalytic perspective, argued that the supposed organic unity of texts exists only in their readers' minds, created as a 'defense against some source of anxiety' (14) and that readers 'act out [their] own lifestyle' (113–114) in their interpretations of texts. Other reader-response critics pointed to the conventions of interpretation that obtain in a given 'interpretive' community, with those conventions rather than individual readings generating meaning. But this interest in the reader's role in the complex realization of meaning was soon relegated to the far background by the impact of another import from Continental Europe which will be discussed in Chapter 5.

SUGGESTIONS FOR FURTHER READING

Robert Scholes's *Structuralism in Literature: An Introduction* (1974) and Jonathan Culler's *Structuralist Poetics: Structuralism, Linguistics and the Study of Literature* (1975) are despite their age still good introductions to structuralism, with Scholes being satisfyingly accessible. The same can be said of two other classic introductions to structuralism, John Sturrock's *Structuralism* (2003) and Terence Hawkes's *Structuralism and Semiotics* (2003). Jonathan Culler's *Structuralism* (2006) collects important structuralist contributions to the humanities and the human sciences. Examples of structuralist analyses of specific genres are Tzvetan Todorov's 'The Typology of Detective Fiction' from 1966 (to be found in his *The Poetics of Prose*, 1971), his *The Fantastic: A Structural Approach to a Literary Genre* (1970), and Will Wright's *Sixguns and Society: A Structural Study of the Western* (1975). An excellent, although admittedly not easy, example of narratological criticism is Gérard Genette's *Narrative Discourse* (1980). Unlike structuralism, whose premises were seriously questioned by later theorists, narratology is still a going concern. (Fairly) recent books that either touch upon or are wholly devoted to narrative theory are Bronwen Thomas, *Narrative: The Basics* (2015), Kent Puckett, *Narrative Theory: A Critical Introduction* (2016), Robyn R. Warhol and Susan S. Lanser (eds), *Narrative Theory Unbound: Queer and Feminist*

Interventions (2017), Matthew Garrett (ed.), *The Cambridge Companion to Narrative Theory* (2018), Genevieve Liveley, *Narratology* (2019), Brian Richardson, *A Poetics of Plot for the Twenty-First Century* (2019), *Queer and Feminist Theories of Narrative*, collected and edited by Tory Young (2021), and the massive *Routledge Companion to Narrative Theory* (2022), edited by Paul Dawson and Maria Mäkelä. Patrick Colm Hogan effectively draws on cognitive studies in his *Affective Narratology: The Emotional Structure of Stories* (2011). *The Return of the Reader: Reader-Response Criticism* (1987) by Elizabeth Freund is a reader-friendly introduction, while *Reader-Response Criticism: From Formalism to Post-Structuralism* (1980), edited by Jane P. Tompkins, gathers important material and comes with a lengthy and excellent introduction by the editor. *Literary Reading: Empirical and Theoretical Studies* (2006) by David S. Miall, who has a long-standing interest in emotional responses to literature, pays particular attention to the empirical side of reader–response research. Ika Willis's *Reception* (2018) is a recent and good introduction to 'reception in the context of literary studies', while it also looks briefly at the reception of some other art forms.

POLITICAL READING
CLASS, GENDER, AND RACE IN THE 1970s AND 1980s

INTRODUCTION

What the major approaches to literature that I have so far discussed have in common is that they focus strongly on literature itself. Richards's practical criticism and the New Criticism limit themselves in their search for a text's meaning to the 'words on the page'. Formalism is primarily interested in what makes literature different from other ways of using language and in the literary reasons for literary-historical change. Structuralism seeks to establish the structures that underlie narratives and that make meaning possible. Conspicuously absent is a serious interest in what many literary academics would now consider very important issues such as the *historical situatedness*, or historical embedment, and the *politics* of literary texts. To what extent is a literary text the product of the historical circumstances in which it was written? The world has gone through enormous socio-economic and political changes in the last millennium. Isn't it reasonable to expect those changes to turn up in our literature? And isn't it at least plausible to assume that those changes have somehow affected the way we experience things? Can the human condition have remained essentially the same? And what sort of view of politics do we find in a given text? Does the text support the socio-economic and political status quo or does it take an openly or more implicitly critical stance?

Before the late 1960s such questions were thought to be irrelevant or even detrimental to reading and to interpretation by the large majority of English and American literary academics. With

DOI: 10.4324/9781003373438-5

only a few exceptions, critics had not much use for historical context and even less for politics. In this chapter on literature and politics I will focus on three major modes of political criticism that became a forceful presence in Anglo-American literary studies in the course of the 1970s: Marxism, feminism, and criticism that concerns itself with racial relations. In Marxism criticism *social class* and *ideology* function as central instruments of analysis, in feminist criticism the concept of *gender* is the crucial critical (and political) instrument, while in criticism concerned with racial relations the fundamental category is of course *race*. I should point out that the 1960s-to-1980s version of these critical approaches, to which I will limit myself in this chapter, are by current standards rather traditional. It must be kept in mind that there are newer versions of these and other critical approaches which have assimilated the so-called *poststructuralist* thought that I will discuss in the next chapter, and which continue political criticism from somewhat different perspectives. For strategic reasons, which will become clear in my discussion of feminism, I will first discuss Marxist literary criticism.

THE POLITICS OF CLASS: MARXISM

To discuss Marxism in the early twenty-first century may well seem strangely beside the point. After all, since the fall of the Berlin Wall in 1989, one self-proclaimed Marxist regime after another has been forced to consign itself to oblivion. And the officially Marxist political parties that for a long time were a serious force in Western European politics have either disappeared or have become marginal. However, Marxism as an intellectual perspective provides a useful counter-balance to our propensity to see ourselves and the writers whom we read as completely divorced from socio-economic circumstances. It also counterbalances the related tendency to view the books and poems we read as originating in an autonomous mental realm, as the free products of free and independent minds.

Marxism's questioning of that freedom is now considerably less sensational than it was in the 1840s and 1850s when Karl Marx (1818–1883) began to outline what is now called Marxist philosophy, although it is still controversial enough. When he noted, in the Preface to his 1859 *A Contribution to the Critique of Political Economy*, that the 'mode of production of material life conditions the general process of social, political, and intellectual life', the Victorian upper class, if aware of this line of thought, would have been horrified, and they would have been outraged by the conclusion that followed: 'It is not the consciousness of men that determines their existence, but their social existence that determines their consciousness' (Marx 1970 [1859]: 3).

What does it mean that the 'mode of production' conditions 'the general process of social, political, and intellectual life'? If people have heard about Marxism, they usually know rather vaguely that it is about how your social circumstances determine much, if not all, of your life. This seems reasonable enough. If you work the night shift in your local McDonald's, for instance, you are unlikely to fly business class to New York City for a week in the Waldorf Astoria or to bid on the next Rembrandt that comes up for sale. But this sort of determinism is perfectly compatible with the idea that we are essentially free. Certain politicians would tell you to get an education, get rid of your provincial accent, buy the right outfit, and start exuding self-confidence. In other words, you have options, like everybody else, and all you have to do is to make the right choices and start moving up the social ladder.

This was not what Marx had in mind. Marxist theory argues that the way we think and the way we experience the world around us are either wholly or largely conditioned by the way the economy is organized. Under a medieval, feudal regime people will have thought and felt differently from the way we think and feel now, in a capitalist economy – that is, an economy in which goods are produced (the 'mode of production') by large concentrations of capital (old-style factories, new-style multinationals) and then sold in a free, competitive, market. The *base* of a society – the way its economy is organized, broadly speaking – determines its *superstructure* – everything that we might classify as belonging to the realm of culture, again in a broad sense: education, law, but also religion, philosophy, political programmes, and the arts.

This implies a view of literature that is completely at odds with the Anglo-American view of literature that goes back to Matthew Arnold. If the way we experience reality and the way we think about it (our religious, political, and philosophical views) are determined by the sort of economy we happen to live in, then clearly there is no such thing as an unchanging human condition.

On the contrary, with, for instance, the emergence of capitalism some centuries ago we may expect to find a new experience of reality and new views of the world. Since capitalism did not happen overnight, we will not find a clean break but we certainly should find a gradual transition to a new more-or-less collective perspective. The term 'collective' is important here. If the economic 'base' indeed determines the cultural 'superstructure', then writers will not have all that much freedom in their creative efforts. They will inevitably work within the framework dictated by the economic 'base'. Traditional Marxism, then, asserts that thought is subservient to, and follows, the material conditions under which it develops. Its outlook is *materialist*, as opposed to the *idealist* perspective, whose claim that the material world is basically subservient to thought is one of the fundamental assumptions of modern Western culture: we tend to assume that our thinking is free, unaffected by material circumstances. In our minds we can always be free. For Marxism, minds aren't free at all, they only think they are.

Capitalism, Marxism tells us, sees labourers in terms of production – as production units, as objects rather than as human beings. Labourers, as Marx himself said, must 'sell themselves' and are, essentially, 'a commodity'. By turning them into things, by *reifying* them, capitalism *alienates* them from themselves. However, this process of reification is not limited to labourers. The capitalist mode of production generates a view of the world – focused on profit – in which ultimately all of us function as objects and become alienated from ourselves.

IDEOLOGY

This leads inevitably to the question of how it is possible that we can be so blind to the real state of affairs around us and so terribly delude ourselves. It also leads to the question of how it is possible that apparently some people are *not* deluded. The answer given to this second question by one important movement within Marxism – so-called 'Western' Marxism – is that we always have a certain margin of freedom. To put that in the terms usually employed in the debates over issues such as freedom of action and thought: within Western Marxism there is room for human agency and subjective consciousness, that is, for action and thought that are not wholly determined by external forces. As a consequence, the super-structure – including, of course, literature and culture in general – also enjoys a certain measure of independence (a point that Marx also makes with regard to art). But to return to our (almost) collective delusion. For Marxism, we are blind to our own condition because of the effects of what it calls *ideology*. We should not confuse the Marxist use of 'ideology' with the way we often use the term: as referring to a set of beliefs that people *consciously* hold – beliefs of which they are aware and which they can articulate. We can for instance speak of the ideology of the free market – referring to a series of arguments that defend free enterprise against state intervention – and also of the communistic ideology that gave the state total control over produc-tion. For Marxists, however, the term is much more encompassing.

In Marxist usage, ideology is what causes us to misrepresent the world to ourselves. As I have just said, for Marxism the basis of any society is its economic organization, which then gives rise to certain social relations – for instance, the class relations between capitalists and workers in nineteenth-century capitalist economies. This socio-economic base then conditions the cultural superstructure. How-ever, there are forces at work that prevent us from seeing this: for instance, the liberal humanist idea that we are essentially free and can remain free as long as we can think. For Marxists, ideology is not so much a set of beliefs or assumptions that we are aware of – although most of them would include consciously held beliefs and assump-tions in their definition of the term – but, more importantly, that which makes us experience our life in a certain way and makes us believe that the way we see ourselves and the world is *natural*. In so doing, ideology distorts reality and falsely presents as natural and harmonious what is artificial and contradictory – the class differences that we find under capitalism, for instance. If we succumb to ideol-ogy, we live in an illusory world, in what in Marxists have often described as a state of *false consciousness*. As we will see later, the idea that we are blind to our own condition is in more than one way vitally important for literary studies.

How is ideology able to hide authentic reality from us? One very influential answer was given by the French Marxist philoso-pher Louis Althusser (1918–90). Althusser's first thesis regarding ideology is that 'Ideology represents the imaginary relationship of individuals to their real conditions of existence' (Althusser 2001 [1969]: 109), which roughly corresponds with what I have just said: ideology distorts our view of our true 'conditions of existence'. His second thesis connects ideology with its social sources. For Althusser ideology works through so-called 'ideological State apparatuses', which, although they may have their own sub-ideology, are all subject to the ruling ideology (from the Marxist perspective, the State is not neutral, but actively supports the capitalist order). Althusser's ideological State apparatuses include organized religion, the law, the political system, trade unions, the educational system, the media – in short, all the institutions through which we are socialized and all the other organizations that have in one way or another been coopted by those institutions. Ideology, then, has a *material* existence in the sense that it is embodied in all sorts of material practices. Althusser mentions some of the practices that are part of

> the *material existence of an ideological apparatus*, be it only a small part of that apparatus: a small mass in a small church, a funeral, a minor match at a sports club, a school day, a political party meeting, etc.
> (Althusser 2001 [1969]: 114)

Ideology is waiting for us wherever we go and everything we do and everything in which we engage is pervaded by ideology. This leads Althusser to the following conclusion: 'It therefore appears that the subject acts insofar as he is acted by the … system' (115). While we believe that we are acting out of free will, we are in reality 'acted by the system'. Within such a perspective there is, at best, little room for freedom.

How can ideology have such immense influence? To answer these questions Althusser draws on the writings of the French psychoanalyst Jacques Lacan (1901–1981), whose work I will discuss in more detail in the next chapter. For Lacan, the processes that we go through when we grow up leave us forever incomplete. Aware of that deep lack – although we cannot name it – and yearning for completion and for wholeness we turn to ideology, which constantly 'hails and interpellates' (addresses) us as 'concrete subjects' – as if we are whole already. In so doing, it may 'interpellate' us in the different social roles that we play, or, as Althusser would say, the different 'subject positions' that we occupy. One and the same woman could be 'interpellated' as a mother, as a member of a particular church, as a doctor, as a voter, and so on. The way ideology addresses us creates those subject positions for us; yet simultaneously those positions are already familiar to us because they are part of what we know. Ideology is not a set of political views, but offers a fundamental coherence and stability, tied up with a specific socio-economic order. Ideology invites us to accept an image of ourselves that is deeply tempting and because we want to be tempted it convinces us that we are whole and real, that we are the 'concrete subjects' we want to be. No wonder, then, that we see whatever ideology makes us see as natural, as belonging to the natural order of things.

At first sight, literature would seem to be on the side of ideology. Critics have for instance tried to show that the apparently objective realism of the mid-nineteenth-century English novel is not so objective at all. They argued that novels like Charlotte Brontë's *Jane Eyre* (1847) and George Eliot's *Middlemarch* (1871–1872), which present their characters as essentially free, even if not all of them make use of that freedom, 'hail' us just like ideology hails us. Such novels invite their readers to become part of a world that is essentially free and to look over the shoulders of people who make autonomous decisions. They create a specific subject position for their readers and give them the illusion that they, too, are free. Just like ideology, such novels give their readers the idea that they are complete: they make them believe that they are free agents, and in that way make them complicit in their own delusion. But that is not the whole story. As the British critic Frank Kermode once noted, 'texts can under Marxist analysis reveal a meaning not intended by their author' (Kermode 1988: 99). This 'theory of discrepancy', already hinted at by Marx himself and put to early use by the Marxist theorist Leon Trotsky in the 1930s, argues that a literary text, no matter how pervasively ideological it would seem to be, will always have cracks in that ideological façade that show a different reality underneath. I will return to that below.

HEGEMONY

Although Althusser's analysis led to valuable insights in the various ways in which literature can conspire with, and simultaneously deceive, its readers, a good many Marxist critics felt uneasy with the deterministic character of his view of ideology. As we have seen, Althusser would seem to leave very little room, or no room at all, for autonomous, non-ideological thought or action, even though in his scheme of things the economic 'base' did not directly determine the superstructure and its numerous institutions, but worked indirectly, through what he called the 'structure in dominance'. With the publication of the writings of the Italian Marxist Antonio Gramsci (1891–1937) in the early 1970s, a modified concept of ideology and of such a structure became available. Gramsci, writing in the 1930s, is fully aware of the power of ideology, which leads to '[t]he "spontaneous" consent given by the great masses of the population to the general direction imposed on social life by the dominant fundamental group' (Gramsci 1998 [1971]: 277). This consent is '"historically" caused by the prestige (and the consequent confidence) which the dominant group enjoys because of its position and function in the world of production' (277). Gramsci's explanation of the power of ideology has the merit of allowing us to resist what he calls the *hegemony* – the domination of a set of ruling beliefs and values through 'consent' rather than through 'coercive power'. Gramsci's 'hegemony' is far less inescapable than Althusser's ideology, even if it, too, establishes and maintains itself through 'civil society' and employs cultural means and institutions. Under hegemonic conditions the majority – usually a large majority – of a nation's citizens has so effectively internalized what the rulers want them to believe that they genuinely think that they are voicing their own opinion, but there is always room for dissent. Gramsci's hegemony, although it saturates society to the same extent as Althusser's ideology, is not airtight and waterproof. We can catch on to it and resist its workings with counterhegemonic actions even if we can never completely escape its all-pervasive influence.

In the United Kingdom, the important Marxist critic Raymond Williams (1921–1988) emphasized this aspect of Gramsci's thought. For Williams 'hegemony is not singular … its own internal structures are highly complex, and have continually to be renewed, recreated and defended … they can be continually challenged and in certain respects modified' (Williams 1996 [1980]: 22). Although the economic 'base' and its 'mode of production' are still important factors, the idea that the 'base' completely determines the cultural 'superstructure' is too simple: 'no mode of production, and therefore no dominant society or order of society, and therefore no dominant culture, in reality exhausts the full range of human practice, human energy, human intention' (26). Marxist critics who follow Williams's more flexible notion of ideology – such as the cultural materialists who I will discuss in Chapter 6 – see literature as an important vehicle for ideology, but are very attentive to the dissenting voices and views that literature may also present.

MARXIST LITERARY STUDIES

This discussion of ideology and hegemony will have made clear that a Marxist perspective leads to an approach to literature that is significantly different from the approaches I have discussed so far. As we have just seen, Marxists may differ on the extent to which the cultural superstructure is determined by the socio-economic base. All Marxist critics agree, however, that in the study of literature the social dimension is absolutely indispensable. Writers can never completely escape ideology and their social background and so the social reality of the writer will always be part of the text.

A central question in Marxist approaches to literature concerns the reliability of literary texts as social 'evidence'. If Charles Dickens's *Great Expectations* (1860–1861) and George Eliot's *Middlemarch* (1871–1872) are conditioned by the capitalist society of Victorian England, what then are we going to find in these novels: a true picture of Victorian England, or an ideologically distorted reflection? In short, is it possible for writers, or for literary texts – this is a crucial distinction, as we will see – to offer objective insights (as Marxists see them): to present history as a struggle between antagonistic classes for economic and social gains and to present contemporary reality in that light?

Over time, Marxist critics have given different answers to this question, although most have been inspired by the notion that the meaning of a literary work must be seen as independent of the political (and ideologically coloured) views of its author. This by now familiar strategy of separating text and author does, however, not separate the text from social reality (as the formalists and the literary structuralists did). On the contrary, the idea is that if we remove the author from the picture – or at least the author's political views – we might get an even better picture of the real world of class conflicts and political tension. This idea has the great merit that it allows Marxist critics to read the work of even the most reactionary authors against the grain of their political views so that their work, too, can be appreciated from a Marxist perspective. The Hungarian critic George Lukács (1885–1971), the most prominent Marxist critic of the inter-war period, holds for instance the novels of Walter Scott, the French writer Honoré de Balzac (1799–1850), and the Russian Leo Tolstoy (1828–1910), none of them known for progressive views, in high regard. In fact, Lukács vastly prefers the panoramic novels of such conservative writers to the fragmentary avant-garde products of the sometimes fiercely leftist artists of the 1920s because it is only in the wide-ranging panorama, and in the merging of individual life stories with the larger movements of history, that the reader is confronted with the historical truth. The work of art must 'reflect correctly and in proper proportion all important factors objectively determining the area of life it represents', and it must, moreover, 'so reflect these that this area of life becomes comprehensible from within and from without, re-experienceable' (Lukács 1970 [1954]: 30). And great literary art succeeds in doing this:

> Achilles and Werther, Oedipus and Tom Jones, Antigone and Anna Karenina: their individual existence ... cannot be distinguished from their social and historical environment. Their human significance, their specific individuality cannot be separated from the context in which they were created.
>
> (Lukács 1972 [1957]: 476)

The narratives in which these characters appear are to some extent independent of their authors' political convictions and accurately reflect historical reality. They effectively overcome their authors' ideological limitations and they do so because they offer a total overview of all the social forces involved, approaching the dialectical thinking in terms of the total social process that Marxism demands.

For the British and American Marxist critics of the 1970s and 1980s, usually influenced by Althusser and his grim view of an enormously powerful ideology, literary texts do not so easily allow us a view of an undistorted reality. I have already mentioned that, following Althusser, critics sought to demonstrate that the great realistic novels of the nineteenth century, just like ideology, address ('hail') their readers and make them complicit in their own ideological delusion. Ideology is seen as such a strong presence in the text that we more or less have to break down its resistance to get at a truer picture of the reality the text pretends to present. However, rather surprisingly, the text itself facilitates that process. As Althusser said in 'A Letter on Art in Reply to André Daspre', which also addresses literature, 'art makes us *see* ... the ideology from which it is born, in which it bathes, from which it detaches itself as art, and to which it *alludes*' (Althusser 2001 [1966]: 152). An important influence on critics of the period (especially British ones) was the French critic Pierre Macherey's *A Theory of Literary Production* (1966; translated in 1978). For Macherey literary works are pervaded by ideology. So in order to get beyond a text's ideological dimension we will have to begin with the cracks in its façade, with those sites where the text is not fully in control of itself (a lack of control summarized in the title of one of Macherey's later essays: 'The Text Says What It Does Not Say'). In order to expose a text's ideology, interpretation must paradoxically focus on what the text does *not* say, on what the text *represses* rather than *expresses*. We find what the text does *not* say in gaps, in silences where what might have been said remains unarticulated, and in 'disparities which point to a conflict of meaning'. Literature, as Macherey puts it, *reveals* the vulnerability of ideology (see Macherey 1978: 59–60). Putting the text on the psychoanalyst's couch, we must probe '*the unconscious of the work* (not the author)' (92), an unconscious to which it has consigned what it cannot say because of ideological repression. Macherey finds the cracks in the text not in its major themes, which are fully controlled by ideology, but in textual elements that are only tangentially related to the main theme (or themes), in the text's 'margins'. Here is where we see ideology, with its suppression of contradiction and exclusion of what is undesirable, actually at work. And since in a literary text the work of ideology is never completely successful, we will find 'the inscription of an *otherness* in the work'. Literary criticism then 'brings out a *difference* within the work by demonstrating that it is *other than it is*' (78).

This leads to a way of reading literature that is completely different from that of the English and American critics of the 1920s and beyond whom I discussed in the first chapter. Macherey and like-minded critics in the United Kingdom, such as Terry Eagleton, were not interested in what makes a text coherent but in what makes it incoherent, in what does not fit or is absent for obscure reasons (see for instance Eagleton's analyses of a number of canonical texts in his *Criticism and Ideology* of 1976).

Let us have a brief look at the British critic Catherine Belsey's Macherey-inspired reading of a number of Sherlock Holmes stories in her *Critical Practice* (1980). Their author, Arthur Conan Doyle (1859–1930), presents his detective hero as unerringly penetrating, a man gifted with a brain that can solve any riddle. The 'project' of these stories – to make everything subject to scientific analysis, as Belsey puts it – would seem to promise a true and unflinching picture of reality. However, if we look closely at the reality that the stories present, we see that their presentation of the real world is strangely deficient. As Belsey demonstrates, the women in these stories and their social position are not subjected to analysis at all. They remain mysterious and opaque. The silence of these stories with regard to their female characters reveals the working of a patriarchal ideology in which the males take centre stage and the women are taken for granted. They may at best provide an occasion for Holmes's intellect to dazzle us.

This may well raise a question: do we need a theoretical concept like ideology to find what other readers might have discovered without its help? In fact, Macherey's own analyses of the fiction of Jules Verne raise the same question. However, we should not underrate the added value of this approach. Whereas a more traditional critic might suppose that in the Holmes example we are dealing with a personal blindness or an unwillingness on the part of the author to present a truer picture of late-nineteenth-century or early-twentieth-century reality, for Marxist critics the omission is not personal at all, but points directly to an impersonal cluster of beliefs and values with an immense social influence. It is this ideology that is the real target of literary investigation, and the aim in this particular case is not to show up Doyle's personal shortcomings, but the differences between ideology and the real world. Through the politics of the text – its ideological dimension – Marxist criticism addresses the politics of the world outside the text.

BAKHTIN

Although perhaps more formalist than Marxist, the work of the Russian critic Mikhail Bakhtin (1895–1975) has more links with the discussion above than with the formalism and structuralism discussed in earlier chapters. Moreover, Bakhtin's work came to the English-speaking world very late, long after its publication in Russian, and was absorbed into the exchanges on literary theory as they then took place. In his first book to be published in English, *Rabelais and His World* (written in the early 1940s and first translated in 1968), Bakhtin argues that in the fiction of the French writer François Rabelais (1494?–1553) we find an opposition between a folk culture characterized by spontaneity and laughter, in the spirit of carnival, and an official culture that in both its religious manifestation (the church) and in its worldly ones (the period's feudal institutions) was not only repressive but also essentially life-denying in its negative attitude towards the bodily functions that folk culture did not work hard to hide from sight. Seeing the annual carnival as the epitome of folk culture, Bakhtin celebrated the 'carnivalesque' in Rabelais, and in early modern culture in general. His positive valuation of the carnivalesque was picked up especially by those critics who saw its potential as a site of resistance against contemporary forms of repression, in particular patriarchy (see below) and the reign of consumer capitalism. These critics found instances of a carnivalesque undermining of (male) authority – an undermining from below through comic reversals or outright laughter – in a wide range of texts.

Bakhtin's seminal contribution to contemporary literary theory, the essay 'Discourse in the Novel', dates from the early 1930s but remained virtually unknown in the English-speaking world until it was published in *The Dialogic Imagination: Four Essays* of 1981. In 'Discourse' Bakhtin argues that the novel, as a literary genre, is inherently plural, that is, always presents a plurality of 'voices'. Since novels with only a single character are exceedingly rare this seems fairly self-evident. But that is not what Bakhtin has in mind. The presence of a variety of characters who all articulate themselves in different ways is 'a mere diversity of voices', not the 'heteroglossia' that is his real interest here. For Bakhtin, a natural language – Russian, English, etc. – is not a seamless unity but a compound of a large number of 'languages': 'social dialects, character-istic group behavior, professional jargons, generic languages, languages of generations ... languages of the authorities, of various circles and of passing fashions' (Bakhtin 1981: 263). And all of these 'social and his-torical voices populating language, all its words and all its forms ... are organized in the novel into a structural stylistic system that expresses the differential socio-ideological position of the author and the hetero-glossia of the epoch' (300). Unlike poetry, in which he sees a unity of style, the novel – '[e]very novel' – is 'a *hybrid*', even if it is 'an inten-tional and conscious hybrid, one artistically organized' (366). Whatever the intention of their authors, novels are arenas, sites where diverse and often competing discourses and ideologies live together in a not necessarily peaceful coexistence. Language itself – every word, every phrase – comes laden with a history that testifies to this. Whatever 'object' language wants to address is 'already as it were overlain with qualifications, open to dispute, charged with value ... It is entangled, shot through with shared thoughts, points of view, alien value judg-ments and accents. The word, directed toward its object, enters a dia-logically agitated and tension-filled environment' (276–277).

When 'Discourse in the Novel' found its way into the debate on lit-erary theory, in the early 1980s, it was immediately harnessed to the cause of the poststructuralist 'decentring' (see the next chapter) that had by then become the hottest topic in literary criticism (especially Amer-ican literary criticism). But compared to the views of, say, Roland Barthes or Jacques Derrida, Bakhtin's 'dialogism' is, as we will see, fairly traditional, even if it offered new insights in the social and historical dimensions of language and the specific character of fiction. For Bakhtin the novel still constitutes a unity kept together through intentional artistic organization. It is a work of art whose creation 'demands enor-mous effort: it is stylized through and through, thoroughly pre-meditated, achieved, distanced' (Bakhtin 1981: 366). To stress this may seem unnecessary, even puzzling, but the following chapters will make clear why it makes sense to emphasize that Bakhtin's work belongs with the more traditional criticism that has been discussed so far.

THE POLITICS OF GENDER: FEMINISM

It is now obvious that it does not make much sense to consider the literature that over the ages has been produced by female writers without taking into account the social realities that female authors have had to face. For one thing, for a very long period women were not really supposed to get an education. It is of course possible to become a writer without a formal education – a fortunate circumstance to which we owe a number of great women writers – but clearly the odds are against members of any group that is discriminated against in this way. The work of female writers has so obviously been under a number of serious historical constraints that it is now hard to understand why the odds they faced were virtually ignored in literary discussions (except by some of these writers themselves: Virginia Woolf, for instance). The answer surely has to do with the general blindness of (male-dominated) Western culture to its treatment of women as second-rate citizens. Moreover, as long as within literary studies interest was virtually limited to the 'words on the page' (Richards, Leavis, the New Criticism), to the underlying structures that made literary meaning possible (the French structuralists), or to ideology and the class struggle as mediated through literary texts (traditional Marxist criticism), the plight of women writers drew little attention.

Most critics now believe that it is impossible to cordon off a given field of interest or study neatly from the rest of the world. For better or for worse, everything seems somehow related to everything else. With regard to the social position of women, and therefore also with regard to the field of female writing, that view is to a large extent due to the feminist movement that began to gain momentum in the course of the 1960s. Curiously, even Marxism, with its wide-ranging historical theorizing, had largely ignored the position of women. With hindsight, this oversight is all the more incomprehensible since some of its key concepts – the struggle between social classes, the blinding effects of ideology – might have been employed to analyse the social situation of women.

The feminist movement, then, put socio-historical circumstances as a determining factor in the production of literature firmly on the map. Feminism was right from the beginning involved in literary studies, and for good reasons. Kate Millett's trailblazing *Sexual Politics* of 1970, for instance, devotes long chapters to the attitudes towards women that pervade the work of prominent twentieth-century authors such as D.H. Lawrence (1885–1930) and Henry Miller (1891–1980). Both were held in high regard by many critics for their daring and liberating depictions of erotic relations. Millett, however, showed that the attitude of their male characters towards women was not emancipated at all: most of the male characters that she examined – and especially those of Miller – were denigrating, exploitative, and repressive in their relations with women. Feminism saw very clearly that the widespread negative stereotyping of women in literature and film (not to mention the internet) constituted a formidable obstacle on the road to true equality. At least as important is that in the work of the male writers she discusses Millett finds a relationship between sex and power in which the distribution of power over the male and female partners mirrors the distribution of power over males and females in society at large. In other words, in terms of power, acts that we usually think of as completely private turn out to be extensions of the public sphere. The private and the public cannot be seen as wholly separate – on the contrary, they are intimately linked. Since this is the case, Millett argues, the private sphere is, just like the public realm, thoroughly political: it is a political arena where the same power-based relations exist as in the public world. Feminism and feminist criticism are profoundly political in claiming that the personal and the political cannot be separated. They are also political in the more traditional sense of trying to intervene in the social order with a programme that aims to change existing social conditions. Feminism seeks to change the power relations between men and women that prevail under what in the late 1960s and the 1970s came to be called *patriarchy*, a term that referred to the (almost) complete domination of men in Western society (and beyond).

FEMINIST LITERARY STUDIES

In its first phase, feminist literary studies focused on 'the woman as reader' and on 'the woman as writer'. The American feminist critic Elaine Showalter, from whom I am borrowing these formulations, put it as follows in her 1979 essay 'Towards a Feminist Poetics':

> The first type is concerned with ... woman as the consumer of male-produced literature, and with the way in which the hypothesis of a female reader changes our apprehension of a given text, awakening us to the significance of its sexual codes. ... Its subjects include

images and stereotypes of women in literature, the omissions of and misconceptions about women in criticism, and the fissures in male-constructed literary history.

(Showalter 1985: 128)

When feminist criticism focuses on 'the woman as writer' it concerns itself with

woman as the producer of textual meaning, with the history, genres and structures of literatures by women. Its subjects include the psychodynamics of female creativity; linguistics and the problem of female language; the trajectory of the individual or collective literary career; literary history; and, of course, studies of particular writers and works.

(Showalter 1985: 128)

The first type of feminist criticism asks questions of the following kind. What sort of roles did female characters play? With what sort of themes were they associated? What are the implicit presuppositions of a given text with regard to its readers? (Upon closer inspection many texts clearly assume that their readers are male – just like those commercials in which fast cars are presented by seductive young women.) Feminist critics showed how often literary representations of women repeated familiar cultural stereotypes. Such stereotypes included the woman – fast car or not – as an immoral and dangerous seductress, the woman as eternally dissatisfied shrew, the woman as cute but essentially helpless child, the woman as unworldly, self-sacrificing angel, and so on. Since the way female characters were routinely portrayed had not much in common with the way feminist critics saw and experienced themselves, these characters clearly were *constructions*, put together – not necessarily by the writers who presented them, but by the culture they belonged to – to serve a not-so-hidden purpose. If we look at the four examples I have given we see immediately that female independence (in the seductress and the shrew) gets a strongly negative connotation, while helplessness and renouncing all ambition are presented as endearing and admirable. The message is that dependence leads to indulgence and reverence while independence leads to dislike and rejection. The desired effect – of which the writer clearly need not be aware – is a perpetuation of the unequal power relations between men and women.

GENDER

To put what I have just sketched in somewhat different terms: this type of feminist criticism leads to a thorough examination of *gender* roles. Gender has to do not with how females (and males) really are, but with the way that a given culture or subculture sees them, how they are culturally *constructed*. To say that women have two breasts is to say something about their biological nature, to say something about what it is to be a female; to say that women are naturally timid, or sweet, or intuitive, or dependent, or self-pitying, is to construct a role for them. It tells us how the speaker wants to see them. What traditionally has been called 'feminine', then, is a cultural construction, a *gender* role that has been culturally assigned to countless generations of women. The same holds for masculinity, with its connotations of strength, rationality, stoicism, and self-reliance. Like femininity, traditional masculinity is a gender role that has far less to do with actual males than with the wishful thinking projected on to the heroes of Westerns, hard-boiled private eyes, and British secret agents. Masculinity, too, is a cultural construction. We can see this, for instance, in one of the traditional representations of homosexuality, in which maleness and masculinity are uncoupled. Although homosexuals are male, they are often portrayed as feminine, that is, as lacking masculinity.

Feminism, then, has right from the beginning focused on gender because a thorough revision of gender roles seemed the most effective way of changing the power relations between men and women. Since no one in their right mind will want to give serious power to a person who must be timid, dependent, irrational, and self-pitying because she is a woman, the effort to purge the culture of such gendered stereotyping is absolutely crucial. Feminism has politicized gender – by showing its constructed nature – and put it firmly on the agenda. Moreover, after its initial focus on the gendered representation of women (and men) in Western culture, it has very effectively widened the issue and shown how often seemingly neutral references, descriptions, or definitions are in fact gendered, and usually according to the same pattern. A masculine gendering is supposed to evoke positive connotations, a feminine gendering is supposed to evoke negative ones. Feminism has shown how this binary opposition is pervasively present in the way we think about nature, emotion, science, action (or non-action), art, and so on.

THE WOMAN AS WRITER

The textual focus that we find in studies of how literary representations of women are gendered also characterizes attempts to establish a specifically female tradition – or specifically female traditions – in writing by women. A famous example with regard to the specificity of nineteenth-century female writing is Sandra Gilbert and Susan Gubar's *The Madwoman in the Attic: The Woman Writer and the Nineteenth-Century Literary Imagination* (1979). For Gilbert and Gubar the restrictions – social and otherwise – that a nineteenth-century female writer faced led to 'an obsessive interest in these limited options'. In the work of these writers that interest expressed itself in an 'obsessive imagery of confinement that reveals the ways in which female artists feel trapped and sickened both by suffocating alternatives and by the culture that had created them' (Gilbert and Gubar 1979: 64). An example is 'the madwoman in the attic' of Gilbert and Gubar's title: the supposedly mad wife that Jane's employer and future husband Rochester keeps locked in the attic in Charlotte Brontë's *Jane Eyre* (1847). Not surprisingly, the attempt to establish a female literary tradition fairly soon led to calls for a specifically female form of literary studies, for ways of reading and theorizing that could tell us how typically female experience has over the ages been reflected in literature written by women.

Female literary studies focused on specifically female themes, genres, even styles, but also on the origins and development of larger female traditions. The female focus of this search for a female literary tradition has greatly benefited literary studies in general. It has rediscovered forgotten female authors, has rehabilitated ignored ones, and, in its efforts to let women speak for themselves unearthed much writing of a personal nature, such as letters, travel journals, and diaries, that has contributed to a redefinition and expansion of the literary field. Feminism has expanded the canon, has rediscovered such forgotten genres as that of the 'sentimental', domestic novel, and, within the larger literary tradition, constructed a dynamic canon of writing by women.

The rediscovery and rehabilitation of authors raises the question of why they had disappeared from sight in the first place. What had eliminated these women writers from the race to lasting literary fame? At first sight the answer is obvious: reviewers and critics must have found their work lacking in quality, as not up to the standards required for admission to the literary pantheon. But that leads to further questions: what exactly were those standards, who had established them, and who were the people who put the work of these female writers to the test? There is an easy general answer to the last two questions: male critics and male reviewers. And so another issue suggests itself: could maleness have been a factor in literary judgments in general? Is it possible that the whole issue of literary value is in some way gendered? Couldn't for instance T.S. Eliot's preference for impersonality, for irony, and for a sort of stoic resignation be seen as typically masculine instead of as generally valid? Couldn't it be possible that the odds have been against female writing all along, not only with regard to opportunities for writing but also with regard to that writing's evaluation? Under the pressure of feminist scrutiny reviewers, critics, and literary academics have been forced to recognize their masculinist prejudices and have, for instance, accepted forms of literary criticism in which the personal experience of the (female) critic is brought to bear upon a text in order to illuminate passages that might otherwise remain obscure.

For the defenders of impersonality in literary matters such practices are downright irresponsible – if not typically feminine, too. Feminism has been hard on the impersonalists. In their use of autobiographical material, female academics have followed a trend set earlier by female writers such as the American poets Sylvia Plath (1932–1963) and Adrienne Rich (1929–2012). Since the mid-1960s women writers, drawing on their personal experiences, have increasingly brought female sexuality, female anguish, childbirth, mothering, rape, and other specifically female themes into their work. Still, the feminist criticism and writing that I have so far discussed are in some ways fairly traditional, for instance in their view of the subject. In this (mostly American) feminist criticism of the 1970s and 1980s the female subject, like its male counterpart, is essentially free and autonomous. Once the social and cultural restraints on women have been lifted, women will be as self-determining as men. Moreover, in its earlier stages this feminism assumes that it speaks for all women, regardless of culture, class, and race. This is undeniably more modest than liberal humanism's (male) assumption that it speaks for all of humankind, but it still ignores the often rather different experience of women who, unlike virtually all early feminists, are not white, heterosexual, and middle class. As early as 1977 the African-American critic Barbara Smith argued that Black women writers were ignored by academic feminism ('Towards a Black Feminist Criticism'). In the wake of Smith's article and of bell hooks's acclaimed *Ain't I a Woman? Black Women and Feminism* (1981) more and more groups of women – African-American women, Chicana women, lesbian woman – began to assert identities of their own and to create separate feminist literary traditions. Smith had in 1977 already taken that initiative with regard to Black female writing, arguing that writers like Zora Neale Hurston, Alice Walker, and Toni Morrison presented Black women who with their folk memories, their special skills, and their intimacy with the natural world were clearly distinct from white women. As a result of these developments American feminism and the feminist literary studies that it had produced began to fragment along lines of ethnic and sexual identity, while its liberalist perspective was also submitted to severe critique.

MARXIST FEMINISM

A similar fragmentation would ultimately destabilize a specifically British offshoot of feminism: Marxist feminism. From a Marxist perspective, history is dominated by a struggle between social classes that will end only when a truly classless society has been achieved. Given the fact that throughout history women have been collectively denied important rights, it was almost inevitable that a Marxist feminism would emerge that saw women as constituting a seriously underprivileged class. Moreover, many Marxist concepts, especially as these were redefined by Louis Althusser, seemed greatly relevant. In particular Althusser's definition of ideology and his concept of *interpellation*, which explains how ideology addresses us in a certain role and draws us into a conspiracy that is ultimately aimed at ourselves, proved useful for feminist literary studies and film studies. As we have seen, for Althusser we experience ourselves as complete and whole individuals ('concrete subjects') only through the internalization of ideology. Althusserian feminism examines how literary texts, films, or commercials 'hail and interpellate' their readers or their audience and 'position' them with regard to gender. Into what position does a text, a film, a rock video, or a commercial try to manoeuvre us through specific strategies of narration, specific shots, and other forms of representation? How does it persuade a female audience to accept a liberal humanist ideology that so clearly disadvantages them? But Althusserian feminism is by no means the whole story. We also find a British Marxist feminism that, in Ruth Robbins's words,

> is interested in the material conditions of real people's lives, how conditions such as poverty and undereducation produce different signifying systems than works produced and read in conditions of privilege and educational plenty. This kind of approach is likely to be most interested in the content of a literary text as symptomatic of the conditions of its production.
>
> (Robbins 2000: 13)

However, after its heyday in the early 1980s, Marxist feminism, too, was increasingly charged with being insensitive to *difference*, and came to be seen as the product of a white academic elite (with its standard middle-class background) and as unacceptably neglectful of the specific social problems – and the way these had been given literary expression – of women who did not belong to the white heterosexual middle class. Black Marxist feminists, for instance, were quick to point out that Black female writers had to cope not only with biases based on gender, but also with an equally crippling racial bias and that an approach that failed to take race into account would never be able to do justice to their work.

THE POLITICS OF RACE

This takes us to a third instrument of analysis that we must look at: that of race. Until the twentieth century, the literatures written in the various Western languages were overwhelmingly the product of white writers, male and female. That picture began to change in the period between the two world wars. In the 1920s African-American writing, flowering in the so-called 'Harlem Renaissance', became almost overnight a permanent force within the field of US literature, and in the1930s and 1940s writers hailing from France's African and Caribbean colonies became a presence on the French literary scene. With the emergence of a Black literary presence race entered the agenda of literary studies. In one sense it also entered literature itself − in the sense that it was now presented from the perspective of non-white writers. Racial discrimination is a recurrent theme in African-American writing, from the fiction and poetry of the Harlem Renaissance, via Ralph Ellison's *Invisible Man* (1952), whose theme is that racial prejudice makes Black people invisible as individuals, to the novels of the Nobel Prize-winning (1993) Toni Morrison. In another sense, however, race was not a new theme at all but had been there all along. As we will see in Chapter 7, race seen through the eyes of Western writers had always been part of Western literature but its presence had gone largely unnoticed, at least by Western readers.

With the idea of *négritude* − which might be translated as 'Blackness' − French-speaking Black writers like Aimé Césaire (originally from Martinique) and Léopold Senghor (from Senegal) in the 1940s and 1950s introduced and developed the idea that literature written by Africans was not merely thematically different from Western literature (in its emphasis on race), but that it was *intrinsically* different because Africans, no matter where they lived, were different from whites. 'Négritude' has been variously defined − at one point Senghor equates it with 'feeling', at another he sees it in terms of a reverent attitude towards life and a desire to find harmony in an integration with the cosmos − and has been severely criticized by African and African-American writers. But the Harlem Renaissance and the development of 'négritude' mark the beginnings of African-American and African or, as the case may be, Caribbean self-definition in the face of a Western racism and of a Western system of colonial oppression that had denied (and continued to deny) substance and validity to non-white cultures and cultural expressions, all of which were considered far inferior to the great achievements of Western culture. Inevitably, that process of self-definition involves a critique of Western representations of Africans and African-Americans, representations that usually repeat the stereotypes that have, for instance, legitimized colonization. That self-definition and the critique of Western representations stand at the beginning of the interrogation and

contestation of Europe's colonial enterprise and its legacy that is
now called postcolonial studies, a relatively new field of literary,
cultural, and political enquiry that will be discussed in Chapter 7.

The mordant critique of colonialism that we find in the 'négritude'
movement — in his *Discourse on Colonialism* we find Césaire stating
that Adolf Hitler already spoke through those who defended colonial
oppression and exploitation (Césaire 1997 [1955]: 79) — found a
highly articulate and influential supporter in Frantz Fanon
(1925–1961), a psychiatrist from Martinique who became
involved in the Algerian resistance to French colonialism. Fanon
merits attention here not only because he called attention to the
debilitating psychological effects of colonialism upon the colonized,
which is a major theme in postcolonial studies, but also because in
The Wretched of the Earth (originally published in French in 1961)
he outlines a theory of what we might call colonial literature —
that is, the literature of the colonized. In that theory he distances
himself from 'négritude'. The idea that all Black people would
have essential features in common, for him mirrors the homo-
genization that Black people have always suffered at the hands of
white culture: 'The Negroes of Chicago only resemble the
Nigerians or the Tanganyikans in so far as they were all defined in
relation to the whites' (Fanon 1963 [1961]: 216). Instead of a
homogeneous 'négritude', he stresses the importance of national
culture for 'the native intellectual'. Fanon distinguishes three phases
in the cultural — including the literary — relations between colonized and colonizer. In the first phase the native intellectual takes
pride in demonstrating that 'he has assimilated' — that is mastered —
'the culture of the occupying power'. In the second phase, 'the
native is disturbed; he decides to remember what he is' (222). He
goes back to his own people, immerses himself in the native culture, and the 'rhyming poetry' of the first phase gives way to 'the
poetic tom-tom's rhythms' (226). In the third phase, the 'fighting
phase', the intellectual and the writer will break out of this
immersion and turn into 'an awakener of the people' and will
produce a 'fighting literature, a revolutionary literature, and a
national literature' (223). For Fanon, writing in 1961 — when
much of Africa was still under colonial rule — national cultures and
literatures play a crucial role in the process of liberation. The
poststructuralist theorizing which emerges in the 1970s and the

postcolonial theory which then follows in the 1980s are hesitant about the merits of the idea of 'nation', of the so-called nation-state which they often associate with forms of oppression. In the historical context in which Fanon is writing, however, the sort of revolutionary nationalism and the corresponding national culture that he has in mind seem almost inevitable, if only for the 'psycho-affective equilibrium' of the colonized.

Fanon's view of the differentiation of African writing – which is united only in its desire to resist colonialism – has set the tone for later theories of African, Caribbean, and African-American writing. Abandoning the idea of a Pan-African cultural identity which is shared by all African peoples and the African diaspora in the Americas, critics have emphasized the specific identities of all the various literatures that Black writers have created. The Caribbean mixture of languages and populations has, for instance, led a number of Caribbean writers to try to theorize Caribbean literature in terms of cross-cultural exchanges. Writers such as the Guyanese novelist Wilson Harris and the Barbadian poet Edward Brathwaite have argued that the literature of the region must be seen as the product of interlocking cultural traditions, of 'creolization' as Brathwaite called it in his 1974 *Contradictory Omens: Cultural Diversity and Integration in the Caribbean*, a study in which he argued that various Black and white cultures, and, to a lesser extent, Indian and Chinese cultures have in a continuous process of exchange created a Caribbean identity and culture. In the later 1980s and 1990s the 'hybridity' that is the result of such processes would become a major theme in postcolonial studies.

AFRICAN-AMERICAN LITERARY STUDIES

The development of African-American criticism, which emerged after the mid-1960s when Black studies entered the university curriculum and when the so-called Black Arts movement got under way, to some extent runs parallel to that of feminist literary criticism. A major objective was to rediscover and rehabilitate forgotten African-American writers – that is, to have them recognized as serious contributors to the American literary heritage. A second objective was to establish a specifically African-American literary tradition, a tradition that formally distinguished itself from white

American writing. The recovery and promotion of forgotten or neglected writers has been successful: all anthologies of American literature now present many African-American writers who were absent from their pre-1980s editions. But the search for a specific African-American literary aesthetic has led to perhaps less definitive results. Although we do now indeed speak of an African-American literary tradition, the question of how this tradition hangs together is still debated. What many African-American texts have in common is the overriding theme of racial discrimination, but it less easy to say what they have in common in terms of form rather than theme.

In the 1960s the Black Arts movement, in the spirit of *négritude*, posited a 'Black aesthetic' that expressed a Pan-African, organic and *whole* sensibility. Led by important writers such as the poet and playwright Amiri Baraka, it focused on creative and political writing and on political intervention through theatrical and other performances. Around the mid-1970s, African-American literary academics began to turn from sensibility to form and to seek the 'Blackness' of African-American literature in its specific strategies and use of language. (The idea that African-American literature could be formally distinct from white American literature is not implausible: if we look at the American music scene we immediately recognize musical forms and genres that are distinctly African-American or that derive from African-American sources.) A number of critics, the most prominent of whom is Henry Louis Gates, Jr, began, in Gates's words, 'to chart the patterns of repetition and revision among texts by black authors'. Gates continues: 'Accordingly, many black authors read and revise one another, address similar themes, and repeat the cultural and linguistic codes of a common symbolic geographic. For these reasons, we can think of them as forming literary traditions' (Gates 1992: 30).

This approach, which combines thematic and formal interests, has in Gates's hands been productive. Central to African-American writing is this practice of repetition and revision which Gates calls 'signifyin(g)', a term which refers to the trickster figure of the 'signifying monkey' of African-American – and more generally African – folktales. A 'black text echoes, mirrors, repeats, revives, or responds to in various formal ways' a textual world of other Black texts. 'Signifiyin(g)' is 'this process of intertextual relation ... the troped revision, of repetition and difference' (Gates 1987: 2).

In the Black vernacular tradition 'signifying' has a range of meanings related to the trickster aspect of this 'signifying monkey'. In African-American culture in general, Gates tells us, 'black rhetorical tropes, subsumed under signifying, would include marking, loud-talking, testifying, calling out (of one's name), sounding, rapping, playing the dozens, and so on' (Gates 1998 [1989]: 904). 'The dozens' – a form of verbal duelling that is an ultimately affectionate exchange of ingenious insults – illustrates Gates's argument that '[t]he Afro-American rhetorical strategy of signifying is a rhetorical act that is not engaged in the game of information giving' (905). Tracing this particular practice to the oral roots of African and African-American literature – in which verbal skills were of course paramount – Gates sees in the 'dozens' one of the elements that are reworked time and again by Black writers, just like Black musicians borrow riffs from each other and from earlier generations of musicians and rework them. The example of 'the dozens' and the trickster connotation of signifying should not create the impression that we find the practice of signifying only in contexts that are ultimately not very serious. The poet T. Tenton Fortune's poem 'The Black Man's Burden', which for Gates 'signif[ies] … upon Kipling's "White Man's Burden"' (908) – the white race's 'duty' to bring 'civilization' to other peoples through colonial rule – sufficiently demonstrates the seriousness of signifying: 'What is the Black Man's Burden / Ye Gentile parasites / Who crush and rob your brother / Of his manhood and his rights?' (For a book-length discussion of 'signifyin(g)' practices see Gates 1988).

Beginning in the 1980s, we also find another major line of inquiry for African-American criticism: what we might call the *construction* of Blackness, the ways in which the dominant white culture and its literary products had over the ages *constructed* Black males and females as different from their white counterparts. Just like women had to live up to the feminine gender roles created by a male-dominated society, Black males and females were confronted with the cultural demands implied by the constructions of Black maleness and Black femaleness that white society imposed upon them. By means of these constructions, white society practically forced Black males and females to live up to the stereotypes that it had itself created. In order to acquire insight into the nature of these highly discriminatory social constructs, African-American criticism analysed representations of Black characters – and of Blackness in general – in 'white' literature (or in Jewish-American literature, as in Bernard Malamud's *The Tenants* of 1971, in a which a Jewish and an African-American writer entertain a volatile relationship in a condemned and otherwise deserted New York tenement).

Like the more traditional forms of feminist criticism, until the 1980s African-American criticism worked with a view of the subject that was not really different from that of white, liberal humanist, criticism. Although far more sensitive to social constraints – and particularly those of race and class – than the average white critic, Black critics, too, saw the subject – Black or white – as an autonomous moral agent, able to transcend the limitations imposed by time, place, and colour. Marxist critics once again were the exception. From a Marxist perspective, the relations between the white majority and the Black minority could be rewritten in terms of class relations, with the Black minority kept subservient by ideology. In a brief discussion of Alice Walker's famous novel *The Color Purple*, bell hooks argues that the novel's heroine, who ends as a successful entrepreneur, stays within an individualist, capitalist framework: 'Breaking free from the patriarchal prison that is her "home" when the novel begins, she creates her own household, yet radical politics of collective struggle against racism or sexism do not inform her struggle for self-actualization' (hooks 1997 [1992]: 222). Like feminism, African-American criticism was strongly affected by the emphasis on difference that emerged in the course of the 1980s. African-American feminists came to see it as male-dominated and focused on specifically male issues, and increasingly pursued their feminist agenda, only to find, like the white feminists, that further fragmentation – for instance lesbians pursuing again another agenda – waited down the line.

SUGGESTIONS FOR FURTHER READING

MARXIST CRITICISM

Raymond Williams's *Marxism and Literature* (1977) shows us a very influential Marxist critic in action. Arguing that we must see literature in 'material' terms, Williams elucidates not only the basic Marxist notions, but also Gramsci's 'hegemony' and his own notion of 'structures of feeling'. In *Marxism and Literary History* (1986) John Frow examines the literary criticism of such prominent Marxist critics as Pierre Macherey, Terry Eagleton and Fredric Jameson. Eagleton's *Ideology: An Introduction* (1991) takes us through the 'ideology' debate from a Marxist perspective. One of the major contributions to that debate, Louis Althusser's 'Ideology and Ideological State Apparatuses' (originally in *Lenin and Philosophy and Other Essays*, 1971) is quite accessible, in spite of its title, and has been widely reprinted. Moyra Haslett's *Marxist Literary and Cultural Theory* (1999) offers a very readable overview of the field. Barbara Foley's *Marxist Literary Criticism Today* (2019) is an excellent and more recent introduction that offers very useful examples of Marxist critical practice. In *The Routledge Companion to Literature and Class* (2022) Gloria McMillan collects some thirty essays that examine – although not necessarily from a Marxist perspective – how social class manifests itself in the most diverse texts.

FEMINIST CRITICISM

Ruth Robbins's *Literary Feminisms* (2000) offers a good and lucid overview, although it does of course not cover the most recent developments, which is also the case with Ellen Rooney's *The Cambridge Companion to Feminist Literary Theory* (2006). Mary Eagleton's *Feminist Literary Theory: A Reader* (3rd edition 2011) collects a large number of important texts, as does Gill Plain and Susan Sellers's *A History of Feminist Literary Criticism* (2012). *Literature and the Development of Feminist Theory* (2015), edited by Robin Truth Goodman traces the interaction between literature and feminist thought from Mary Wollstonecraft to the present time. 'Part Two: The Text' of Goodman's *The Bloomsbury Handbook of 21st Century Feminist Theory* (2019) deals with current feminist literary theorizing while the essays collected in Jennifer Cooke's *The New Feminist Literary Studies* (2020) exemplify the state of the art in feminist criticism. In *Gender: The Basics* (2nd edition 2018), Hilary Lips discusses a concept that has permanently changed literary criticism.

The seminal text of Black feminist criticism is Barbara Smith's 'Towards a Black Feminist Criticism' (1977). Barbara Christian's *Black Feminist Criticism: Perspectives on Black Women Writers* (1985), Hazel Carby's *Reconstructing Womanhood: The Emergence of the Afro-American*

Woman Novelist (1987), and Susan Willis's Marxist *Specifying: Black Women Writing the American Experience* of the same year, illustrate the emergence of a forceful Black feminist criticism in the mid-1980s. Cheryl Wall's *Changing Our Own Words* (1989) and Henry Louis Gates's *Reading Black, Reading Feminist* (1990) are very useful collections of Black feminist criticism. Barbara Christian's later criticism is collected in *New Black Feminist Criticism, 1985–2000* (2007). For a more general Black feminism, see the work of bell hooks (*Ain't I a Woman? Black Women and Feminism*, 1982; *Feminist Theory: From Margin to Center*, 1984), Audre Lorde's *Sister Outsider: Essays and Speeches* (1984), Patricia Hill Collins's *Black Feminist Thought: Knowledge, Consciousness and the Politics of Empowerment* (2nd edition 2000), and Jacqueline Bobo's *Black Feminist Cultural Criticism* (2001). Valerie Lee's *The Prentice Hall Anthology of African American Women's Literature* (2006) presents all the major voices while Karla Kovalova's *Black Feminist Criticism: Past and Present* (2016) discusses the evolution of Black feminist criticism since the 1990s.

AFRICAN-AMERICAN CRITICISM

Houston A. Baker, Jr's *Long Black Song: Essays in Black-American Literature and Culture* (1972) collects early but still worthwhile essays in a then developing field. Robert Stepto's *From Behind the Veil* (1979, revised in 1991) is a classic of African–American criticism, dealing with Black literature from slave narratives to Ralph Ellison's *Invisible Man* (1952). *Blues, Ideology, and Afro-American Literature: A Vernacular Theory* (1984) by Houston A. Baker, Jr sees the Black literary tradition as shaped by the conditions of slavery and in interaction with the blues. Henry Louis Gates, Jr's *Figures in Black: Words, Signs and the 'Racial' Self* (1987) and his *The Signifying Monkey* (1988, republished with a new foreword in 2014) together constitute what is probably the most successful effort to theorize a specific African–American writing tradition. *African American Literary Criticism, 1773–2000* (1999), edited by Hazel Arnett Ervin enables us to follow the development of African-American criticism, as does Winston Napier's *African American Literary Theory: A Reader* (2000). *The Cambridge Companion to the African American Novel*, edited by

Maryemma Graham (2004) is brought up to date by Cameron Leader-Picone's *Black and More than Black: African American Fiction in the Post Era* (2019). Mark Christian Thompson's *Phenomenal Blackness: Black Power, Philosophy, and Theory* (2022) discusses, among many other things, 'Literary Negro-ness' and 'Black aesthetic theory'.

THE POSTSTRUCTURALIST REVOLUTION

POSTSTRUCTURALISM

The Russian formalists saw their theorizing as a scientific discipline and in the 1960s theorists like Barthes and Todorov felt the same about narratology. As Todorov said in his *Grammaire du Décameron*: 'this work belongs to a science which does not yet exist, let us say *narratologie*, the science of narrative' (Todorov 1969: 10). The Marxist critics of the 1970s and 1980s, most of them followers of Althusser and convinced that Marxism was firmly grounded in science, likewise felt that their work had scientific status. In her *Critical Practice* of 1980 the prominent British critic Catherine Belsey speaks of Althusserian criticism as a 'scientific practice' which produces 'knowledge of the text' (Belsey 1980: 138). On the other side of the political spectrum, Leavis and the New Critics deeply distrusted science, but that did not prevent them from holding truths that they, too, considered unassailable.

When Belsey published a revised edition of her book in 2002 all references to science and scientific grounding had disappeared. The former belief in a science of criticism – which the even more prominent British critic Terry Eagleton had also briefly embraced – was gone. Criticism, or, as Belsey calls it critical practice is now just that – and not a 'scientific' practice. A major difference between that second edition of Belsey's book and the first is that Jacques Derrida, barely mentioned in the earlier version, now has his own chapter, while Michel Foucault, who in the first edition only features in the 'Further reading' category, is now a significant

DOI: 10.4324/9781003373438-6

presence. Indeed, three years after the publication of the second edition Foucault's work would be a major point of reference in Belsey's *The Subject of Tragedy* (1985). By the mid-1980s belief in the scientific character of literary studies and in unassailable truths had virtually disappeared. What had happened?

The answer to that question can be brief: 'poststructuralism'. In the 1960s and 1970s a number of French theorists developed rather diverse lines of thought that in the US were soon brought together under the heading poststructuralism, which certainly was convenient but did not do justice to the diversity of their ideas (and also led to rather inconclusive discussions about the degree to which some of those theorists were truly poststructuralist). So what is poststructuralism? This time there is no brief or easy answer. It is easier to say what the theorists in question had in common. Derrida, Foucault, Roland Barthes, who in his *S/Z* of 1970 had abandoned narratology's scientific aspirations, the psychoanalyst Julia Kristeva, the philosophers Gilles Deleuze and Jean-François Lyotard, and a number of lesser-known French intellectuals, whatever their differences, were in agreement about the pre-eminence of sign systems, and in particular language, in the creation of meaning. But they also agreed that structuralism had a fatal flaw: it had taken for granted that the analysis of structures would lead to objective knowledge. The so-called poststructuralist theorists argued that objective knowledge is impossible. We ourselves inevitably function within structures that create meaning and we cannot stand outside and above our tool of analysis – language – so that theoretically our efforts at understanding are always compromised. This has far-reaching consequences. It means that truths cannot be absolute and timeless but are, instead, a matter of perspective. Moreover, since no condition is ever permanent, all perspectives have a limited time span. We live in an endless succession of processes. Poststructuralism, then, seeks out and questions all forms of *essentialism*, including humanism which it accuses of holding essentialist views of an unchanging human nature and human freedom which ignore to what extent we are the product of language and of our unconscious drives. There is no such thing as a free, self-determined subject that has a direct access to meaning – or to itself. There is no *presence* since everything is always mediated by language or other sign systems. Poststructuralism's radical questioning of things does not necessarily mean that it opposes them. What it questions is their claims to permanence – to lasting truth – and to purity. There is nothing that is not affected by its context and by history. Even scientific 'facts' have a context and a history and are the indirect product of the value that we attach to science. That does not mean we should reject them but we should treat all claims based on them with caution. Poststructuralism's questioning also does not rule out political positions. It rejects the absoluteness of values, but not values per se, although it will always be on its guard against essentializing tendencies. Finally, poststructuralists are interested in art because of its ambiguities and often undecidable meanings which resist traditional approaches.

DECONSTRUCTION

Two poststructuralists – who both rejected the label – had an enormous impact on literary studies: Jacques Derrida and Michel Foucault. Indeed, the 1970s, when Derrida's *Speech and Phenomena* (1973) and *Of Grammatology* (1976) appeared in translation and when Foucault's work came to be noted, can be seen as a sort of watershed in English and American criticism. Let us first consider Derrida's so-called *deconstruction*, a term he also was not happy with, although he did use it (as 'de-construction') in an early publication.

Derrida's impressive body of writing offers a relentless questioning, and destabilizing, of such notions as truth, meaning, authenticity, identity, purity, closure, frames, borders – in short, of everything that would seem to smack of essentialism. This discussion will restrict itself to what are probably the most relevant of Derrida's arguments for the study of literature. Let us begin with his claim that language is always subject to what, with a neologism, he calls *différance*. We know that the link between a word and what it refers to is a matter of convention and is basically arbitrary. So why doesn't that bother us? The answer is pretty simple: we are not interested in such possible complications because we see language as an instrument, as a tool that makes it possible for us do something: to express ourselves. And we feel that it serves us pretty well. But such a practical argument does not hold water with theorists.

Derrida *is* bothered by the arbitrary nature of the words we use and by the fact that language never touches the real world. There is no single word that is the way it is because it cannot be another way, because its shape is wholly determined by what it refers to. If we would have such a word, determined by something in the real world, it would constitute an absolute fixed and 'true' element within the linguistic system, so that we might then possibly build more and more words around it and in that way anchor language firmly in the real world. Reality would then determine language. As it is, however, we have to work with meanings that are produced with the help of 'difference'. In language we find only differences without positive terms, as Saussure put it. For Derrida, that state of affairs has far-reaching consequences. First of all, because the meaning that we attach to words is the product of difference, that meaning is always contaminated. Think of a traffic light: we all know the 'meaning' of red, amber, or green. But it never occurs to us that those meanings are not 'pure'. When we see red we do not consciously think of amber and green, but one might argue that amber and green are in a sense present in red. Together, the three constitute a differential structure and it is the structure – including amber and green – that gives red its meaning. After all, in other contexts, red may have a completely different meaning. The red of roses has for centuries stood for love, and encouraged going on rather than stopping. The red of traffic lights, then, carries the 'traces' of amber and green within it, and is not pure, unadulterated red. Derrida argues that the same holds for words: every single word contains traces of other words – theoretically of all the other words in a language:

> the movement of signification is possible only if each so-called 'present' element, each element appearing on the scene of presence, is related to something other than itself, thereby keeping within itself the mark of the past element, and already letting itself be vitiated by the mark of its relation to the future element, this trace being related no less to what is called the future than to what is called the past, and constituting what is called the present by means of this very relation to what it is not.

(Derrida 1996 [1982]: 32)

The process that gives words their meaning never ends. The words we say or read never achieve complete stability, not only because they are related to, and take part of their meaning from, the words that have just preceded them, but also because their meaning will always modified by whatever follows. The word that is next to the word we are looking at, or a word later in the same sentence, or even paragraph, will subtly change its meaning. Meaning, then, not only is the product of difference but is also always subject to a process of deferral. Derrida captures this in a self-coined term, *différance*, that contains both the idea of difference and the deferral of meaning. Clearly, *différance* stands in the way, to say the least, of all attempts at definitive interpretation, at *closure*. As Derek Attridge put it, 'effecting closure in this discourse about the significance of a literary text is always a violent act, enforcing a limit upon what could go on endlessly' (Attridge 2018: 103). If we look closely enough we will always see that 'closure' is impossible. As the prominent deconstructionist critic J. Hillis Miller remarked, 'Deconstruction is not a dismantling of the structure of a text but a demonstration that it has already dismantled itself' (Miller 1976: 341).

Nothing is safe from Derrida's critique of things we take for granted. Writing about signatures (in his 'Signature Event Context' of 1971) he points out that in order to be authenticated a signature must be repeated – 'iterated' – with another signature that is both same and other. But signatures may be expertly falsified so that what must guarantee authenticity may itself not be authentic at all. Like *différance*, 'iterability', a fundamental aspect of language, has far-reaching consequences:

> The iterability of the mark does not leave any of the philosophical abstractions ... intact ... Once it is iterable, to be sure, a mark marked with a supposedly 'positive' value ('serious', 'literal', etc.) can be mimed, cited, transformed into an 'exercise' or into 'literature,' even into a 'lie' – that is, can be made to carry its other, its 'negative' double.

> (Derrida 1988 [1977]: 61)

For Derrida, 'iterability alters', and because it 'alters' it 'unavoidably generates' 'undecidability' as the critic Cary Wolfe tells us (Wolfe 2010: 12).

There is no escaping this condition because, as Derrida puts it, 'il n'y a de hors-texte' – there is nothing that is 'outside-text' (Derrida 1976 [1967]: 158). That has often been taken to mean 'that language (or "discourse") goes all the way down, that "reality" is itself a discursive (that is to say, fictive) construct' (Norris 2003: 227), but that is not what Derrida means to say. The point is that we must use language if we want to deal with the world even if we fully recognize that the independent 'play' of language escapes our control and will have its way with what we say or write. The best we can do is to be continually on our guard and not succumb to *logocentrism*, the naïve and mistaken notion that language gives us direct and uncomplicated access to reality.

BINARY OPPOSITIONS, REVISITED

What helps us to do so is that language betrays itself. Because there is always an excess of meaning no text will ever present a completely coherent whole. This is where deconstruction comes in. As the American critic Barbara Johnson described it: 'The deconstruction of a text does not proceed by random doubt or arbitrary subversion, but by the careful teasing out of warring forces of signification within the text' (Johnson 1980: 5). For deconstructionist critics texts create hierarchies. Some things are presented as central, others as marginal. Some things are portrayed positively, others negatively. Such oppositions often take the form of binary oppositions. Quite often these oppositions are implicit or almost invisible – they may be hidden in a text's metaphors, for instance – or else only one of the terms involved is explicitly mentioned. That explicit mention, then, evokes the other, absent term. Rather general sets of oppositional terms include good/evil, same/other, truth/falsehood, presence/absence, masculine/feminine, thought/feeling, mind/matter (or body), nature/culture, pure/impure, and so on and so forth. A notorious oppositional set within Western culture is white versus Black. One of these terms always functions as the centre – it is *privileged*, in poststructuralist terms, and is, because of its supposed *natural* status, not questioned. Some terms have always been privileged – truth, purity – others may either be found in the centre or in the margin. In literary history we find texts that privilege 'thought' and 'rationality' but in the work of the Romantic poets 'feeling' occupies the centre.

As I have just suggested, the privileging of certain terms can easily escape our notice. Take for instance words like 'Discman' and 'Gameboy', now obsolete, just like the gadgets they refer to (a portable CD player and a portable videogame player, respectively). The second, non-privileged and inferior pole of the opposition is even absent here. We may never have realized it, but 'Discman' and 'Gameboy' set up an opposition between masculine and feminine. Why is a 'Discman' not a 'Discwoman' or a 'Discgirl'? Why is a 'Gameboy' not a 'Gamegirl'? In all probability the companies in question used the 'man' in 'Discman' and the 'boy' in 'Gameboy' to give their products a positive image that would boost sales. In any case, we have implicit binary oppositions in which the masculine term is the 'privileged' one.

Quite often such binary oppositions are tied up with negative stereotyping, repression, discrimination, social injustice, and other undesirable practices and might even be said to perpetuate them actively. And so deconstruction, which sees itself as politically progressive, sets out to deconstruct them, to demonstrate that they are not natural but that they are *constructions*. What is more, deconstruction argues that in binary oppositions we do not only find an oppositional relationship between the two terms involved, but also a strange complicity. Take for instance the seemingly wholly natural – that is, not constructed – opposition light versus darkness. Arguably, light needs darkness. If there were no darkness, we would not have light either because we would not be able to recognize it for what it is. Without darkness, we would in one sense obviously have light – it would be the only thing around – but we would not be *aware* of light. We would not have the *concept* of light so that what we call light (which implies our awareness that there is also the possibility of non-light) would not exist. One might argue, then, that the existence of darkness (that is, our awareness of non-light) creates the concept of light. Paradoxically, the inferior term in this oppositional set – if we assume, because of its cultural connotations, that darkness is the inferior term – turns out to be a condition for the opposition as such and is therefore as important as the so-called privileged one. The two terms in any oppositional set are defined by each other: light by darkness, truth by falsehood, purity by contamination, the rational by the irrational, the same by the other, nature by culture. If there were no purity, we would have no concept of impurity and would presumably not deplore it (if we do). Once difference – the relationship between two such terms – has given rise to meaning, we privilege one pole of the oppositional axis at the cost of the other. Even if the terms involved seem at first sight wholly neutral – light / darkness, for instance – our metaphorical operations will set up a positive and a negative pole. Some privilegings will strike most of us as wholly reasonable – good versus evil, or truth versus falsehood – while others have done incalculable damage – white versus Black, masculine versus feminine. But whatever the effect of binary oppositions, they are constructions that always have their origin in difference. And the terms in question will always be involved in each other. There is no purity, there is only hybridity and heterogeneity.

LITERARY DECONSTRUCTION

Deconstruction analyses and dismantles texts or, more usually, parts of texts in order to reveal their inconsistencies and inner contradictions. No matter whether a text is literary or non-literary, it can always be shown to rely for its internal stability on rhetorical operations that mask the text's origin in difference and also mask the endless proliferation of meaning (*dissemination*) that is the result of *différance*. As I have already pointed out, texts never achieve *closure* – which quite literally means that their case can never be closed: there is no final meaning, the text remains a field of possibilities. In Jeremy Hawthorn's apt formulation: 'Thus for Derrida the meaning of a text is always unfolding just ahead of the interpreter, unrolling in front of him or her like a never-ending carpet whose final edge never reveals itself' (Hawthorn 1998: 39).

In some ways, deconstructionist reading practice resembles the New Critical reading for juxtapositions, tensions, inversions, and the like. Just as the New Criticism did, deconstruction depends on close reading. However, while the New Critics emphasized the ultimate coherence of what they considered successful literary works (coherence being one of their touchstones), deconstructionist criticism seeks to expose the cracks in the façade, to reveal where and how the text works against what at first sight would seem to be its meaning. In her reading of Herman Melville's *Billy Budd* (1891, first published in 1924), in which a young sailor (Billy) is hanged because he has inadvertently killed the master-at-arms Claggart, who has falsely accused him, Barbara Johnson sees a whole series of binary oppositions:

> the fate of each of the characters is the direct reverse of what one is led to expect from his 'nature.' Billy is sweet, innocent, and harmless, yet he kills. Claggart is evil, perverted, and mendacious, yet he dies a victim. Vere [the captain in charge of the ship] is sagacious and responsible, yet he allows a man whom he feels to be blameless to hang.
>
> (Johnson 1980: 82)

However, the relations between these opposites, and the characters that embody them, turn out to be complex and paradoxical: 'Claggart, whose accusations of incipient mutiny are apparently false and therefore illustrate the very double-facedness they attribute to Billy, is negated for proclaiming the lie about Billy which Billy's act of negation paradoxically proves to be the truth' (86). It is not only that the opposites shift within the structure, they also would seem to collapse into each other. Either/or turns into both/and. Johnson concludes that in *Billy Budd* we have a 'difference' that effectively prevents closure.

Derrida's own reading of the very short story 'Before the Law' by Franz Kafka (1883–1924) emphasizes the same lack of closure. In Kafka's story a man arrives at the door that gives access to the law. He is not allowed to enter but hears from the doorkeeper that he may perhaps enter later and had better not use force because there are many more doors, and many more doorkeepers that are even more powerful than this first one. He waits all his life and finally, just before he dies, asks the doorkeeper why he is the only one who has sought admittance. Answering that this particular door was meant for him only, the doorkeeper shuts the door on the dying man. Derrida sees the story as exemplifying *différance*:

> After the first guardian there are incalculably many others, perhaps without limit, and progressively more powerful and therefore prohibitive, endowed with the power of delay. Their potency is *différance*, an

interminable *différance* .... As the doorkeeper represents it, the discourse of the law does not say 'no' but 'not yet,' indefinitely.

(Derrida 1987 [1985]: 141)

The discourse of any given text forever tells us 'not yet' in our search for definitive meaning.

Deconstruction has come in for a good deal of criticism. It has been argued, for instance, that ultimately all deconstructionist interpretations are similar, because they always lead us to the impossibility of final meanings. This is undeniably true, but it disregards the fact that before a deconstructionist reading arrives at that point, it has uncovered the structures that operate in a text and shown us how these structures can be dismantled by making use of the text itself.

To other critics of deconstruction, its intellectual underpinnings – Derrida's critique of logocentrism – seems extremely far-fetched. You might for instance grant Derrida's original point of departure, and agree that language is based on difference and hovers over the world without ever actually touching solid ground, but reject his conclusions: why would that invariably lead to a surplus of meaning that fatally affects the texts we produce? From a pragmatic perspective language would seem to do its work reasonably well. However, even for those critics who prefer a pragmatic position deconstruction has its uses. It is, for instance, perfectly possible to approach the 'warring forces of signification' that deconstruction habitually finds from a modified humanistic perspective. Such a humanism might argue that although ideally free and rational agents, in actual practice we are to a considerable extent determined by, for instance, our cultural environment. The revelation that the hierarchical relations that we can discover in texts have a cultural origin and always serve to inflict injustice upon the 'inferior' party can only be a step towards a better world in which the full humanity of every single human being is recognized and respected.

Such adaptations of deconstruction, and of poststructuralism in general, are particularly useful for those critics who want to be politically effective. *Différance* will affect whatever we say and there is no getting away from its lack of closure and from undecidability. But for politically motivated criticism the absence of solid ground is a poor starting point. If I want to achieve certain political ends there is not much help in the thought that all meanings – including the values that have led to my political stance – are the result of difference and have no solid foundation. To be fair, Derrida was deeply committed to justice and argued that only the most stringent critique of logocentrism and all other forms of essentialism could lead to genuine justice.

IMPLICATIONS

While for the structuralists the structures they described were objectively present in the texts they dealt with, for deconstructionist critics such a structure is an arrangement produced by a reader who has temporarily stopped the infinite flow of meanings that a text generates. A text is not a structure, but a chain of signs that generate meaning, with none of these signs occupying a privileged, anchored (and anchoring) position. Language is 'a system where the central signified, the original or transcendental signified, is never absolutely present outside a system of differences', as Derrida put it in his seminal essay 'Structure, Sign, and Play' (Derrida 2000 [1970]). From the perspective of poststructuralism the subject is to a large (although never knowable) extent the product of linguistic and cultural structures (even if their exact nature can never be established). As Roland Barthes wrote in 1970 with regard to reading: 'This "I" which approaches the text is already itself a plurality of other texts, of codes which are infinite, or more precisely, lost (whose origin is lost)' (Barthes 1975 [1970]: 10). The implication is that, like those texts, we cannot have a stable core. This is of course not how we experience ourselves and it is a view of the subject that is certainly not uncontested. In any case, since the 1970s the liberal humanist subject, with its self-determination, moral autonomy and coherence, has been a major target for poststructuralist critique.

For Eliot, Richards, Leavis, and the New Critics the literary text had timeless significance because it put us in touch with the essence of what it means to be human – with the 'human condition'. Literature referred to unchanging truths and values. For the poststructuralists, literature can do no such thing. All we have are interpretations of literary texts and, like structures, interpretations are mere freeze-frames in an endless flow of signification. There is,

however, one important difference between one category of literary texts and other forms of language use: there are literary texts
that confess to their own impotence, their inability to establish
closure. To Derrida and to poststructuralists in general such texts are
far more interesting than texts that try to hide their impotence
such as philosophical texts or realistic novels that claim to offer a
true representation of the world. If deconstruction deals with such
a text it will expose the 'warring forces of signification' that it tries
to hide and show how it creates the suggestion that the author is in
full control of the text (and that its readers are in control of
themselves). And it will try to show how the text generates an
infinite flow of meaning. We have arrived, as the French critic
Roland Barthes put it somewhat dramatically in 1968, at 'the death
of the author', which simultaneously is 'the birth of the reader'
(Barthes 2000 [1968]: 150).

FOUCAULDIAN POWER

In deconstructionist criticism the dismantling of oppositions and the
exposure of hidden hierarchies and relations of power is generally
limited to the text at hand. Although the interrogation of power on a
wider scale is implicit in Derrida's deconstruction of logocentrism –
the belief that language can give us access to truth – the interest in
power and its workings that dominates the poststructuralist criticism
of the 1980s and 1990s, and that is still very much with us, derives
mainly from the work of Michel Foucault. During his career as a
cultural historian Foucault wrote books on the historical trajectory of
the concept of madness, on the origin and rise of clinical medicine, on
the rise of other forms of knowledge in the domain of the human
sciences and on the way these sciences established their authority, and
on the emergence of the modern prison system, before turning to the
history of 'sexuality' (not as a biological force but as dealt with, as
managed, by culture) in his last books. In so doing, Foucault does not
focus on agency, on the individual intentionality of those involved in
these historical developments, but on *discourses*, a notion which he
gradually develops, and which he increasingly sees as instruments of
power and repression until, towards the end of his career, he would
seem to allow the possibility of escape from such repression – not
through individual agency, but through resistance that has its source

in a specific subject position. For Foucault the humanist concept of the self-determined, autonomous individual or subject who is gifted with reason is a temporary illusion that, after a life span of some centuries, will disappear again. Each of us is the effect of discursive operations rather than in control of them.

For Foucault the apparently humanitarian rationality that we already see at work in early modern culture and that was at the heart of Enlightenment thinking has created bodies of knowledge that in the name of discipline and order marginalize or even exclude groups such as the 'insane', the 'criminal', the 'abnormal', the 'sick'. These new bodies of knowledge – which included psychiatry, criminology, medicine, and (human) biology – and the social policies that emerged from them, and that were meant to impose discipline and order, are essentially repressive. They have led to a self-imposed submission to social control and have turned out to be straitjackets that, strangely enough, we would seem glad to put on. Foucault's 'archaeologies' seek to show how power was at work in the seemingly 'objective' vocabularies, such as the terms that define abnormality or madness, developed by the various branches of the human sciences as these constituted themselves in the aftermath of the Enlightenment. And they seek to show how repressive measures taken to deal with sources of social disruption such as madness, criminality, other forms of deviant behaviour, and contagious diseases, have gradually pervaded modern society.

THE PANOPTICON

In a section called 'Panopticism' in his book *Discipline and Punish: The Birth of the Prison* (1975, translated in 1977), Foucault gives a succinct account of how in early modern society leprosy and the plague – both highly contagious diseases – were dealt with. Lepers were simply excluded from social intercourse to minimize the risk of infection. However, with regard to the plague, which always affected large numbers of the population, other measures were necessary. And so seventeenth-century society did its utmost to contain the plague through confining people to their houses, once the disease had manifested itself. But such a drastic measure demands constant surveillance: 'Inspection functions ceaselessly. The gaze [of surveillance] is alert everywhere' (Foucault 1977

[1975]: 195). This imprisonment by way of precaution is for Foucault typical of how in the modern world the individual is constantly monitored, inspected:

> This enclosed, segmented space, observed at every point, in which the individuals are inserted in a fixed place, in which the slightest movements are supervised, in which all events are recorded ... in which the individual is constantly located, examined and distributed among the living beings, the sick and the dead – all this constitutes a compact model of the disciplinary mechanism.
>
> (Foucault 1977 [1975]: 197)

The 'political dream' of the plague is 'the penetration of regulation into even the smallest details of everyday life' (198). It must not be thought that in such attempts to confine the plague one powerful group of citizens controls another, powerless one. There is with regard to power not a 'massive, binary division between one set of people and another' (198), but a distribution of power through many channels and over a large number of individuals.

It is the detailed regulation and constant surveillance that were mobilized against the plague that in the nineteenth century begins to be applied to 'beggars, vagabonds, madmen, and the disorderly' – in short, 'the abnormal individual'. The instrument that the authorities responsible for this use is 'that of binary division': 'mad/sane; dangerous/harmless; normal/abnormal' (199). Foucault's metaphor for this new sort of social regulation is that of the *Panopticon*, a type of prison designed by the English philosopher Jeremy Bentham in the late eighteenth century. This ideal prison consisted of a ring of cells that was built around a central point of observation from which one single guardian could survey all the cells – which were open to inspection – on a given floor.

However, the prisoner cannot see the supervisor. He never knows if he is being watched. This is for Foucault the 'major effect' of the Panopticon:

> to induce in the inmate a state of conscious and permanent visibility that assures the automatic functioning of power. So to arrange things that the surveillance is permanent in its effects, even if it is discontinuous in its action; that the perfection of power should tend to

render its actual exercise unnecessary; that this architectural apparatus should be a machine for creating and sustaining a power relation
independent of the person who exercises it; in short, that the inmates
should be caught up in a power situation of which they themselves
are the bearers.

(Foucault 1977 [1975]: 201)

And so a 'real subjection is born mechanically from a fictitious
relation' (202). For Foucault the Panopticon stands for the modern
world in which we are 'the bearers' of our own figurative, mental,
imprisonment. We are complicit in our own bondage.

At first sight this may not seem very plausible, so let me give an
example. Before sexology entered the scene in the nineteenth century homosexual acts were just that: discrete acts that in most places
were against the law but that did not say much about the offender.
With the advent of sexological discourse what had seemed to be discrete sexual acts were traced back to an underlying, unchanging,
homosexual nature. It was no longer just acts, but personalities that
were deviant. Given the strongly negative connotations surrounding
this new 'personage', young males must have started to monitor
themselves and, if necessary, to repress undesirable feelings. Foucault
argues that over the last two centuries a whole army of psychiatrists,
doctors, sociologists, psychotherapists, social workers, and other self-
appointed guardians of 'normality' has sprung up to create a stifling
apparatus of social surveillance in which, as we will see in a moment,
language plays a major role.

Let us briefly look at a novel that illustrates Foucault's idea of
surveillance and self-surveillance. Although it pre-dates Foucault's
work, Ken Kesey's *One Flew Over the Cuckoo's Nest* (1962)
describes a truly Foucauldian world. The novel takes place in a
mental institution that is run by a woman ('Big Nurse') whose
weapons are surveillance and inspection. The patients regularly
take part in group sessions in which they must reveal their problems – ostensibly for therapeutic purposes but in reality because
the humiliation of public confession keeps them subservient and in
line. One of the major surprises of the novel is that many of the
inmates have not been committed at all, but have come to the
institution on a wholly voluntary basis. They have had themselves
committed because the outside world's insistence on 'normality'

and its definition of normality have convinced them that they are abnormal and need treatment. They have, in other words, subjected themselves to the authority of the human sciences. They have, first of all, accepted and completely internalized *a discourse* about normality for which the human sciences are mainly responsible; secondly, they have literally turned their minds and bodies over to one of its institutions. (For Foucault the operations of power often involve the body – it includes bio-power, as we have already seen in the case of contagious diseases.) The only 'patient' who is sure that he is absolutely sane has escaped this discourse about normality and its disciplining power because he has never gone to school or church – two regulating and 'normalizing' institutions. Ironically, unlike most of the others, he is not free to go.

DISCOURSES

In its policing of 'abnormal' behaviour, the authority of the human sciences derives from what they claim to be *knowledge*. Such a cluster of claims to knowledge in a particular field is what Foucault calls a *discourse*. In his *The Archaeology of Knowledge* (1972) Foucault tells us that a discourse is 'a series of sentences or propositions' and that it 'can be defined as a large group of statements that belong to a single system of formation' – a so-called discursive formation. Thus, he continues, 'I shall be able to speak of clinical discourse, economic discourse, the discourse of natural history, psychiatric discourse' (Foucault 1972: 107–108). His type of history – which he terms 'genealogy' – must first of all 'account for the constitution of knowledges, discourses, domains of objects etc. without having to make reference to a subject' (117). Foucault is interested in the rules and the conditions that make it possible for 'propositions' to acquire the status of knowledge and the authority that comes with it. These rules determine what counts as knowledge with regard to the field in which they operate and thus – as in the case of clinical medicine or psychiatry – establish bodies of 'knowledge' that apply to us all. Because of their claims to expertise such discourses then go on to determine the way we talk and think about the field in question (sexuality, for instance, or mental illness) and as often as not persuade us to keep ourselves and others under constant surveillance. Like language in general they operate independently of any individual intention and perpetuate themselves through their users. Since we are all instruments of the discourses that we have internalized, we ourselves constantly reproduce the 'historical unconscious' of our period, its 'episteme', and we reproduce the power of its discourses, even in our intimate relations. It is important to keep in mind that for Foucault such discourses are *constructions* whose truthfulness is in any case not relevant for the way they acquire and exert their power. What is crucial is that knowledge or, to be more precise, knowledge that is accepted as such, is inextricably entangled with power. Knowledge defines and categorizes others and is only one step away from surveillance and discipline. Occasionally, it seems to have more positive effects. To stay with the field of sexuality: the 'discovery' that there are men who have a 'homosexual personality' has led to disciplining and stigmatizing, but may also be said to have contributed to the creation of homosexual communities, to solidarity at the personal level, and even to collective action at the political level. Foucault calls our attention to examples of '"reverse" discourse' (his term) leading to actual resistance. Still, a reverse discourse makes use of the same vocabulary and of the same categories that the discourse itself uses, and thus runs the risk of affirming that discourse's validity. As I have already mentioned, in his late work Foucault seems to suggest that we may see through the constructed nature of discourses and involve ourselves in 'the endeavor to know how and to what extent it might be possible to think differently, instead of legitimating what is already known' (Foucault 1985: 9). But that is not a return to the autonomous, self-determining subject of humanism.

Foucault's power clearly has much in common with Althusser's 'ideology' and Gramsci's 'hegemony' because it, too, rules by consent. Just like 'ideology' or 'hegemony' it derives its strength from the fact that we deeply believe what it tells us, giving us a sense of belonging and contributing to our well-being:

If power were never anything but repressive, if it never did anything but to say no, do you really think one would be brought to obey it? What makes power hold good, what makes it accepted, is simply the fact that it doesn't only weigh on us as a force that says no, but that it traverses and produces things, it induces pleasure, forms knowledge, produces discourse.

(Foucault 1980: 119)

Foucault's exploration of discourses as vehicles for power has been immensely productive in the study of literature. After all, he locates power firmly in language, and language is the business of literary studies. Deconstructionism is certainly not blind to the fact that language is tied up with power – its dismantling of binary oppositions testifies to that. Foucault, however, places language in the centre of *social* power and of social practices. The social role of language – including literature – and its power is the starting point for the various trajectories within literary studies that I will discuss in the chapters that follow.

POSTSTRUCTURALISM AND PSYCHOANALYSIS

We have just encountered the 'historical unconscious' of a period and in the discussion of literary criticism based on Althusser's critique of ideology we have met with the 'unconscious' of the literary text. But what is the unconscious? The answer must be speculative since it escapes our conscious awareness, but it is nonetheless one of the central concepts in the psychoanalytic theories of Sigmund Freud (1856–1939), for whom it is that part of our mind that against our wishes preserves whatever we want to forget and seek to *repress*: traumatic or shameful experiences, undesirable urges, unwholesome impulses that we must suppress because they would take us into forbidden territory. One of those unwelcome desires is the hypothetical erotic interest of little boys in their mother (Freud connects this with the Greek myth in which Oedipus unknowingly marries his mother) which they give up when they realize that they are in direct competition with their father and are on their way to a confrontation they must lose. If you cannot beat them, join them; and so the little boy decides to be like his father – simultaneously accepting social authority – and will eventually direct his erotic interests at other women. Little girls, as disappointed by their mothers' lack of a penis as by their own, turn to their father – who possesses one – and will eventually give up their desire for a penis and want a baby instead. (Freud's account of the little girl's development – and of women's sexuality – has not unreasonably infuriated many female writers; see for instance Kate Millett's *Sexual Politics*.) All of these traumatic disappointments are relegated to the unconscious.

Still, although our conscious mind vigorously polices the border with the unconscious – whose traumas and unfulfilled desires always want to remind us that they are still there – the unconscious has ways of getting past its vigilance. It first of all manifests itself in unguarded moments, in slips of the tongue, for instance, or in unintended puns, or in our dreams. But the unconscious also slips through, according to Freud, in language that we see as figurative – symbols, metaphors, allusions, and the like. The unconscious can for instance hide a repressed desire behind an image that would seem to be harmless – a trick that Freud called *displacement* – or it can project a whole cluster of desires upon an image in a manoeuvre that Freud called *condensation*: a dream figure can for instance combine characteristics of a number of people we know. The language that we use may always have hidden meanings of which we ourselves have no conscious awareness. If we repress our hatred for a person who usually wears red, we may accidentally say 'dead' instead of 'red' in a conversation, or we may dream that a red car is flattened in a traffic accident.

Although we have no access to our unconscious it is a considerable influence in our day-to-day activities. That is dramatically the case if a repressed traumatic experience breaks into our consciousness and we are forced to relive – and perhaps for the first time fully understand – an extremely disturbing event (a delay of impact that Freud called *Nachträglichkeit* – literally, 'afterwardsness'). It should be clear that Freud's psychoanalysis presents a view of the subject that is radically at odds with the liberal humanist view of the subject as an ultimately free, coherent, and autonomous moral agent. For Freud, the subject is irreparably split and at odds with itself.

Psychoanalytic criticism focuses on 'cracks' in the text's façade, on what slips through authorial control, and seeks to bring to light the unconscious traumas or desires of either the author, or of the characters that the text presents. Shakespeare's *Hamlet*, for instance, has been a popular target of psychoanalytic criticism. It does not ignore what the text ostensibly would seem to be about, but its real interest is in the hidden agenda of the language that the text employs, in its tropes, metaphors, and symbols. Freud's theories no longer find much support in the medical world, where biological psychiatry has effectively displaced Freudian psychoanalysis. However, the proposition that the language of a literary work has both a conscious and an unconscious dimension and that the text's unconscious finds ways to get past the censorship exercised by its conscious dimension is a powerful interpretative tool and has been very attractive to a wide variety of critics.

LACAN

Freudian psychoanalysis has been heavily criticized for its sexist character, but perhaps even more so for its claims to universal validity. Freud's suggestion that his Oedipal model of infantile development is of all times and all places has become increasingly unacceptable, not in the least for poststructuralist theorists. As a consequence, many critics interested in psychoanalysis turned to Jacques Lacan, whose work avoids the fixed developmental scheme that Freud proposed and instead proposes a *relational* structure that allows for difference and change. This is not to say that Lacan's brand of psychoanalysis has fared better than that of Freud in contemporary medicine. As a prominent psychoanalytic critic recently said, 'psychoanalysis as reinvented by Lacan became a tool to study culture ... exiled from psychiatric practice and enthroned in humanities departments' (Camden 2022: 2). She also tells us that literary studies have 'veer[ed] away from ... psychoanalysis in particular' (2), but Lacan's considerable influence cannot be ignored.

For Lacan, too, the subject is split beyond repair. But in Lacanian theory that split is not the result of an Oedipal conflict, but of the infant's entry into the slippery world of language. In Lacan's terminology, the infant leaves the world of the *imaginary* – a state in which it cannot yet speak, is subject to impressions and fantasies, to drives and desires, and has no sense of limitations and boundaries – and enters the *symbolic*, in which the *real* – the real world which we can never know – is symbolized and represented by way of language and other representational systems. (We cannot know the 'real' because it can never be fully represented – it is beyond language.) This entrance into the 'symbolic' necessitates an acceptance of the language and of the social and cultural systems that prevail in the child's environment. It implies the acceptance of limitations and prohibitions. Lacan calls the massive configuration of authority that works through language the *nom du père*, the name of the father, in recognition of the patriarchal character of our social arrangements. The same recognition leads him to speak of the *phallus* as the signifier that signifies that patriarchal character. (Note that he avoids the term 'penis' because in Lacan's conception of things male dominance is a cultural construction and not a biological given. The phallus is thus always symbolic.) Hence the term *phallocentric*, which is of feminist origin and denotes the (false) assumption that maleness is the natural, and in fact only, source of authority and power.

We go from the Imaginary to the Symbolic through the 'mirror stage' in which we are confronted with the 'mirror' image that the world gives back to us. But that image, just like the image that we see in an actual mirror, is a distortion that leads to a 'misrecognition'. Still, that misrecognition is the basis for what we experience as our identity. For Lacan, we need the response and recognition of the outside world to develop a self. Our 'subjectivity' is construed in interaction with 'others', that is, individuals who resemble us in one way or another but who are also irrevocably different. We become ourselves by way of the perspectives and views of others, a process in which language plays a crucial role so that we may be said to be constructed in language. This happens under the 'gaze' of the 'Other' or 'great other' ('*grande autre*'). This 'Other' – 'the locus from which the question of [the subject's] existence may be presented to him' – is not a concrete individual, although it may be embodied in one (father or mother, for instance), but stands for the larger social order, for what we call 'reality'. We become subjects through a literal subjection to an existing order. Since our identity is constituted in interaction with what is outside of us and reflects us, it is *relational* – a notion that introduces the idea of difference into the process of identity construction. At the same time, we are positioned amid the relational systems created by language. As a result, identity is not something fixed and stable, it is a *process* that will never lead to completion. It is, moreover, not the authentic self of humanism, an authentic self that we know and that allows us to make decisions based on what we truly are. For Lacan our identity is the product of acts of misrecognition and will never fully satisfy us.

With the transition from the *imaginary* to the *symbolic*, in which we submit to language and reason and accept 'reality' as it is, we lose that feeling of wholeness, of undifferentiated being, that, as in

Freudian theory, will forever haunt us. Because we do not have access to this pre-verbal self we live ever after with a lack. This loss of our original state results in *desire*, in an unspecific but deep-felt longing that cannot be fulfilled by an identity that is the result of misrecognition, but can only (temporarily) satisfy itself with symbolic substitutes. Even what we call 'love' is only a substitute.

Lacan's view of the conscious and the unconscious has for many critics been more attractive than Freud's. Freud sees the repression that leads to the formation of the unconscious in terms of the nuclear family, even if he is of course aware that that family is embedded in a much larger social order (he speaks of the 'prevailing cultural super-ego'). Lacan, however, sees that repression as the direct effect of entry into the social order. For Lacan, there is a direct connection between the repressive character of language and culture and the coming into being of the unconscious. If we see 'ideology' in psychoanalytic terms, that is, as the conscious dimension of a given society, then we may posit a social unconscious where everything that is ideologically undesirable and that ideology therefore represses – exploitation, social inequality, unequal opportunity, lack of freedom, discrimination – is waiting to break to the surface. We may then examine the language that ideology uses for tell-tale cracks in its façade. The social unconscious will just like our individual unconscious succeed in getting past the censor. This is, as we have seen, the presupposition of the literary-critical practice of Pierre Macherey and the critics who followed his example (see Chapter 4).

As I have already suggested in my discussion of Althusser (also in Chapter 4), Lacan's psychoanalytic model has also been invoked to explain the hold ideology has over us. Ideology gives us the illusion that it makes us whole; it would seem to neutralize the desire that results from our entry into the 'symbolic'. Lacanian criticism sees this repeated on a smaller scale when we read literary texts and is interested in the ways in which narrative structures and rhetorical operations try to give us that sense of wholeness while the text's unconscious works against that effort. Apart from that, it explores how Lacan's view of identity construction may shed new light on literary characters. However, although Lacanian psychoanalysis has led to classic interpretations such as Shoshana Felman's (1982) reading of Henry James's *The Turn of the Screw* (1898), it has perhaps been more influential on the level of theory. We have already seen how it can be invoked to theorize the power of ideology and in Chapter 7, on postcolonial studies, we will see how Lacan's thesis that we develop our identity by way of 'others' can be used to analyse the relations between colonizer and colonized.

FRENCH FEMINISM

In the wake of Lacanian psychoanalysis a number of influential French feminists developed the notion of an *écriture féminine*, a feminine or female practice of writing that will escape the restrictions imposed by 'the phallocratic system' that for them dominates Western culture. As Hélène Cixous put it:

> In philosophy woman is always on the side of passivity. Every time the question comes up; when we examine kinship structures; whenever a family model is brought into play; in fact as soon ... as you ask yourself what is meant by the question 'What is it'; as soon as there is a will to say something. A will: desire, authority, you examine that, and you are led right back – to the father. ... And if you examine literary history, it's the same story. It all refers back to man, to *his* torment, his desire to be (at) the origin. Back to the father. There is an intrinsic bond between the philosophical and the literary ... and phallocentrism.
>
> (Cixous 2000 [1975]: 265)

For Cixous, this never-ending privileging of the masculine, which results from what she calls 'the solidarity of logocentrism and phallocentrism', damages us all, females and males alike, because it curbs the imagination and is thus gender-blind in its oppressiveness. '[T]here is no *invention* possible', Cixous argues, 'whether it be philosophical or poetic, without the presence in the inventing subject of an abundance of the other, of the diverse' (269). But how to tap this 'other', this 'diversity'?

In another 1975 essay, 'The Laugh of the Medusa', Cixous suggests that laughter, sex (if not policed by patriarchal heterosexuality), and writing may have liberating effects. Aware that writing usually serves the consolidation of patriarchal power, Cixous then proposes what she calls *écriture féminine*:

> It is impossible to define a feminine practice of writing [*écriture fémi-nine*], and this is an impossibility that will remain, for this practice can never be theorized, enclosed, encoded – which doesn't mean that it doesn't exist. But it will always surpass the discourse that regulates the phallocentric system; it does and will take place in areas other than those subordinated to philosophico-theoretical domination.
>
> (Cixous 1981 [1975]: 253)

For Cixous *écriture féminine* is radically different from phallocentric writing because it inscribes the female body – 'Write yourself. Your body must be heard' – and female being in its texts. It is a sort writing practice that 'surpasses' what Lacan calls the Symbolic and that we may associate – but not identify – with his Imaginary. Cixous chooses to call the radically subversive writing that she has in mind feminine or female because the forces of repression are so clearly male, although she would seem to suggest that males, too, can escape this 'philosophico-theoretical domination'. I should perhaps add that not all French feminists shared Cixous's views and that she was accused of essentializing a stereotypically anti-rational women's nature that some of her Parisian colleagues were decidedly unhappy with.

Julia Kristeva (1941–), literary critic and psychoanalyst, stays close to Lacan with her concepts of the 'symbolic' and the 'semiotic' – which is a version of Lacan's 'Imaginary'. For Kristeva, what has been repressed and consigned to the 'semiotic' finds its way into the not yet fully regulated language of children, into poetry, into the language of mental illness – into all uses of language that for whatever reason are not fully under control of the speaker or writer. 'symbolic' and 'semiotic' language are never to be found in their 'pure' state: all language is a mixture of the two:

> These two modalities are inseparable within the *signifying process* that constitutes language, and the dialectic between them determines the type of discourse (narrative, metalanguage, theory, poetry, etc.) involved; in other words, so-called 'natural' language allows for different modes of articulation of the semiotic and symbolic.
>
> (Kristeva 1984 [1974]: 24)

Semiotic purity is only possible in 'nonverbal signifying systems' such as music. Whenever we use language, both our conscious (which participates in the 'symbolic') and our unconscious (Kristeva's 'semiotic') mark it with their presence.

The sort of writing that Cixous and Kristeva have in mind is fairly rare in the history of literature. We might perhaps think of James Joyce's *Finnegans Wake* (1939) or of Virginia Woolf's *The Waves* (1931). The attitude that it presupposes, however, is much less rare nowadays. In *Surfacing* (1972), by the Canadian writer Margaret Atwood, we find a young woman caught in a rational, patriarchal, and often exploitative world exemplified by her lover, her father, and other male characters. During a trip to the wilderness, ostensibly in search for her missing father, she gradually strips herself of the perspective and the accoutrements of the rational modern world. Not accidentally, a dive deep into a pristine lake — into what hides under the surface — is the novel's turning point. When she figuratively resurfaces at the end of the novel from a brief period of almost complete surrender to instincts, she will always take the experience and the resulting knowledge with her.

POSTMODERN CRITICISM

Postmodern criticism started as the response of American critics to a new mode of writing that took matters of authorial control, coherence, and unity far less seriously than modernist writing had done, and that as often as not undermined its own authority by flaunting its constructed status and by incorporating wholly unrealistic if not downright zany scenes and events. This so-called postmodern fiction first made its mark around 1960 (see, for example, Thomas Pynchon's *V.*, 1962), rose to prominence in the 1970s (Pynchon, *Gravity's Rainbow*, 1973; Robert Coover, *The Public Burning*, 1977), became the dominant mode of the late twentieth century and is still a lasting influence (Angela Carter, *Nights at the Circus*, 1984; Paul Auster, *City of Glass*, 1985; J.M. Coetzee, *Foe*, 1987; Mark Z. Danielewski, *House of Leaves*, 2000; Nicola Barker, *In the Approaches*, 2014). From the late 1970s onwards, critics began to use an amalgam of poststructuralist ideas and assumptions in their analyses of postmodern fiction, one result of which was that the terms postmodern and poststructuralist soon became interchangeable. In fact, 'postmodernism' practically displaced 'poststructuralism', witness such books as Steven Best and Douglas Kellner's *Postmodern Theory: Critical Interrogations* (1991) in which we meet Derrida, Foucault, Gilles Deleuze, and Jean Baudrillard – the last two will return below – or Michael Drolet's *The Postmodernism Reader: Foundational Texts* (Drolet 2003) in which we find the same line-up, supplemented with other poststructuralist theorists.

Postmodern criticism took from poststructuralist theorists its emphasis on language and on the problematic status of meaning, which it saw as inherently unstable and uncontrollable, a perspective that seriously questioned traditional forms of representation, such as realism in fiction. It saw the universal claims of Enlightenment thinking and liberal humanism as a form of (unfounded) essentialism and as covertly totalitarian. It rejected the humanist view of the subject as coherent and self-determined, seeing the subject instead as the unsteady product of (often conflicting) discourses, a position that had little patience with such notions as originality and creativity. In a later stage it developed an interest in how language was instrumental in establishing and perpetuating power relations and in processes of marginalization. It is fair to say that since the turn of the millennium postmodern criticism's once dominant position has considerably weakened, but it is not yet a spent force, while much of its theoretical repertoire has, in modified form, found its way into the more recent developments in literary studies that will be discussed in later chapters.

Let me now look briefly at some poststructuralist theorists who played a more modest role than Derrida and Foucault in postmodern criticism. The French philosopher Jean-François Lyotard, who had borrowed the term 'postmodern' from American criticism, contributed considerably to its popularity with his influential *La Condition postmoderne* (1979), translated into English as *The Postmodern Condition* (1984). Lyotard (1924–1998) argued that the reign of what he called 'grand narratives' or 'metanarratives' was over, to be replaced by the far more modest and benign rule of limited, local narratives. Such grand, all-encompassing explanations and theories as religions, philosophical systems (including Marxism), psychoanalytic models (Freud, Lacan), ideologies (free-market capitalism), socio-political projects (the Enlightenment narrative of never-ending progress and future social harmony), had been exposed as fictions, as the mere narratives that they are, and had run their course. Extremely simplified, Lyotard said, postmodernism was an 'incredulity towards metanarratives' (Lyotard 1984: xxiv). Recognizing that in the absence of metanarratives there is no way to reconcile diametrically conflicting and equally weighted 'local' narratives, he accepted that the postmodern condition inevitably involved incommensurability, and would produce unsolvable dilemmas. In other words, like Derrida's deconstruction, Lyotard's postmodernism led in the direction of undecidability.

For Lyotard, the dilemmas that the postmodern condition threw up were real enough. For another theorist, Jean Baudrillard (1929–2007), they were both real and what he called 'hyperreal'. Which is to say that they were real to the parties involved and yet, simultaneously, unreal because reality itself had at some point become unreal, a simulation. Somewhere along the way, because of the ubiquitous commodification caused by free-market capitalism, we had become inauthentic, mere copies that simulated an originality and authenticity that we did not know was forever gone (the 1999 film *The Matrix* and its sequels come to mind). An equally pessimistic diagnosis of the postmodern condition was offered by the American Marxist critic Fredric Jameson, another important voice in what briefly was an intense discussion. Jameson suggested that the postmodern condition, which he, too, attributed to the ever more powerful march of capitalism – he defined postmodernism as 'the cultural logic of late capitalism' – had led to what he called a 'waning of affect'. Whereas before the advent of postmodernity we still had known authentic emotions, we now experienced mere 'intensities'.

More tenuously connected to postmodernism than the other French theorists who were associated with the term was the philosopher Gilles Deleuze (1925–1995), who wrote part of his oeuvre in collaboration with the psychoanalyst Félix Guattari (1930–1992). Deleuze's radical decentrings – some of his openly proclaimed aims are the subversion of Western philosophy and the 'liquidation of the principle of identity'- and his concept of the 'rhizome' clearly have elements in common with his colleagues. The 'rhizome', a mode of lateral growth that 'has no beginning or end', and 'is always in the middle, between things' (Deleuze and Guattari 1986 [1980]: 21), is contrasted with the rooted, the vertical, the arboresque that he sees as controlling Western thinking and social organization. Radically opposed to the hierarchical and to the rooted, the fixed, in whatever form, Deleuze advocates 'deterritorialization', 'flows', 'nomadic' thinking. Deleuze and Guattari enjoyed a brief vogue in Anglophone literary theory through their concept of 'minor' literatures, proposed in *Kafka: Towards a Minor Literature* (published in French in 1975). A minor literature deterritorializes the major language in which it is written. Because it is written from a marginalized position, 'in it language is affected with a high coefficient of deterritorialization' (Deleuze and Guattari 1986: 16). It is thus inescapably political and speaks for the marginalized minority as such, not simply for its individual authors, and is even 'a revolutionary force for all literature' (19).

Postmodernism as an intellectual enterprise may almost be equated with the various poststructuralist positions that were first articulated in the 1960s and took in particular American literary criticism by storm in the 1970s and 1980s. It is only as a diagnosis of a supposed cultural malaise – usually seen as involving an extreme form of relativism and a mindless celebration of corporate capitalism – that it has no direct connections with poststructuralism. Indeed, such diagnoses tend to come from political conservatives who abhor poststructuralism – which they see as a radically relativist and renegade mode of thought that seeks to destroy the values underpinning Western culture – or from Marxists such as Jameson (or his British colleague Terry Eagleton) who see it as the product of an unfettered capitalism that can no longer be controlled.

SUGGESTIONS FOR FURTHER READING

Jacques Derrida's writings are notoriously difficult. However, 'Différance', in the opening section of his *Margins of Philosophy* (1984), is a reasonably accessible discussion of this central concept. Another text that might serve as an introduction to Derrida's critique of logocentrism is 'Structure, Sign, and Play in the Discourse of the Human Sciences' (1970), reprinted in many anthologies of literary theory, including David Lodge and Nigel Wood's *Modern Criticism and Theory: A Reader* (2000; 3rd edition 2014). Roland Barthes's 'The Death of the Author' and his 'From Work to Text', which focus on literary writing, must also be recommended. Originally published in *Image–Music–Text* (1977), the essays are also available in *The Rustle of Language* (1986). Deconstructionist readings of texts are never easy. Derrida's discussion of Kafka's 'Before the Law' (1987) is fairly accessible and gives a good impression of his interpretative practice. Another good starting point is Barbara Johnson's discussion of Melville's *Billy Budd*, which I have briefly mentioned and which is to be found in her *The Critical Difference* (1980). Jonathan Culler's *On Deconstruction: Theory and Criticism after Structuralism* (1984) offers a thorough but relatively difficult overview. More recent and quite accessible introductions are Catherine Belsey's *Poststructuralism: A Very Short Introduction* (2002), James Williams's *Understanding Poststructuralism* (2005) and, especially recommended, Leslie Hill's *The Cambridge Introduction to Jacques Derrida* (2007). David J. Gunkel's *Deconstruction* (2021) is a rather idiosyncratic but useful recent introduction.

The Foucault Reader, edited by David Rabinow (1984), is an excellent selection, with an emphasis on Foucault's later work. The interviews that are included serve as brief and lucid introductions to his thought. Another collection, *Power/Knowledge: Selected Interviews and Other Writings, 1972–1977* (1980), edited by Colin Gordon, also contains helpful characterizations of his work by Foucault himself (see 'Two Lectures' and 'Truth and Power'). Foucault's famous discussion of 'panopticism' was originally published in Part III of his *Discipline and Punish* (1977). Lisa Downing's *The Cambridge Introduction to Michel Foucault* (2008) offers a very good introduction to Foucault's work. *Michel Foucault: Key Concepts* (2011), edited by Dianna Taylor, collects twelve essays on Foucault's central themes. In his *French Theory: How Foucault, Derrida, Deleuze, and Co. Transformed the Intellectual Life of the United States* (2008) François Cusset gives a very informative account of the meteoric rise of poststructuralist thought in American academic institutions.

A good and accessible introduction to psychoanalytic criticism is Mathew R. Martin's *Psychoanalysis and Literary Theory* (2023). *The Cambridge Companion to Literature and Psychoanalysis* (2022), edited by Vera Camden, offers, apart from its useful introduction, examples of psychoanalytic criticism in action. Malcolm Bowie's *Lacan* (1991) is still an excellent introduction to the complexities of Lacan, as is Sean Homer's *Jacques Lacan* (2005). Lacan's own writings are notoriously difficult. Bruce Fink provides a very helpful guide to Lacan's famous discussion of *Hamlet* in his 'Reading Hamlet with Lacan'

(1996). Lacanian criticism is usually not easily accessible either. A relative exception, however, is provided by Linda Ruth Williams's Lacanian readings in her *Critical Desire: Psychoanalysis and the Literary Subject* (1995).

Literary Feminisms by Ruth Robbins (2000) gives a very readable account of French feminism in relation to in particular Lacanian psychoanalysis. *Between Feminism and Psychoanalysis* (1990), edited by Teresa Brennan, collects fifteen essays on French feminism by major feminist critics. A more recent collection is *The French Feminism Reader* (2000) edited by Kelly Oliver.

For a lively overview of the strategies of postmodern novels, see Brian McHale, *Postmodernist Fiction* (1987). For the more thematic aspects of postmodern writing see Linda Hutcheon's *A Poetics of Postmodernism: History, Theory, Fiction* (1988). Ian Gregson's *Postmodern Literature* (2004) is a very readable account of postmodern fiction. Fredric Jameson's *Postmodernism, or, the Cultural Logic of Late Capitalism* (1991) is a hugely influential Marxist analysis of contemporary culture, including both postmodern literature and criticism. Hans Bertens's *The Idea of the Postmodern* (1995) discusses the rise of 'postmodern' and 'postmodernism' as critical concepts in literature, the arts, architecture, and the social sciences. Finally, Christopher Butler's *Postmodernism: A Very Short Introduction* (2002) and Simon Malpas's *The Postmodern* (2005) are excellent introductions to postmodern thought and postmodern cultural practice.

LITERATURE AND CULTURE
CULTURAL STUDIES, THE NEW HISTORICISM, CULTURAL MATERIALISM

CULTURAL STUDIES

In his *Culture and Anarchy* Matthew Arnold, whose formative influence on English and American literary studies I have discussed in the first chapter, sees as one of the sources of the 'anarchy' of his title a working class which 'assert[s] an Englishman's heaven-born privilege of doing as he likes' (Arnold 1971 [1869]: 105). Unfortunately, this sense of personal freedom does not lead the working class towards 'the best that had been thought and said', but to activities and pastimes that in their brashness and thoughtless vulgarity are the antithesis of culture. *Culture and Anarchy* sets up an opposition between culture – which for Arnold means implies coherence and order – and chaos and lawlessness. The term 'culture' is explicitly reserved for what most literary academics would now consider to be a rather narrowly defined 'high culture' – the culture of a specific elite.

The opposition between a superior high culture and a vulgar, commercial, and exploitative mass culture that always threatens its existence runs like a red thread through pre-1970s English and American criticism. It is, in fact, this opposition between high culture and the various – and socially dominant – ways of life or cultures that threaten it that gave English Studies its extraordinary self-confidence. The idea that high culture is essentially different from other forms of culture and that it has an inherently oppositional role to play with regard to other cultural expressions,

DOI: 10.4324/9781003373438-7

explains the missionary zeal and the moral urgency that we so often encounter in classic English and American criticism. For Leavis, the guardians of Arnold's 'best' — first of all, the literary critics — had the moral duty to defend high culture and to offer the sort of cultural critique that would maintain its standards and expose the inferiority of other cultural expressions. *Culture and Environment*, published by Leavis and Denys Thompson in 1921, is a case in point.

However, although it had strong opinions about lower-class and mass culture (which are not necessarily the same), traditional criticism did not much to examine and understand it. This changed in the late 1950s with the English critic Richard Hoggart's *The Uses of Literacy: Aspects of Working-Class Life with Special Reference to Publications and Entertainments* (1957), which offered a warm, autobiographical account of Yorkshire working-class culture of the 1930s and 1940s combined with a close reading of popular magazines of the period, and with Raymond Williams's *Culture and Society, 1780–1950* (1958), which traces the idea of culture as it developed in England from the late eighteenth century to (almost) the time of writing. Both Hoggart and Williams were literary academics, with Hoggart representing a leftist humanist perspective and Williams a moderately Marxist one, and both emphasized the valuable and life-enhancing qualities of cultures, in particular working-class culture, that from the perspective of high culture were generally condemned. Here is an example of Hoggart's evaluative but sympathetic attitude. Admitting that the more genuinely working-class magazines and the fiction that they print for their primarily female readers 'are in some ways crude', Hoggart goes on to stress that 'they still have a felt sense of the texture of life in the group they cater for' (Hoggart 1971 [1957]: 121). In fact, '[t]he strongest impression, after one has read a lot of these stories, is of their extraordinary fidelity to the detail of the readers' lives' (126). 'Most of the material is conventional,' Hoggart tells us, 'that is, it mirrors the attitudes of the readers; but those attitudes are by no means as ridiculous as one might first be tempted to think' (122). Working-class culture is simple, often even 'childish', but it is genuine and affirmative, and it also plays a valuable role in the lives of millions of people.

Still, although it does not hesitate to step across the barrier dividing literature from what we might call pulp fiction, in an important way

Hoggart's book repeats the traditional juxtaposition of authenticity and inauthenticity that we have already seen in D.H. Lawrence and F. R. Leavis. While for Hoggart the older and more traditional working-class magazines convey authenticity (a 'felt sense of ... life'), the newer ones tend to succumb to a sensationalism that is a sure sign of the postwar commodification of the genre at the expense of honesty and sincerity. A new, manipulative mass culture created by corporate interests and directed at the passive consumer is taking the place of an older popular culture that came from below and in which there was still a bond, a system of shared values.

In Williams we find similar echoes of the ideal of an organic and shared culture. 'We need a common culture', Williams tells us in the concluding chapter of *Culture and Society*, 'because we shall not survive without it' (Williams 1961 [1958]: 304). Like so many other critics, Williams finds this common culture in literature and the other arts: 'in the arts of a period ... the actual living sense, the deep community that makes the communication possible, is naturally drawn upon' (Williams 1965 [1961]: 64–65). He is fully aware that in any given society we will find more than one single culture – which in his use of the term signifies 'a whole way of life' – but the coexistence of several different cultures does not rule out a common culture: 'In our culture as a whole, there is both a constant interaction between these ways of life and an area which can properly be described as common to or underlying both' (Williams 1961 [1958]: 313). The further development of that common culture (about which Williams would later change his mind) is then described as a process of organic growth aided by its members: 'The idea of a common culture brings together ... at once the idea of natural growth and that of its tending' (322).

What we see is that the basis for cultural critique has shifted from literature to culture. Hoggart uses an older, more authentic and organic working-class culture to expose the mercenary outlook of the new culture that is in the process of replacing it. Williams puts his hope in a common culture, based on working class-values such as democratic solidarity – 'the basic collective idea' that finds expression in, for instance, trade unions and cooperative ventures – as the place from which to critique the free market ideology of capitalism which alienates people from their true selves. Both radically expand the field of study for literary criticism, while they stay true to Leavis's notion that criticism – which now includes cultural criticism – should position itself in opposition to those socio-economic forces that threaten authentic life and its modes of expression and to single out those literary texts and cultural products that resist the instrumentalization of reason and its corollary, the prioritizing of profit.

Although in their ideal of authenticity and organic coherence Hoggart and Williams belong to what for many critics writing today is an older intellectual dispensation, with their work and that of Stuart Hall – whose *The Popular* Arts (1964), written with Paddy Whannel, offers close readings of television programmes and other forms of popular culture – what we now call 'cultural studies' became a legitimate interest of Anglo-American literary academics. That interest got a further boost when in the early 1970s French structuralist approaches to culture, such as Roland Barthes's *Mythologies* (1957), with its analyses of the most diverse cultural phenomena, became available in English. In the course of the 1970s and 1980s the question of culture, and in particular that of a culture that could offer resistance to an apparently omnipresent capitalist order – a place in which cultural critique could be lived or from where it could be offered – became ever more important. One reason for this was the ever-increasing dominance of everyday life by the corporate media – which soon became a major object of study for cultural studies – another was the influence of first Althusser and Gramsci and then Foucault. Althusser's state apparatuses, Gramsci's notion of hegemony, and Foucault's discourses suggested that cultural practices constituted a form of power with enormous influence. Power was no longer exclusively defined in military, economic, or political terms, but was discovered in activities that had always seemed innocuous or even diverting. Cultures and subcultures stood accused of being the carriers of undesirable ideologies.

A third reason for the ever increasing importance of culture (and of cultural studies) was the insight, derived from structuralism and poststructuralism, that all cultures, no matter how seemingly authentic, were constructions. And if cultures were constructed, they could be contested, perhaps even changed. Williams, influenced by Gramsci, who had argued that resistance to the dominant culture was a valid option, developed a theory of culture that recognized both the power of the dominant culture to win consent without the use of force and a self-determination that made resistance possible: 'no dominant culture in reality exhausts human practice, human energy, human intention' (Williams 1996 [1980]: 43) True to his Marxist leanings Williams saw such self-determination not in terms of liberal humanism, as an autonomous, individual act, but as the product of social forces. In any case, whatever their philosophical persuasion, the emergence of cultural studies as a new discipline offered critics instruments to talk about power and the relationship between culture and power that literary criticism had lacked.

Given its background in oppositional criticism, cultural studies was eager to find resistance to the pressure of hegemonic culture in niches and subcultures that at first seemed wholly commodified and to show how the creative and subversive appropriation and reworking of hegemonic culture – by for instance women or minority artists – could be a positive source of pleasure. And so, for a while, cultural studies sought political subversion in practically every subculture, and tended to see hybridity – the coming together of elements taken from two or more cultures in one new (sub) culture – as oppositional in itself, as a form of resistance to a homogeneous corporate culture. In the course of the 1980s, spurred on by the feminist movement, by Britain's changing demographics, and by critiques such as the one articulated in Paul Gilroy's *There Ain't No Black in the Union Jack: The Cultural Politics of Race and Nation* (1987), gender, race, and ethnicity were added to the agenda. And so was the construction of identities and the role that power plays in such constructions. With the explosive growth of interest in Derrida, Foucault, and other theorists, the problem of identity formation had become a hot topic, and culture obviously played a major role in the constitution of us subjects.

Although cultural studies, in Simon During's words, 'does consistently drift back towards the interpretative and empathetic methods of traditional hermeneutic disciplines, including the literary criticism to which it owes so much' (During 2005: 8), its focus, then, is definitely not literature, but the vastly larger world of contemporary culture. But cultural studies would require a book in itself and so we return to the more manageable world of literary theory.

THE NEW HISTORICISM AND CULTURAL MATERIALISM

The constructed character of culture and its annexation by literary studies are central in two modes of criticism that became prominent in the 1980s: the new historicism, which was American in origin and has remained largely American, and cultural materialism, which was, and is, mainly British.

Before I discuss them separately, let me make clear what these critical approaches have in common. First of all, both brought to the then still traditional study of Renaissance literature, in particular the work of Shakespeare, poststructuralist notions of the self, of discourse, and of power. In so doing the new historicism leaned more towards Foucault in its focus on power, on the discourses that serve as vehicles for power, and on such issues as the discursive construction of identity, while cultural materialism leaned more towards the Marxism of Raymond Williams (who had coined the term 'cultural materialism' in his 1977 *Marxism and Literature*) and its focus on ideology, on the role of institutions, and on the possibilities for subversion (or dissidence, as some cultural materialists prefer to call it).

The new historicism and cultural materialism reject both the autonomy and individual genius of the author and the autonomy of the literary work and see literary texts as absolutely inseparable from their historical context. The role of the author is not denied, but it is to a large extent determined by historical circumstances. As the prominent new historicist critic Stephen Greenblatt has put it: 'the work of art is the product of a negotiation between a creator or class or creators, equipped with a complex, communally shared repertoire of conventions, and the institutions and practices of society' (Greenblatt 1989: 12). The literary text, then, is always part and parcel of a specific cultural, political, social, and economic dispensation. Far from being untouched by the historical moment of its creation, the literary text is directly involved in history. Instead of transcending its own time and place, as traditional Anglo-American criticism had argued (and was still arguing), the literary text is a time- and place-bound verbal construction that is always in one way or another political. Because it is inevitably involved with ideologically charged discourses, it cannot help being a vehicle for power. As a consequence, and just like any other text, literature does not simply reflect relations of power, but actively participates in the consolidation and/or construction of discourses and ideologies, just as it functions as an instrument in the construction of identities, not only at the individual level – that of the subject – but also at the level of the group or even that of the national state. Literature is not simply a product of history, it also actively *makes* history. Because they do not see literature as a special category of essentially a-historical texts, new historicists and cultural materialists treat literary texts in the same way as they treat other texts. For their specific purposes – to trace and bring to light relations of power and processes of ideological and cultural construction – there is no difference between literature and other texts, no matter whether these are religious, political, historical, or simply documentary in nature. Finally, acting on their conviction that culture, including all beliefs and values, is a construction, the new historicists and cultural materialists are willing to grant that their own assumptions must also be constructed and may therefore be deconstructed. But that does not prevent them from taking up political positions that are motivated by a political vision. The prominent new historicist critic Catherine Gallagher has argued that new historicist and cultural materialist thought must be seen as a continuation of certain strands within the New Left of the late 1960s (Gallagher 1989). As we will see, with regard to new historicist practice – as opposed to theory – not everybody accepts that claim at face value.

THE NEW HISTORICISM

If the new historicism and cultural materialism have so much in common what could possibly distinguish them? One distinctive feature is the role that subversion, or dissent, is allowed to play in them. As the British cultural materialist Catherine Belsey has argued, the new historicism's view of culture 'allows no space for dissent. Instead, minor revolts simply offer occasions for extending social control; crime legitimates an extension of the police' (Belsey 2005: 29). But let us first look at the new historicism's own history.

Although the term had been used before, the new historicism received its current meaning in 1982, when the prominent critic Stephen Greenblatt used it to describe recent work of himself and others on the Renaissance period. Most commentators situate its origin in 1980, though, when Greenblatt published his book *Renaissance Self-Fashioning: From More to Shakespeare* and when another prominent new historicist, Louis Montrose, argued for the presence of power in a genre usually not associated with its exercise, that of the pastoral. Following Foucault in his assumption that 'social relations are, intrinsically, relations of power', Montrose examined the role of Elizabethan pastorals in 'the symbolic mediation of social relationships' in his essay '"Eliza, Queen of Shepeardes," and the Pastoral of Power' (Montrose 1994 [1980]: 88). *Renaissance Self-Fashioning* argues that 'in the sixteenth century there appears to be an increased self-consciousness about the fashioning of human identity as a manipulable, artful process' (Greenblatt 1980: 2). This should not be taken to mean, however, that it was possible for Renaissance individuals to 'fashion' themselves fully and authentically. In the epilogue to *Self-Fashioning* Greenblatt tells us that in writing the book 'the human subject itself began to seem remarkably unfree, the ideological product of the relations of power in a particular society' (256). In short, there is good reason to accept John Brannigan's definition of the new historicism as 'a mode of critical interpretation which privileges power relations as the most important context for texts of all kinds' and his claim that '[a]s a critical practice it treats literary texts as a space where power relations are made visible' (Brannigan 1998: 6). In this Foucauldian context, power works through discourses and, like ideology, gives the subject the impression that complying with its dictates is the natural thing to do and thus a free, autonomous decision. The new historicists see literature as actively involved in the making of history through its participation in discursive practices. Louis Montrose's 1983 essay '"Shaping Fantasies": Figurations of Gender and Power in Elizabethan Culture' discusses a wide range of texts – including autobiography, travel writing and a Shakespeare play – to examine how representations of Queen Elizabeth I – the 'shaping fantasies' of his title – contribute to the creation of the essentially political cult of the 'virgin queen'.

The new historicism pays special attention to thus far hidden and unsuspected sources of, and vehicles for, power and on the question of how power has worked to suppress or marginalize rival stories and discourses. It has a distinct interest in the disempowered, the marginalized, those whose voices we hardly ever, or never, hear. Although it depends on the close reading of texts, its methods may be said to be anthropological rather than literary critical or historical. History, such as the socio-economic circumstances of a specific literary text's creation, is not read to illuminate literature, nor is literature read to shed a direct light on history. Rather, the historical period in question is seen as a network of intersections, including economic relations, whose various discursive manifestations – all the texts that have come down to us – need detailed attention and need to be brought into contact with each other so that the power relations and the forces operating in that culture may be brought to light. This means that it does not much matter from which point we try to access it – the earlier new historicism of the 1980s is famous for opening its enquiries with seemingly anecdotal material that is later on shown to have great relevance. Since under the regime of a specific hegemony (to use Gramsci's term) or dominant ideology everything is interrelated and since no specific body of texts has a privileged status, we can always start wherever we want to start in our explorations. Any text may lead us into the network of texts that is all that we have of a historical period. In its rather loose methodology the new historicism is indebted to the American anthropologist Clifford Geertz, not only because of his insistence that all culture is 'manufactured' and for all practical purposes without origins – in line with the poststructuralist view of culture – but also because of his method of 'thick description', that is, analysis by way of minutely observed social and cultural practices that have been recorded in great detail.

It is the influence of Foucault that has elicited a good deal of criticism. Foucault's views of power and its effectiveness have been widely, and inconclusively, debated, but no matter how we finally judge those views there are passages in his work that suggest a deep pessimism regarding the possibility of resistance. In a seminal new historicist essay, 'Invisible Bullets' (1981), Stephen Greenblatt echoes Foucault's pessimistic strain and argues that Renaissance subversion inevitably played into the hands of power. In fact, power *needs* subversion and actively produces it: 'subversiveness is the very product of that power and furthers its ends' (Greenblatt

1981: 48). This pessimism is not necessarily shared by all new historicists and I should in all fairness say that Greenblatt has also defended himself against charges such as the cultural materialist Alan Sinfield's claim that the new historicism works with an 'entrapment' model of culture that leaves no room for effective action and change. Still, although he argues that '[a]gency is virtually inescapable' (Greenblatt 1990: 74), Greenblatt immediately goes on to sketch a very limited horizon for agency:

> new historicism, as I understand it, does not posit historical processes as unalterable and inexorable, but it does tend to discover limits or constraints upon individual intervention: actions that appear to be single are disclosed as multiple; the apparently isolated power of the individual genius turns out to be bound up with collective, social energy; a gesture of dissent may be an element in a larger legitimation process, while an attempt to stabilize the order of things may turn out to subvert it.
>
> (Greenblatt 1990: 74–75)

The new historicists are of course aware that the at best limited freedom of the subject did not stop with the Renaissance period. As Louis Montrose has put it: 'I have a complex and substantial stake in sustaining and reproducing the very institutions whose operations I wish to call into question' (Montrose 1989: 30). However, as he suggests, although the 'possibility of political and institutional agency cannot be based upon the illusion of an escape from ideology', an *awareness* of the omnipresence and power of ideology, no matter how imperfect, may allow us some freedom: 'A reflexive knowledge so partial and unstable may, nevertheless, provide subjects with a means of empowerment as agents' (30). Apart from that, 'confrontations within or among ideologies' (30) may make room for relatively independent thought and action.

Let me conclude this section with a few observations. I have up till this point created the impression that the new historicism is concerned only with the Renaissance. Although it did indeed first emerge within Renaissance studies, where it caused a true revolution, by the mid-1980s new historicist approaches had spread to the study of other periods and in the 1990s they were virtually everywhere. Second, in the later 1980s and early 1990s, the dividing lines between the new historicism (and cultural materialism) on the one hand, and feminism and the newly emerging field of postcolonial studies on the other, began to fade.

Greenblatt's *Marvellous Possessions: The Wonder of the New World* of 1991, for instance, operates in a field of enquiry that we would now call postcolonial studies. It examines the role that 'wonder' plays in the response of European explorers and travellers to the New World. He characteristically sees that wonder as 'an agent of appropriation' (Greenblatt 1991: 24), in the sense that the expressions of wonder that we find in those (written) responses function as an instrument of power. Under Greenblatt's scrutiny, 'European representational practice' turns out to have played a vital role in the process of colonization that followed exploration and travel. Although its focus is on the Europeans and not on the new worlds and new peoples that give rise to European wonder – as is usually the case in the postcolonial studies that I will discuss in the next chapter – *Marvelous Possessions* is as much a postcolonial study as it is new historicist.

The new directions we find in 1990s new historicism can be interpreted as a sign of the times, as testimony to the sudden, and pervasive, influence of the new field of postcolonial studies, but it is also a response to serious critique. Feminist and other critics had begun to object to the steamroller effect of the new historicism's view of power – to how in new historicist criticism structures of power flattened and homogenized all subjects that lived within them so that differences in class, sex, and race practically disappeared from view. Responding to such criticisms, the new historicism had begun to take such differences into account in its analyses of the way subjects are constructed. But the theorizing of sex and race that came in the wake of poststructuralism will have to wait until the next chapters.

CULTURAL MATERIALISM

Cultural materialist criticism established itself permanently in the field of literary studies in the mid-1980s, with the publication of Jonathan Dollimore's *Radical Tragedy: Religion, Ideology and Power in the Drama of Shakespeare and his Contemporaries* (1984), of Catherine Belsey's *The Subject of Tragedy: Identity and Difference in Renaissance Drama* (1985), and of two collections of essays: *Alternative Shakespeares* (1985) edited by John Drakakis, and *Political Shakespeare: Essays in Cultural Materialism* (1985) edited by Jonathan Dollimore and Alan Sinfield. Like the new historicism, cultural materialism saw literature as part of a much wider context. As Dollimore and Sinfield put it in their introduction to *Political Shakespeare*, '[a] play by Shakespeare is related to the context of its production – to the economic and political system of Elizabethan and Jacobean England and to the particular institutions of cultural production (the church, patronage, theatre, education)' (Dollimore and Sinfield 1985: viii).

Cultural materialism focused on the ideological forces at work in Shakespeare's plays, and in early modern literature generally. But it also studied contemporary performances of the plays, including their screen versions, and analysed how Shakespeare's work had been hijacked by conservative critics and educators, how it was presented in secondary school curricula and in higher education, and how Shakespeare or his work were used for commercial purposes such as advertising and merchandising. Cultural materialists agree that literary texts will at first sight seem supportive of the dominant ideology of their time, but see that ideology as less pervasive than their new historicist colleagues do. One of their main interests was the way in which the dominant social order sought (and seeks) to legitimize itself, for instance through the construction of socially marginalized groups as 'other' – a practice that led to an early interest in issues of gender and race and would substantially contribute to the rise of queer studies. Although Foucault is an obvious influence in their work, cultural materialism follows Williams in his argument that the dominant, hegemonic culture is never the only player in the cultural field, even if it is by far the most powerful. Since cultures are always in process there will always be the remains of an older culture that is on its way out and the first signs of a new, emergent culture. So while cultural materialist analyses of literary texts bring to light how these texts function as instruments of a dominant socio-cultural order, they also show how the apparent coherence of that order is threatened from the inside, by inner contradictions and by tensions that it seeks to hide.

Alan Sinfield's discussion of Shakespeare's *Othello* in his *Faultlines: Cultural Materialism and the Politics of Dissident Reading* (1992) is a case in point. In the patriarchal culture that the play presents

Desdemona is bound to obey her father, and the role of obedient daughter should in the normal course of things lead her to follow his wishes in her marital choice. However, in the early modern period we also find an increased emphasis on the idea that marriage should be personally fulfilling. This 'contradiction in the ideology of marriage' – one of Sinfield's 'faultlines' – allows Desdemona to disregard her father's wishes and to marry a man who is totally unsuitable from the perspective of the social group to which she belongs. As a result, the social order comes under immediate pressure. I should hasten to point out that for Sinfield Desdemona is not a free, autonomous agent in the dissident choice that she makes. It is the faultline in question that creates what Sinfield calls 'dissident potential'. Dissidence is not so much a matter of individual agency but is produced by the inner contradictions that characterize any social order.

Since such faultlines are to be found in all cultures, it is only natural that they should turn up in literary texts – *especially* in literary texts, in fact, because literature offers a place where contradictions and tensions can be addressed and worked through. Focusing on the cracks in the ideological façade that texts offer, cultural materialism reads even the most reactionary texts against the grain, offering readings of dissidence that allow us to hear the socially marginalized and that expose the ideological machinery that is responsible for their marginalization and exclusion. Cultural materialists are also interested in the way in which traditional humanist criticism has obscured the presence of ideological faultlines in those texts. Dollimore's *Radical Tragedy* argues (among many other things) that the traditional interpretations of the Jacobean tragedies that he discusses – including Marlowe's *Dr Faustus* and Tourneur's *The Revenger's Tragedy* – have ignored how the plays undermine humanist assumptions because they focus exclusively on what fits the humanist framework.

Cultural materialism reads texts for signs of subversion and political dissidence and sees those (often controversial) readings of texts from the past as political interventions in the present. Its critical practice not only tries to offer alternative understandings of the past but equally, and overtly, tries to effectuate political change in the present from a broadly socialist and feminist point of view. (Catherine Belsey's discussion, in *The Subject of Tragedy*, of the various literary – and non-literary – representations of the six-teenth-century murderer-by-proxy Alice Arden immediately announces cultural materialism's stake in feminism.) As Dollimore and Sinfield polemically announce in their introduction to *Political Shakespeare*:

> Cultural materialism does not, like much established criticism, attempt to mystify its perspective as the natural, obvious or right interpretation of an allegedly given textual fact. On the contrary, it registers its commitment to the transformation of a social order which exploits people on grounds of race, gender and class.
>
> (Dollimore and Sinfield 1985: viii)

Because of its double focus on the past and on contemporary pol-itics, cultural materialism is deeply interested in the ways in which literature from the past, say the works of Shakespeare, has been made to function in later periods and in our contemporary culture. As Dollimore and Sinfield point out, 'culture is made continuously and Shakespeare's text is reconstructed, reappraised, reassigned all the time through diverse institutions in specific contexts. What the plays signify, how they signify, depends on the cultural field in which they are situated' (viii). Cultural materialism could, for instance, ask which Shakespeare plays, or parts of plays, feature on secondary school reading lists. Which plays do we find within university curricula? Which sonnets are standardly anthologized? Which plays are still performed, and where, and within what context? How do we read the film version of *Richard III* (1998) which lifts the play right out of its historical period and has its protagonist set up a monstrously fascist regime in 1930s Great Britain? In other words, how is 'Shakespeare' constructed, and from what ideological position?

In one of the essays collected in *Political Shakespeare* Sinfield concludes that '[i]n education Shakespeare has been made to speak mainly for the right', adding that 'that is the tendency which this book seeks to alter' (Dollimore and Sinfield 1985: 135). For cul-tural materialists ideology takes on a tangible, material form in institutions like the university, the museum, the army, the school, the church, the labour unions and other organizations. And ideol-ogy becomes material in the ways in which images and representations from the past are used to promote it – in for instance the merchandising of the product called 'Shakespeare' (and other big sellers in the heritage industry) and in the use of 'Shakespeare' in commercials. In *Faultlines* Sinfield shows how a reference to Shakespeare's Globe Theatre, evoking the continuity of British tradition, is used by a manufacturer of defence equipment to promote itself and its wares. From the perspective of cultural materialism, contemporary culture is a battlefield where an omnipresent conservative ideology must constantly be challenged.

The acrimony of the debate that followed cultural materialism's emergence in the mid-1980s testifies to the effectiveness of its intervention, although it also demonstrates the strength and number of those literary academics who prefer a more traditional, and still broadly humanist, approach – especially to Shakespeare ('The Bard'), whose work was the focus of a protracted battle. In the early 1990s cultural materialism expanded its original interests and incorporated issues of empire and sexuality (feminism had been on its agenda from the beginning). Jonathan Dollimore's *Sexual Dissidence: Augustine to Wilde, Freud to Foucault* (1991) and Alan Sinfield's *The Wilde Century: Effeminacy, Oscar Wilde and the Queer Moment* (1994) and his *Cultural Politics – Queer Reading* of the same year exemplify this development, but the so-called 'queer theory' that we see in the making in these texts – and in a wide range of other texts from around the same time – will have to wait until Chapter 8. Cultural materialism's emphasis on the historical and material conditions of the production and reception of texts has remained influential, especially in Britain, but as time went on its political interventions largely lost their effectiveness.

SUGGESTIONS FOR FURTHER READING

John Brannigan's *New Historicism and Cultural Materialism* (1998) is an excellent early introduction while Kiernan Ryan's *New Historicism and Cultural Materialism: A Reader* (1996) presents important intellectual sources and examples of critical practice. Brief but to the point is Louis Montrose's 'New Historicisms' (1992). H. Aram Veeser's collection *The New Historicism Reader* (1994) brings together a number of important examples of the new historicism in action. Excellent examples of new historicist readings are Stephen

Greenblatt's 'Invisible Bullets' and Louis Montrose '"Eliza, Queene of Shepeardes," and the Pastoral of Power'. Greenblatt and Christine Gallagher's *Practicing New Historicism* (2000) offers essays on a wide range of topics. *The Greenblatt Reader* (2004), edited by Michael Payne, collects Greenblatt's most important writings in a single volume.

Ryan presents an excerpt from Alan Sinfield's *Faultlines* that wonderfully exemplifies cultural materialism's interest in dissidence. The second chapter of Sinfield's *Cultural Politics – Queer Reading* (1994; 2nd edition 2005) is a lively introduction to cultural materialism. Also very readable is the polemical introduction to Jonathan Dollimore and Alan Sinfield's *Political Shakespeare: New Essays in Cultural Materialism* (1985), a book that with its interest in 'Shakespeare' in the twentieth century also illustrates cultural materialism's contemporary focus. Andrew J. Milner's *Re-imagining Cultural Studies: The Promise of Cultural Materialism* (2002) and Alan Sinfield's *Shakespeare, Authority, Sexuality: Unfinished Business in Cultural Materialism* (2006) brought cultural materialism into the twenty-first century. Neema Parvini's *Shakespeare and Contemporary Theory: New Historicism and Cultural Materialism* (2012) takes issue with what Parvini sees as cultural materialism's determinism and denial of agency. In his *Shakespeare and Cultural Materialist Theory* (2017) Christopher Marlow offers an excellent recent introduction to cultural materialism and the new historicism

Simon During's *Cultural Studies: A Critical Introduction* (2005) is a somewhat unorthodox, but highly readable and very well-informed introduction to cultural studies and his *The Cultural Studies Reader* (3rd edition 2007) collects almost forty major contributions to the emergence and rise of the discipline. Other good introductions are David Oswell's *Culture and Society: An Introduction to Cultural Studies* (2006), Michael Ryan's *Cultural Studies: A Practical Introduction* (2010) and Chris Barker and Emma Jane's *Cultural Studies: Theory and Practice* (5th edition 2016). *Introducing Cultural Studies* (3rd edition 2017) by Brian Longhurst *et al.* offers a very comprehensive and thorough overview of the field.

POSTCOLONIAL CRITICISM AND THEORY

INTRODUCTION

As we have seen in Chapter 4, in the 1920s and 1930s, with the Harlem Renaissance and with the introduction of the concept of *négritude* – the idea that all Africans and people of African origin somehow participated in a collective consciousness – 'race' began to be a factor of importance in literary studies. Refusing to be defined, on the basis of race, by the dominant white culture, African-American and French-speaking writers from Africa and the Caribbean began to define themselves and their culture in their own terms. After the Second World War, this project of cultural self-definition developed alongside the project of political liberation and self-determination that we find in the American Civil Rights movement and in the demands of Asian, African and Caribbean colonies for political independence and nationhood. This should not create the impression that cultural self-definition and political self-determination moved along two parallel lines that never met. On the contrary, the one cannot be separated from the other. The African-American Black Arts movement saw itself as the cultural wing of the political Black Power movement of the 1960s and we have seen how Frantz Fanon, a radical critic of colonialism, saw national cultures – and in particular national literatures – as important instruments in the struggle for political independence. Cultural self-definition and political self-determination were two sides of the same coin.

The desire for cultural self-determination, that is, for cultural independence, is one of the driving forces behind the literatures

DOI: 10.4324/9781003373438-8

that in the 1960s and 1970s sprang up in the former colonies. Wilson Harris (Guyana), Yambo Ouologuem (Mali), Chinua Achebe (Nigeria), Wole Soyinka (the winner of the 1986 Nobel Prize for literature, also from Nigeria), Derek Walcott (the 1992 Nobel laureate, from Santa Lucia), and a wide range of other writers created novels and poems that respond to, and reflect, their immediate cultural environment. In their response to specific cultural contexts, these texts signal the emergence – and in some cases, where a literary tradition had already developed, the confirmation – of new national literatures. The desire to draw directly on one's own culture is defended vigorously in an essay called 'Colonialist Criticism' that Chinua Achebe first presented in 1974 (see Achebe 1995). Arguing that the 'universal' qualities that Western criticism expects from literature are not so much 'universal' as 'European' in a universal disguise, he attacks the idea that literary art should transcend its time and place. Paradoxically, his own *Things Fall Apart* from 1958, which describes the effects of colonialism on an Igbo community in moving detail, has spoken to large audiences all over the world.

As its title indicates, *Things Fall Apart* is written in English, as are the large majority of literary works written in the former British colonies. That is not self-evident: English is usually the second language of these writers, in particular in Africa. The choice for English, then, is a conscious choice, and one that is not uncontroversial. The Kenyan novelist Ngugi wa Thiong'o, for instance, argued in the 1970s that the continued use of the language of the colonizer – leading to what he called 'Afro-Saxon' literature – is a form of self-inflicted neo-colonization and so he turned to Gikuyu, his native language, for the novels which have been translated as *The Devil on the Cross* (1980, translation 1982) and *Matigari* (1986, 1989). However, even if African writers use English, they often let the rhythms and idioms of their own language be heard because the defamiliarization that results from such a practice automatically draws our attention to the non-English linguistic and cultural context of their work – as in Ken Saro-Wiwa's ironically titled novel *Sozaboy: A Novel in Rotten English* (1985). But how should we classify such novels? We cannot very well claim that *Things Fall Apart*, although written in English and dealing with British colonialism, belongs to English literature, just as we cannot seriously claim that Derek Walcott's epic poem *Omeros* (1990) is English. In recognition of this new situation, in which writing in English from the former colonies – including India, Pakistan, Sri Lanka, and other Asian colonies – has proved itself as vital and as important as the literature written in England itself, we now usually speak of 'literatures in English' rather than of 'English literature' if we want to refer to English-language writing from the United Kingdom and its former colonies.

COMMONWEALTH LITERARY STUDIES AND EUROCENTRISM

When in the later 1960s it first became clear that the former colonies were busy producing literatures of their own, the idea that 'English literature' was mutating into 'literatures in English' of which the literary production of England was only one – although still very important – strand, was still unthinkable. Instead, English critics interested in the writings that came out of the former colonies developed the idea of a 'Commonwealth literature': the English-language literature of the dependencies and former colonies that, with Great Britain at its centre, formed the so-called Commonwealth of Nations, or British Commonwealth. With hindsight, we can see that the idea of a Commonwealth literature followed the hierarchy of the political Commonwealth in that it placed the literature of Great Britain at the centre of this otherwise rather loose configuration. Although Commonwealth literary studies rarely said so explicitly, English literature and English criticism set the norm.

In its early stages, the study of Commonwealth literature was traditionally humanistic. Although it tried to do justice to the widely varying historical and cultural contexts of Commonwealth literature – and to explain those to British readers – its critical practice often assumed that its moral and aesthetic framework had universal validity because it rested upon the foundation of an unchanging, universal human condition. Because that is the case, it could without much further thought be applied to the work of writers ranging from Jamaica to Nigeria and from India to New Zealand. A writer like Chinua Achebe was not primarily seen as Nigerian, or even African, but as contributing to a humanistic

English literary tradition. It was in fact this idea that all Commonwealth writers were working within the English tradition that gave the otherwise hopelessly heterogeneous field of Commonwealth studies a semblance of unity.

At that time, admission to the ranks of English literature might still have counted as an official stamp of approval for writers from former colonies like Australia or Canada. However, African, Asian, and Caribbean Commonwealth writers were on the whole not happy with the Western or *Eurocentric* perspective of Commonwealth criticism, not least because their memories of colonial rule had not invariably convinced them of British civilization's humanistic superiority. In the course of the 1970s their objections – voiced in Achebe's 'Colonialist Criticism' and other critiques – began to find a serious echo in the writings of a number of British literary academics who had themselves begun to question the supposedly universal validity of humanist values. These critics argued, first, that overseas writers must be seen within the specific context of the culture of which they were part and which informed their writing and, second, that that culture was not inferior to, but only different from, the culture of the mother country. This new approach also exposed and contested the ideological underpinnings of the colonialist enterprise (in what was called 'colonial discourse analysis'), and in one important version argued that the relationship between the former colonial powers and their colonies could most rewardingly be analysed with the help of Marxist concepts (with the colonized as the oppressed class). Looked at from this perspective all these 'literatures in English' become the site of a struggle over ideology. From this Marxist perspective the work of Commonwealth writers was either involved in an ideological resistance against (neo-)colonial forces or else ideologically complicit with them (the work of the Trinidadian Nobel Prize winner V.S. Naipaul has, for instance, been accused of such complicity).

POSTCOLONIAL STUDIES

In the last forty years, the question of how we should read writers that, like the Commonwealth writers, write in a European language but are geographically and often ethnically not European, has become more and more pressing. We now find African writers writing in English, French, Afrikaans, and Portuguese, and Caribbean writers writing in English, French, Dutch, and Spanish. These writers may still live in their home country or they may have moved to the *metropolis*, that is, the centre of cultural power in a specific colonial relationship – London, and by extension all of England, for the Commonwealth nations, Paris (or France) for the French-speaking colonies. However, wherever they live, the question of how we should read them remains the same. There is now, moreover, a new category of writers that confronts us with the same question. All industrialized Western nations have in the postwar period absorbed substantial numbers of immigrants: from former colonies, from regions with high unemployment, from places with dictatorial regimes, and from war zones like Vietnam, Afghanistan, Somalia, Iraq, or Syria. The sons and daughters of these immigrants, and by now their grandchildren, have begun to contribute to the literatures of the places where they have grown up. In so doing they only rarely completely forsake their cultural heritage. Although German-born and educated, German writers of Turkish descent will often work on the line where the culture of their parents (or grandparents) and the majority culture meet.

In a nation shaped by immigration like the United States such meetings of culture and the cultural displacements that usually follow from them are standard fare, from the encounters of Native American and English culture in James Fenimore Cooper's early nineteenth-century Leatherstocking novels to, for instance, the uneasy negotiations between traditional Chinese and modern American culture that we find in Maxine Hong Kingston's *The Woman Warrior* (1976). The literature of the US now includes Chinese-American, Japanese-American, Dominican-American (Junot Díaz, *The Brief Wondrous Life of Oscar Wao*, 2008), Nigerian-American (Tope Folarin, *A Particular Kind of Black Man*, 2019), and many other hyphenated literatures. In Europe, however, encounters with non-Western cultures and the consequent displacements are relatively new.

In the course of the 1980s Commonwealth literary studies and colonial discourse analysis became part of the then emerging and now vast field of literary, cultural, anthropological, political, economic, and historical inquiry into the consequences of Western colonization that we call postcolonial studies. Whereas Commonwealth literary studies tacitly assumed common ground between the cultural products of the former colonies and the culture of the *metropolis*, postcolonial theory and criticism emphasizes the tension between the metropolis and the (former) colonies, between what within the colonial framework were the metropolitan, imperial centre and its colonial satellites. At the heart of postcolonial studies we find a trenchant critique of Eurocentrism – with its division of the world into 'modern' Europeans and backwards 'others' – and a strong focus on those who in one way or another have become the victims of Eurocentric thought (its utilitarian rationality), attitudes (racism), politics (military expansion), and exploitation (economic or otherwise). In the field of literary studies it has led to new readings of virtually all canonical works (Shakespeare's *The Tempest*, Joseph Conrad's *Heart of Darkness*, and E.M. Forster's *A Passage to India*, with their non-European dimension, were obvious candidates for such new readings) and to a revision and expansion of the canon. This expansion is partly the result of the incorporation of non-European texts that fit the older canon's expectations (and might have been incorporated a good deal earlier), but it also results from a new appreciation of genuinely different aesthetic traditions.

Postcolonial theory and criticism radically questions the aggressively expansionist imperialism of the colonizing powers and in particular the system of values that supported imperialism and that it sees as still dominant within the Western world. It studies the process of cultural displacement that inevitably followed colonial conquest and rule and its consequences for personal and communal identities, and it studies the ways in which the displaced have offered resistance to colonization. In one of its most important versions, postcolonial theory sees such displacements, and the ambivalences and hybrid cultural forms to which they lead, as vantage points that allow us to expose the internal doubts and the instances of resistance that the West has suppressed in its homogenizing and globalizing course and to deconstruct the seamless façade that the combination of imperialism and capitalism has traditionally striven to present. Homi Bhabha, one of the most prominent postcolonial theorists, has put it this way:

> Postcolonial perspectives emerge from the colonial testimony of Third World countries and the discourses of 'minorities' within the geopolitical divisions of east and west, north and south. ... They

> formulate their critical revisions around issues of cultural difference, social authority, and political discrimination in order to reveal the antagonistic and ambivalent moments within the 'rationalizations' of modernity.
>
> (Bhabha 1992: 438)

Here, the postcolonial perspective, just like that of 'the marginal' in general, is a 'substantial intervention into those justifications of modernity – progress, homogeneity, cultural organicism, the deep nation, the long past – that rationalize the authoritarian, "normalizing" tendencies within cultures in the name of national interest' (Bhabha 1990: 4). For Bhabha, the postcolonial perspective has a disruptive potential because the effects of colonialism are similar to what we find in the analyses of the human predicament offered by poststructuralist theory:

> the encounters and negotiations of differential meanings and values within 'colonial' textuality, its governmental discourses and cultural practices, have enacted, *avant la lettre*, many of the problematics of signification and judgment that have become current in contemporary theory – aporia, ambivalence, indeterminacy, the question of discursive closure, the threat to agency, the status of intentionality, the challenge to 'totalizing' concepts, to name but a few.
>
> (Bhabha 1992: 439)

Bhabha might have added the 'problematic' of 'otherness' – which he mentions later in the essay from which I am quoting – and which remains a vexing problem: how to deal with *real* otherness, with the absolute 'incommensurability of cultural values and priorities' (439) that has often characterized colonial encounters? Even postcolonial studies, no matter how emphatic, has struggled with such concepts as the 'sacred' and 'ancestral land' and with the role of non-Western religions in struggles for independence.

Not all postcolonial theorists and critics would agree with Bhabha's suggestion that we can already find poststructuralist themes and perspectives in colonial situations and that, in a sense, the experience of the colonial subject and especially the migrant are emblematic for the way we experience ourselves in the early twenty-first century – as 'living on the borderline of the "present"'

(Bhabha 1994: 1). They would, however, surely agree with his claim that 'the language of rights and obligations' that operates in the various Western cultures 'must be questioned on the basis of the anomalous and discriminatory legal and cultural status assigned to migrant, diasporic, and refugee populations' (Bhabha 1992: 441).

Bhabha's reference to migrants and refugee populations might raise a not unimportant question. What exactly may postcolonial studies rightfully claim as its historical and geographical scope? Some critics have vigorously defended the inclusion of white set-tler colonies such as Australia, New Zealand, and Canada, arguing that their inhabitants, too, have suffered displacement and margin-alization at the hands of imperialism and have had to develop cul-tural identities against the odds of imperial relations. Others have argued that white settler colonies cannot fruitfully be put in one and the same scholarly framework with for instance Kenya or India because the question of race does not feature in the relations between white overseas subjects and the metropolis. Those critics claim instead that in settler colonies the postcolonial approach is only relevant for the encounter between (white) settlers and indi-genous populations (such as the New Zealand Maori).

And what about the historical range of postcolonial studies? Does colonization start in the wake of Columbus's first voyage to the Americas? Or should we see the late medieval Anglo-Norman conquest and consequent occupation of Ireland already within the framework of colonizing imperialism? There is no easy answer to such questions. However, all postcolonial theorists and critics would agree that they are engaged in a reassessment of the tradi-tional relationship between the metropolis and its colonial subjects and in the radical deconstruction – either along poststructuralist or along more traditional lines – of the imperialist perspective. They agree in their focus on colonial (and neocolonial) repression, on resistance to colonization, on the respective identities of colonizer and colonized, on patterns of interaction and cultural exchange in the colonies, on postcolonial migration to the metropolis, on post-independence hybridity, and other consequences of colonialism. Central to these interests are issues of race, indigeneity, language, gender, identity, class, and, above all, power, which often finds expression in sexual terms. Postcolonial theorists and critics would also agree on the relevance of their enterprise for the world of the early twenty-first century, from which colonies may have dis-appeared, but in which neocolonial relations abound – not only between Western nations and their former colonies, but also within those nations, between national majorities and ethnic minorities.

ORIENTALISM

With all due respect for the pioneering work done by postcolonial writers such as Edward Brathwaite, George Lamming, Wilson Harris, Chinua Achebe, and Wole Soyinka, postcolonial studies in its current form starts in 1978, with the publication of the Palesti-nian-American critic Edward Said's book *Orientalism*. Drawing primarily on Foucault, Said's study deeply influenced the agenda of the study of non-Western cultures and their literatures and pushed it in the direction of what we now call postcolonial theory.

Orientalism is a devastating critique of how through the ages, but particularly in the nineteenth century – the heyday of imperialist expansion – Western texts have represented the East, and more spe-cifically the Islamic Middle East (for the sake of convenience I will here refer to 'the Orient' or 'the East'), and how they were complicit in that imperialism. Using mostly British and French 'scholarly works ... works of literature, political tracts, journalistic texts, travel books, religious and philological studies' (Said 1991: 23), Said exam-ines how these texts either implicitly or explicitly *construct* the Orient through imaginative representations (in for instance novels), through seemingly factual descriptions (in journalistic reports and travel writ-ing), and through claims to knowledge about Oriental history and culture (in histories, anthropological writings, academic studies). Together, all these texts constitute a Foucauldian discourse – a col-lection of related written and visual representations, reports, studies, claims, and the like, that constitutes a discursive field within which 'knowledge' concerning a particular subject matter is constructed: 'without examining Orientalism as a discourse one cannot possibly understand the enormously systematic discipline by which European culture was able to manage – *and even produce* – the Orient politically, sociologically, militarily, ideologically, scientifically and imaginatively during the post-Enlightenment period' (3). For Said, Orientalism's 'imaginative geography' has legitimized Western imperialism in the eyes of Western governments and their electorates and it has also insidiously worked to convince the East that Western culture represented universal civilization. Accepting Western culture could only benefit the East's citizens and would make them participants in the most advanced civilization the world had ever seen.

For Said, Western representations of the Orient, no matter how well-intentioned, have always contributed to this damaging discourse. Even those Orientalists who were clearly in sympathy with Oriental peoples and their cultures – and Said finds a substantial number of them – have unintentionally contributed to Western domination. So instead of disinterested objectivity we find representations pervaded by Western subjectivity – not to mention outright, even if unconscious, fantasy – that have effectively paved the way for military domination, cultural displacement, and economic exploitation. Although we 'ought never to assume that the structure of Orientalism is nothing more than a structure of lies or myths', Said argues that 'Orientalism is more particularly valuable as a sign of European-Atlantic power over the Orient than it is as veridic discourse about the Orient' (Said 1991: 4). I should perhaps say at this point that in later publications, and in response to criticism, Said has presented a less homogeneous picture of Orientalism, while he has also acknowledged the importance of the response of native writers to the West's Orientalism. There is no doubt, however, that *Orientalism*, whatever its shortcomings may have been, revolutionized the way Western scholars and critics looked at representations of non-Western subjects and cultures.

Said's book also drew attention to the way in which the discourse of Orientalism serves to create the West just as it creates the East. West and East form a binary opposition in which the two poles define each other (see Chapter 5). The inferiority that Orientalism implicitly attributes to the East, in spite of its acknowledged achievements, simultaneously serves to construct the West's superiority. As Said puts it, 'European culture gained in strength and identity by setting itself off against the Orient as a sort of surrogate and even underground self' (Said 1991: 3). The supposed sensuality, irrationality, primitiveness, and despotism of the East constructs the West as rational, democratic, and progressive. The West always functions as the 'centre' so that the East's 'other', simply through its existence, confirms the West's centrality and superiority.

Not surprisingly perhaps, the opposition that the West's discourse about the East sets up makes use of another basic opposition, that between the masculine and the feminine. Naturally the West functions as the masculine pole – enlightened, rational, entrepreneurial, disciplined – while the East is its feminine opposition: irrational, passive, undisciplined and sensual. Once we have been alerted to this opposition we have no trouble finding it exemplified. Here is a passage from *A Short Walk in the Hindu Kush* (1958), a classic of travel writing by the English writer Eric Newby:

> there was a sudden outburst of screams and moans from the other side of the road, becoming more and more insistent and finally mounting to such a crescendo that I went to investigate.
>
> Gathered round a well or shaft full of the most loathsome sewage was a crowd of gendarmes in their ugly sky-blue uniforms and several women in a state of happy hysteria, one screaming more loudly than the rest.
>
> 'What is it?'
>
> '*Bābā*,' said one of the policemen, pointing to the seething mess at our feet and measuring the length of quite a small baby. He began to keen; presumably he was the father. I waited a little, no one did anything.
>
> This was the moment I had managed to avoid all my life; the rescue of the comrade under fire, the death-leaper from Hammersmith Bridge saved by Newby, the tussle with the lunatic with the cut-throat razor.
>
> Feeling absurd and sick with anticipation I plunged head first into the muck. It was only four feet deep and quite warm but unbelievable, a real eastern sewer. The first time I got hold of something cold and clammy that was part of an American packing case. The second time I found nothing and came up sputtering and sick to find the mother beating a serene little boy of five who had watched the whole performance from the house next door into which he had strayed. The crowd was already dispersing; the policeman gave me tea and let me change in the station house but the taste and smell remained.
>
> (Newby 1974 [1958]: 62–63)

Admittedly the irony of Newby's highly entertaining book is also, and consistently, directed at the author himself – and at his companion – but in emergencies it is their character that makes the difference. We also see this in a more recent, and, with regard to the representation of the East, far more sophisticated travel book, *The Places in Between* (2004) by the British politician Rory Stewart, who in the winter of 2002 walked through the wilds of Central Afghanistan from Herat to Kabul (and who, one might add, exemplifies empire in his personal history: born in Hong Kong and raised in Malaysia and Scotland). Stewart is a highly empathic outsider, who even speaks the language, but in his fascinating narrative he is a beacon of reason in an unpredictable, dangerous, and often medieval world.

Race, ethnicity, and the dominant position of the *metropolis* were already well established on the literary-critical agenda when *Orientalism* appeared, as was the study of Commonwealth writing and that of English literature dealing with colonial relations, like E. M. Forster's novel *A Passage to India* (1924). Said, however, was the first to draw on the new French theory and on the recently discovered Gramsci in dealing with what are now called post-colonial themes. *Orientalism* offered a challenging theoretical framework and a new perspective on the interpretation of European writing about the East (and other non-European cultures) and, perhaps even more importantly, of writing produced under colonial rule. Whereas in the study of Commonwealth writing novels from, say, India, Pakistan, or Kenya, were seen to have heterogeneous, discrete, backgrounds, each with its own particulars, now all such novels could be read within one unifying theoretical framework. Said's book also highlighted the role of Europe's cultural institutions (the universities, literature, newspapers, museums, to mention only a few) in its military, economic, and cultural domination of non-European nations and peoples and asked questions that we still ask concerning literature's role in past and present racial, ethnic, and cultural encounters. As a matter of fact, our questions have since 1978 only proliferated.

COLONIZED AND COLONIZER

One question that *Orientalism* does not address but that is central to the work of Homi Bhabha is what happens in the cultural interaction between colonizer and colonized. In earlier writings on colonialism, such an interaction was denied. Aimé Césaire, for instance, claimed in his 1955 *Discourse on Colonialism* that between colonizer and colonized there is '[n]o human contact, but relations of domination and submission which turn the colonizing man into a classroom monitor, an army sergeant, a prison guard, a slave driver, and the indigenous man into an instrument of production' (Césaire 1997: 81). British and French official accounts of colonial life standardly presented a wholly different, and benign, view of colonialism, but saw as little interaction between colonizer and colonized as Césaire. The colonizer remained his civilized and disciplined European self even in the most trying circumstances. The West has always been convinced that its presence overseas greatly affected the 'natives' (telling itself that the smartest and most sensitive of them immediately started scrambling to adopt Western ways and values), but has never been comfortable with the idea that its sons and daughters might in their turn be affected by the cultures they encountered. It is mostly in literature that we find alternative perspectives. In Joseph Conrad's *Heart of Darkness* (1899) the colonial experience has the effect of turning the ivory collector Kurtz into a megalomaniacal barbarian, and in E.M. Forster's *Passage to India* (1924) two British women suffer experiences in India that permanently unsettle them.

For Bhabha, who is a major theorist of the subjectivities of colonizer and colonized, their encounter always affects both. Said's *Orientalism* analyses the process by which Orientalist discourse sets up a binary opposition between Europe and the Orient, between colonizer and colonized, but Bhabha sets out to deconstruct that opposition, at least on the level of the subjects involved. As I have mentioned above, colonialism, with the displacements and terrible uncertainties that it brings, is such a radically unsettling 'affective experience of marginality' (Bhabha 1992: 438) that the colonized subject's plight can be seen as prefiguring poststructuralist decentring. But the colonial experience also affects the colonizer. More specifically, for Bhabha the colonizer cannot escape a complex and paradoxical relationship with the colonized. Drawing on psychoanalytic views of the way identity gets constructed, Bhabha offers us analyses in which the identity of the colonizer – in Bhabha's work the British colonizer of India – cannot very well be separated from that of the colonized. Instead of being self-sufficient with regard to his identity ('his' because colonialism is an almost exclusively male enterprise), the colonizer at least partly constructs it through interaction with the colonized. The colonizer's identity has no 'origin' in himself and is not a fixed entity, but is unsettled, a product of relations. The identity of the colonizer as colonizer can only become a 'reality' after the colonial contact which truly confirms it.

Bhabha sees signs of the colonizer's partial dependency on none-too-friendly 'others' – and the resulting inherent uncertainty – in a whole range of phenomena. Racial stereotyping, for instance, first of all repeats this process of identity-creation in that it construes not only those who are stereotyped, but also the stereotyper himself, in opposition to the stereotyped. It functions to construe or confirm the stereotyper's identity. However, the repetitiveness of acts of stereotyping points to a continuing uncertainty in the stereotyper: apparently the stereotyper has to convince himself over and over again of the truthfulness of the stereotype – and thus, by extension, of his own identity. The self-confidence of the colonizer is further undermined by what Bhabha calls *mimicry* – the always slightly alien and distorted way in which the colonized, either out of choice or under duress, will repeat the colonizer's ways and discourse. We see this exemplified, for instance, in Wole Soyinka's plays *The Road* (1965) and *Death and the King's Horseman* (1975) or in V.S. Naipaul's significantly titled novel *The Mimic Men* (1967). In mimicry the colonizer sees himself in a mirror that slightly but effectively distorts his image – that subtly and unsettlingly 'others' his own identity. And mimicry may play a part in 'sly civility', a seemingly submissive attitude that still succeeds in conveying the colonized's sense of independence, if not superiority. Colonial power's lack of complete control is also the result of acts of conscious resistance on the part of the colonized. In the physical encounter between colonizer and colonized the latter may for instance refuse to meet his oppressor's gaze and in so doing reject 'the narcissistic demand that [he] should be addressed directly, that the Other should authorize the self, recognize its priority, fulfill its outlines' (Bhabha 1994: 98). Almost eighty years after the end of Dutch colonial rule over the Dutch East Indies, now Indonesia, the Dutch language still has the expression 'Oost-Indisch doof' – deaf in the East Indies way – which means that an addressee has perfectly heard and understood a question or an order, but simply refuses to acknowledge it, thus forcing the speaker, who is fully aware of that refusal, to repeat him- or her-self – a procedure that over time becomes highly embarrassing.

Perhaps the most influential of Bhabha's contributions to post-colonial theory is his notion of *hybridity*. In his rather inhospitable prose, 'hybridity is a problematic of colonial representation and individuation that reverses the effects of the colonialist disavowal, so that other "denied" knowledges enter upon the dominant dis-course and estrange the basis of its authority' (Bhabha 1994: 115). While Said's *Orientalism* keeps the spheres of colonizer and colo-nized rather firmly apart, Bhabha, with his interest in their inter-action, sees important movements going both ways. Shifting his focus from 'the noisy command of colonial authority' and 'the silent repression of native traditions', to 'the colonial hybrid', Bhabha argues that the cultural interaction of colonizer and colo-nized leads to a fusion of cultural forms that from one perspective, because it signals its 'productivity', confirms the power of the colonial presence. However, as a form of mimicry it simulta-neously 'unsettles the mimetic or narcissistic demands of colonial power' (112). Hybridity 'intervenes in the exercise of authority not merely to indicate the impossibility of its identity but to represent the unpredictability of its presence' (114). Like most of Bhabha's notions, hybridization and hybridity – which seems to present an in-between position, halfway between two cultures of equal weight and power – thus get positive connotations. In fact, Bhab-ha's application of poststructuralist theorizing to colonial and post-colonial relations has more in general positive overtones. Some critics have objected that this is armchair theorizing which in its 'reconciliatory' approach (Simon During) takes the sharp edges of the colonial encounter and cannot have much relevance in the analysis of the everyday practice of colonial rule. For them, post-structuralist theory leads Bhabha to see the identity and position of the colonizer as far too precarious and to see those of the colonized in a far more positive light than is warranted. The gun you are carrying as a fledgling colonizer may not fundamentally strengthen your identity, but it may give it enough of a boost to disregard all signs of mimicry that you are likely to encounter. There will have been examples of the permanent state of anxiety that Bhabha ascribes to the colonizer but it should probably not be generalized. Other critics have objected to what they see as Bhabha's tendency to romanticize the in-between position, the 'double conscious-ness' – Bhabha's term – of the colonized and of migrants who, because they are by definition between cultures, are granted an awareness of relativity and an insight into their own and others' positions that may not come as naturally or be experienced as positively as Bhabha would seem to think. In Chinua Achebe's *Things Fall Apart* such a double consciousness is seen as divisive and destructive. As one of the wise elders in the novel says, 'The white man is very clever. He came quietly and peaceably with his religion. We were amused at his foolishness and allowed him to stay. Now he has won our brothers, and our clan can no longer act like one. He has put a knife on the things that held us together and we have fallen apart' (Achebe 1976 [1958]: 124–125). In the historical and partly autobiographical novel *Bumi Manusia* (1980; *This Earth of Mankind*) of the Indonesian author Pramoedya Ananta Tur, a young boy belonging to the Javanese aristocracy is delighted to be admitted to a Dutch school only to discover that what he gains in knowledge is outweighed by the loss of his original identity while he will never gain real access to the colonizer's world. In Kiran Desai's *The Inheritance of Loss* (2006), too, 'in-betweenness' is not a viable option and its main character returns in disillusionment to the Indian subcontinent (where he is subsequently robbed of all his American savings). A 'double consciousness' may surely bring the broadened perspective that Bhabha associates with it, but it might just as well be a painful rather than enlightening condition. And of course it may be both. A final point of critique concerns the level of abstraction at which Bhabha's work often operates. Marxist and feminist critics have argued that there can be no such thing as a generalized encounter between colonizer and colonized. To them a theory that addresses the colonial situation without paying serious attention to the differences between men and women and to socio-economic circumstances cannot do justice to the hetero-geneity of the colonial encounter. For Marxist critics especially, Bhabha's overriding interest in the psychoanalytic dimension of that encounter – the subjectivities involved – while disregarding its economic framework is a serious deficiency. However, Bhabha's focus on interaction and his notion of hybridity have sharpened our awareness of what actually happens (or may happen) in the colonial or postcolonial situation. Whereas Said prompts us to question Western representations of the East, Bhabha asks us to submit the actual encounter between West and East – in his case India – to the closest (psychoanalytic) scrutiny.

THE SUBALTERN

Postcolonial Marxists such as Aijaz Ahmad have perhaps unfairly suggested that Bhabha and other 'Westernized' non-Europeans are hardly in the best position to speak for the colonized and neo-colonized masses. The third postcolonial theorist I will consider here, Gayatri Chakravorty Spivak, has no trouble admitting that her position as an academic working in the West separates her from the masses of India, her country of origin. At the same time, however, she has drawn our attention to that large majority of the colonized that has left no mark upon history because it could not, or was not allowed to, make itself heard. Many millions have come and gone under the colonial dispensation without leaving a trace: men and even more so women. Since colonized women almost by definition went unheard within their own patriarchal culture, they were doubly unheard under a colonial regime. Spivak can be said to be the first postcolonial theorist with a feminist agenda. That agenda includes the complicity of female writers with imperialism. 'It should not be possible to read nineteenth-century British fiction without remembering that imperialism, understood as England's social mission, was a crucial part of the cultural representation of England to the English', Spivak tells us in her 1985 essay 'Three Women's Texts and a Critique of Imperialism' (Spivak 1995a: 269). Noting that '[t]he role of literature in the production of cultural representation should not be ignored', she goes on to analyse, in terms of cultural representation, Charlotte Brontë's *Jane Eyre* (1847) and the way in which it chooses to present the 'Creole' Bertha Mason – the mad wife of Jane's future husband Rochester. For Spivak, too, the so-called 'metropolitan' subject defines itself either explicitly or implicitly through its encounter, real or imagined, with the non-European 'other'. Spivak's insistence on the importance of feminist perspectives is part of a larger role that she has played since the 1980s: that of the theoretical conscience of postcolonial studies. Freely drawing on Marxism, feminism, and deconstruction, her work has as much addressed theoretical shortcomings in postcolonial theorizing, and what she sees as simplifying approaches of 'otherness', as it has focused on postcolonial issues itself.

Spivak represents the voice of difference among the major postcolonial theorists. In spite of their poststructuralist sources of inspiration, Said and Bhabha do not focus upon the question of difference. However, feminist scholars have argued that for instance female representations of the Orient are different from male ones. Mary-Louise Pratt's *Imperial Eyes* from 1992 tells us that travel writing by women about the non-West must be distinguished from travel writing by men. Following Said's example, Bhabha makes no such distinction between men and women in his theorizing of the interaction between colonizer and colonized. Said and Bhabha also largely ignore cultural difference. Setting up his opposition between Europe and the Orient, Said is not much interested in the differences between the various European cultures – Protestant or Catholic, liberal or authoritarian – that are his target in *Orientalism* and Bhabha writes as if the interaction of colonizer and colonized can be completely separated from the cultures involved. Spivak, however, is attentive to difference, to heterogeneity, even within feminism itself: she has taken Western feminism to task for operating within a horizon determined by white, middle-class, and heterosexual preoccupations.

As we might expect from a theorist who is sensitive to difference, social class – which also plays not much of a role in Said or Bhabha – is one of Spivak's major analytic categories. Of all postcolonial theorists, Spivak has most consistently focused on what the so-called Subaltern Studies Group of Indian historians – borrowing the concept and the term from Antonio Gramsci – has called the *subaltern:* the category of those in the most precarious social positions (in the military terms that are always appropriate to the colonial situation, the lowest ranks). Spivak, too, employs the term to describe the lowest and least powerful layers of colonial and postcolonial (or, as many would say, neo-colonial) society: the homeless, the unemployed, the subsistence farmers, the day labourers. She is aware, however, that categorizations by way of class, too, tend to make difference invisible and 'insist[s] that the colonized subaltern *subject* is irretrievably heterogeneous' (Spivak 1995b: 26). One result of this attentiveness to difference is Spivak's focus on the female subaltern, a very large – and of course differentiated – category among the colonized that, she argues, has traditionally been doubly marginalized: 'If, in the context of colonial production, the subaltern has no history and cannot speak, the subaltern as female is even more deeply in shadow' (28).

This focus does not mean that she speaks for – or has the intention of speaking for – the female subaltern. Rather, she is motivated by the desire to save the female subaltern from misrepresentation. In a famous essay from 1988, 'Can the Subaltern Speak? Speculations on Widow Sacrifice' (expanded in her *Critique of Postcolonial Reason*, 1999), Spivak, in the wider context of a critique of what she sees as appropriations of the colonial subject, examines the nineteenth-century controversy between the colonized Indians and their British colonizers over what she calls 'widow-sacrifice': the burning of widows on the funeral pyres of their deceased husbands. Spivak concludes that neither party allowed women – the victims of this practice – to speak. The British texts construct a position for the woman in which she is made to represent Western individualism and, by implication, a superior Western civilization that emphasizes modern freedom, while the Indian ones present her as choosing for duty and tradition. Although both parties claim that they have them on their side, the women themselves remain unheard.

Spivak combines an emphasis on gender and class as a differentiating factor with a deconstructionist approach to texts and to identity. In one way the decentred subject of deconstruction serves her purpose well: it radically undermines all essentialist pretensions on the part of colonizer and neo-colonizer and it equally undermines essentialist leanings of postcolonial theory, for which she has little patience. In her analyses of, and attacks on, forms of renascent essentialism she again acts as postcolonial theory's poststructuralist conscience. On the other hand, decolonized nations and cultures, just like the political movements of the decolonized, arguably need some sort of identity that does not immediately deconstruct itself. A political platform that takes itself apart in public cannot be very effective. In her earlier work, Spivak's solution to this dilemma is what she calls a '*strategic* use of positivist essentialism' that is not afraid to put forward a clear political agenda but remains fully aware of its constructed underpinnings. But here, too, she has moved towards what one might with some trepidation call a more traditional position, telling us that after she gave up her 'strategic use of essentialism', she found a new strategy: 'learning to learn from below' (Spivak 2000: 326).

POSTCOLONIAL STUDIES IN THE TWENTY-FIRST CENTURY

As this call for a political strategy illustrates, postcolonial studies soon ranged far and wide beyond its original literary provenance. It now discusses contemporary events and developments in post-colonial cultural studies and postcolonial media studies; it has pushed back its historical interest to the medieval period (the Crusades and their encounters with the Muslim world) and even to antiquity; it studies religions and concepts of the sacred which it has long ignored; it has taken aboard the ecological effects of colonialism (following up on Alfred W. Crosby's *Ecological Imperialism: The Biological Expansion of Europe, 900–1900* of 1986); it examines how the body has been a site of oppression (and of resistance); it has discovered and opened a fruitful dialogue with Latin American studies; it studies postcolonial films, dance, and sports, and it has more recently included the original colonizing nations in its interests. As Ato Quayson remarked, with reference to 'diasporic writing', which by now has become the object of the subdiscipline of diaspora studies, 'we find that Britain, Germany, France, and the Netherlands may be productively understood as themselves being postcolonialized by people from their erstwhile margins' (Quayson 2012: 366). This should not surprise us, of course. Colonization affects the whole life world of the colonized but is also a contributing factor in the constitution of the colonizer's subjectivity. Postcolonial studies has also become sensitive to the ways in which in many postcolonial societies attitudes and practices that postcolonial critics would strongly condemn in the western world – such as the stigmatization and criminalization of homosexuality – are very much alive.

Although in the field in which postcolonial studies originated, that of literary studies, Said, Bhabha and Spivak remain important, postcolonial studies in its current, much more encompassing, incarnation can be said to have moved away considerably from its

Foucauldian inspiration, even if in some areas it remains very much aware of poststructuralist concerns (as for instance in studies of the postcolonial body) and even if its textual focus once again proved very relevant when Orientalism resurged after 9/11 (see Makdisi 2019). This broadening of the field led to criticisms of postcolonial studies' earlier, primarily literary bias and what was seen as its pre-occupation with theoretical issues. Already in for instance *Postcolonial Studies and Beyond* of 2005 we find a politely phrased critique: a 'keynote' of the volume, the editors tell us, 'is the reassertion of a certain historical urgency that may have been leached from post-colonial studies during its period of theoretical refinement and institutional consolidation' (Loomba et al. 2005: 5). For many of the contributors to *Postcolonial Studies and Beyond* some of the central assumptions of postcolonial studies will have to be rethought. Its 'refinement' and 'consolidation' have harmed its political relevance and its focus on texts and subjectivities will not enable postcolonial critics to arrive at an understanding of the processes of globalization that have followed in the wake of decolonization and that arguably constitute one of the most important developments of the last forty years. Other critics, focusing on indigenous peoples and their plight, point out that these as often as not defend homogeneous identities, myths of origin, a bond with land regarded as sacred, and other values that they see as essential to their survival but that cannot very well be reconciled with poststructuralist assumptions (see for instance Stam and Shohat 2012).

Some critics claim that colonialism was more ambivalent than postcolonial studies has been willing to admit and call for a balanced approach to its history and legacy. In an exchange on the state of postcolonial studies Simon During argued that 'colonialism involved expropriation after expropriation, oppression after oppression, atrocity after atrocity. Nonetheless, even among those very aware of this, it has long been recognized that there is also a strong case for arguing that empire brought benefits to its subject peoples too. Marx himself came early to this cause' (During 2012: 333). Others, like Benita Parry – another participant in this exchange – reject this position as 'accommodationist' (Parry 2012: 352) and defend what During calls an 'anticolonialist' line, with a strong focus on political economy. Especially Parry and Robert Young (the latter in *Postcolonialism: A Very Short Introduction*, 2nd edition 2021, and other books) have worked to ask attention for 'a politics grounded in the material, social and existential' as Parry put it in a 2002 article (Parry 2002: 77). (Young, by the way, should also be mentioned for his positive valuation of such 'traditional' issues as religion, nationalism, and pan-Africanism.) There is, then, no shortage of views on colonialism or on the colonial subject, whose subjectivity and agency – or lack of it – are still hotly disputed. But I should not hide that outside the somewhat closed world of Western theory there is also serious doubt as the importance of all this. As Simon Gikandi, an expert on African and Caribbean literature observed not too long ago, 'the institutional authority of postcolonial theory often appears divided: it is celebrated in European and North American institutions of interpretation as a significant addition to poststructuralist or postmodern conversations, but it is treated with hostility or benign neglect in the postcolonial world' (Gikandi 2011: 163). From this perspective, postcolonial studies is most of all Europe trying to come to terms with its own past.

But let me return to postcolonial writing. In her overview of postcolonial literature in English, C.L. Innes tells us that '[c]ritics have sometimes described postcolonial literatures as very roughly falling into several phases: literature of resistance; literature of national consolidation; literature of disillusion and/or neocolonialism; post-postcolonial literature; and diaspora literature' (Innes 2007: 17). It is indeed easy enough to find, for instance, novels that exemplify these phases, even in the career of one single novelist. Achebe's *Things Fall Apart* fits well into the resistance phase, while his *Anthills of the Savannah* (1987), like Ngugi's *Petals of Blood* (1977), with its emphasis on Nigeria's internal tensions and its corruption, exemplifies post-independence disillusionment – just like NoViolet Bulawayos's *Glory* (2022), which offers scathing criticism of Zimbabwe, and other recent novels. Wole Soyinka's memoir *Aké* (1981), which celebrates Yoruba culture, might on the other hand be seen as representing the literature of national consolidation. We also find texts that with great and almost mocking self-confidence deal with colonization and its aftermath. Here are the first two stanzas of the Jamaican poet Louise Bennett's 'Colonization in Reverse', published in 1966, four years after Jamaica's independence:

> Wat a joyful news, Miss Mattie,
> I feel like heart gwine burs'
> Jamaica people colonizing
> England in reverse.
> By de hundred, by de t'ousan
> From country and from town,
> By de ship-load, by de plane-load
> Jamaica is Englan boun.

Not surprisingly, hybridity is a recurrent motif, especially in diaspora literature. V.S. Naipaul's *The Enigma of Arrival* (1987), Kiran Desai's already mentioned *The Inheritance of Loss* (2006), and a host of other novels in English, French, German, and Dutch have a hybrid postcolonial or diasporic identity as a central theme. Under the influence of theorists like Bhabha, the postcolonial in general was often 'associated', in Elleke Boehmer's terms, 'with metropolitan, diasporic, migrant and minority spaces for which the nation as a horizon of expectation had retreated' (Boehmer 2005: 247). But in the twenty-first century many postcolonial writers are moving, or have moved, away from such spaces, which evoke images of in-betweenness and alienation. Contemporary African novelists 'work', to quote Boehmer again, 'to build local "structures of feeling" positioned at several removes from the dominant North, drawn from their life worlds' (250) and they 'turn increasingly towards local audiences and narrative traditions, and away from the implied European reader' (251). In the work of such novelists both 'colonial' and 'postcolonial' lose much of their relevance.

SUGGESTIONS FOR FURTHER READING

The importance of postcolonial theory and criticism in contemporary literary studies is reflected in the number of good introductions and guides that have appeared in the last thirty years. Bart Moore-Gilbert's *Postcolonial Theory* (1997) is an excellent introduction to postcolonial studies' major theorists and to the tensions between theory and criticism. Ania Loomba's *Colonialism/Postcolonialism* (2nd edition 2005) complements Moore-Gilbert because of the attention that she pays to questions of gender and sexuality, while the second edition of Leela Gandhi's *Postcolonial*

Theory: A Critical Introduction (2019) brings things up to date. The historian Robert Young's *Postcolonialism: An Historical Introduction* (2001) and Benita Parry's *Postcolonial Studies: A Materialist Critique* (2004) criticize the dominant poststructuralist orientation of much early work in postcolonial studies from a Marxist perspective. Postcolonial literature is discussed in Elleke Boehmer's *Colonial and Postcolonial Literature: Migrant Metaphors* (2nd edition 2005), Alison Donnell's *Twentieth-Century Caribbean Literature* (2006), S. Patke Rajeev's, *Postcolonial Poetry in English* (2006), *The Cambridge Companion to Postcolonial Literary Studies* (2004), edited by Neil Lazarus, *The Cambridge History of Postcolonial Literature* (2012), edited by Ato Quayson, *A Concise Companion to Postcolonial Literature* (2014), edited by Shirley Chew and David Richards, and *The Cambridge Companion to the Postcolonial Novel* (2015), also edited by Quayson. *After Said: Postcolonial Literary Studies in the Twenty-first Century* (2019), edited by Bashir Abu-Mannen, brings the discussion of postcolonial literary criticism up to date.

The Post-Colonial Studies Reader (2nd edition 2005) edited by Bill Ashcroft, Gareth Griffiths, and Helen Tiffin, *Postcolonial Studies: An Anthology* (2016), edited by Pramod K. Nayar, and *Reading Postcolonial Theory: Key Texts in Context* (2016), edited by Bibhash Choudhury, between them collect practically all the major contributions to postcolonial studies. The third edition of *Post-Colonial Studies: The Key Concepts* (2013), edited by Bill Ashcroft, Gareth Griffiths and Helen Tiffin, offers brief and lucid discussions of not just the key-concepts, but also covers an impressive list of minor terms. Graham Huggan's *The Oxford Handbook of Postcolonial Studies* (2013) is a massive collection of essays that illustrates the impressive range of postcolonial studies.

SEXUALITY, LITERATURE, CULTURE, AND QUEER STUDIES

LESBIAN AND GAY CRITICISM

Sexuality and literature first became an issue within the feminist movement. In its early stages, feminism spoke, or at least seemed to speak, on behalf of all women. A common female front against what looked strongly like a common oppression seemed only natural. In the course of the 1970s, however, various groups within the feminist movement began to express their dissatisfaction with a collective feminism that they increasingly saw as shaped by the interests of the dominant group within the movement: white, middle-class, college-educated, and heterosexual women. As a result, the groups that did or could not identify with this mainstream image gradually broke away to formulate their own feminisms. These breakaway communities included groups of Black feminists, Chicana feminists, and, most important for this chapter, lesbian feminists. For a good many lesbian feminists the subversiveness of mainstream feminism did not extend to sexuality. While mainstream feminists questioned traditional views of gender, they failed to question similarly traditional views of same-sex relations. As a result, lesbian feminism turned away from mainstream feminism to pursue its own, separate path, which would soon fork again, with for instance Chicana writers like Gloria Anzaldúa and Black writers like Audre Lorde claiming specific identities for the groups they represented.

Lesbian feminism in turn led to lesbian literary criticism. Jeanette H. Foster's encyclopaedic *Sex-Variant Women in Literature* of 1956 was more of an immense inventory than literary criticism, but in 1975 Jane Rule published her pioneering *Lesbian Images* and with

DOI: 10.4324/9781003373438-9

Lillian Faderman's comprehensive *Surpassing the Love of Men: Romantic Friendship and Love Between Women from the Renaissance to the Present* (1981) lesbian criticism definitively established itself. However, the vanguard of critics that tried to lay out the ground rules for a specific lesbian criticism found that a focus on lesbianism in literature runs into serious practical problems. In the words of one critic:

> What is a lesbian text? Is it one describing lesbian relationships? Is it one written by a lesbian author? Is it one in which hidden kinds of pleasure are offered to an implied lesbian reader? Are texts lesbian if neither author nor content are *explicitly* lesbian? How much of a text has to be about lesbianism to be regarded as 'lesbian'?
>
> (Humm 1995: 162)

And what, for that matter, is a lesbian exactly? The answer might seem fairly straightforward, but it is easy enough to ask questions that complicate the picture. For instance, are sexual acts a necessary condition? Should we consider a woman who has felt a strong and lifelong attraction to other women but has never acted upon it as a lesbian? If not, we will disqualify a good many women who in their own time never had an opportunity to follow their sexual preference, but who, if they were alive today, would openly live with a female lover. This problem leads us to two important issues. The first is the issue of sexual identity. The phrase 'life-long attraction' strongly implies that this woman's erotic orientation is simply programmed into her. But does that really have to be the case? For many radical lesbians of the early 1970s, lesbianism was a matter of choice – a political anti-patriarchal choice. Or is lesbianism a matter of socialization – of the individual experiences that some of us go through and that turn us into lesbians? The same questions may be raised with regard to homosexuality.

The other issue that is raised by my introduction of the woman who does not act upon her lesbian inclinations is that of visibility – or, rather, invisibility. Gender and race are visible and recognizable categories. There are exceptions, of course. There are men who choose to dress like women and every racial minority has members who can 'pass', that is, successfully pose as members of the majority. But on the whole gender and race are obvious. Sexual orientation, however, is not visible. What is more, since it is only really visible at those moments when it is actively acted upon, it can be kept hidden even from one's immediate social environment. So how do we establish which writers have been gay or lesbian when it was impossible for them to reveal their sexual identity in their writings? How can we reconstruct a gay or lesbian literary tradition and, on the basis of such a tradition, a lesbian aesthetic? I will look here at the answers given by lesbian criticism, not because it is in any way superior to gay criticism, but because it has a longer independent history. As Julie Rivkin and Michael Ryan have observed, '[m]ore so than Gay Studies, Lesbian Studies has demonstrated a tendency towards separatism, perhaps because as women, lesbians suffer a double oppression' (Rivkin and Ryan 1998: 677). It will be clear, though, that there are many parallels between lesbian and gay criticism.

LESBIAN WRITING

Lesbian criticism, then, faces a number of very specific problems. One way around them is to opt for lesbian *readings*, that is, for interpretations that leave unresolved the question whether a given author, or character, or situation, really *is* lesbian, but instead create the possibility for lesbian recognitions and moments of identification. This does of course not mean that lesbian criticism can make no firm claims and is never more than a reading strategy that could be easily dismissed by people who take a dim view of everything that is not solidly anchored in textual 'evidence'. There is a fast-growing body of texts – most of them dating from the last forty years – that clearly announce themselves as lesbian. But a lesbian reading strategy is a complementary and necessary instrument. Especially in the case of texts published before the twentieth century, when lesbianism was largely unmentionable, lesbian readings of close friendships between single women have led to often revealing new appreciations of the plays, novels, and poems in question. (The same goes for gay criticism: a well-known example is Alan Sinfield's reading of the poems in which the Victorian poet Alfred Tennyson nostalgically remembers his very intimate friendship with a long dead friend; see Sinfield 1986.) Such new lesbian interpretations have led to the identification of texts that together can be said to create a sort of lesbian literary tradition – or at least a tradition of texts that would seem to invite a lesbian reading. Simultaneously, lesbian criticism has drawn our attention to the way that lesbians have traditionally been portrayed in mainstream texts. As might be expected, lesbians (and homosexuals) have standardly been pictured as 'other' and have served to define and confirm the heterosexuality of the centre.

But on what grounds can critics defend a lesbian reading of a text that is in no way explicitly lesbian and that until forty years ago was never considered within a lesbian framework? Lesbian and gay critics generally agree that lesbian and gay writers work from a special awareness of the constructedness of language and culture and of the fact that the constructions that they see in operation can be contested. It is a reasonable assumption that such an awareness would lead to a specific sensibility. After all, lesbian and gay writers have until recently been forced either to hide their sexual orientation altogether from their audience or to present it so indirectly that only the initiates were in a position to recognize it. *Á la récherche du temps perdu*, Marcel Proust's early twentieth-century great novel cycle, offers a famous example. The girl Albertine, with whom Proust's novelistic alter ego falls in love, was in the reality of Proust's life a boy. Lesbian and homosexual writers saw themselves forced to disguise same-sex relationships as heterosexual ones. Because of such suppressions even the most realistic mode of writing must always have been more than slightly unreal and false for lesbian and gay writers. Naturally, then, we find lesbian writers gravitating away from realism towards other modes of writing. For Terry Castle, writing in 1993, lesbian fiction should never be read as straightforward realism: 'Even as it gestures back at a supposedly familiar world of human experience, it almost invariably stylizes and estranges it – by presenting it parodistically, euphemistically, or in some other rhetorically heightened, distorted, fragmented or phantasmagoric way' (Castle 1993: 90). Moreover, we may expect to find gender ambiguities, role playing that involves gender, and other coded references – such as certain recurrent symbols – to the fact that not everything is what it would seem to be to the unsuspecting reader. More in general, according to this view of lesbian (and gay) writing, the writer's constant awareness of the gap between their own reality and that of the repressive heterosexual majority, coupled with the necessity – which often still applies – to keep that private reality secret, leads to an all-pervasive sense of irony and theatricality (with the exceptions that keep essentialism at a distance confirming the rule). Here we are moving towards that 'blurring of boundaries between self and other, subject and object, lover and beloved' that by the early 1990s for many lesbian critics had come to constitute 'the lesbian moment' in literary texts (Zimmerman 1992: 11). We are, in fact, moving towards what we now call 'queer theory', in which such a blurring of boundaries has a significance that far exceeds specific lesbian or gay conditions.

THE PRODUCTION OF SEXUALITY

Queer theory – which has turned a term that traditionally disparages homosexuality into a proud banner – comes in more than one form. However, all modes of queer theory, to which the remainder of this chapter will be devoted, are indebted to Michel Foucault's multi-volume *History of Sexuality* (1976–84) and his argument that especially 'deviant', that is, non-heterosexual, forms of sexuality play a prominent role in the organization of Western culture. Although 'perversion' is actively marginalized, it is discursively central: the effort to police 'perversion' through a discourse on sexuality that continuously puts it in a negative light paradoxically keeps it in the centre of attention. For Foucault, Western culture has turned sexuality into a discourse that enables it to constantly monitor us and to exercise power: if we do not internalize its sexual rules and police ourselves, then it can step in and force us to conform.

In *An Introduction* (1976, later retitled *The Will to Knowledge*), the first volume of his *History*, Foucault argues that homosexuality and homosexuals date from the 1870s (a claim that would seem to be supported by the fact that the term 'homosexual' was coined in 1869). It is easy to misunderstand this. Foucault does not mean to say that sexual acts that we would now call homosexual acts were unknown before the 1870s. What he is saying is that in the later nineteenth century sexual acts between men were no longer seen as incidental to their lives, that is, as acts that anyone might engage in under certain circumstances, but as expressions of their *identity*. For the first time, Foucault tells us, homosexual acts were seen as part of the essential *nature* of the men involved, as the result of an inclination that was always there. Whereas before that turning point a man who had sex with another man – a so-called 'sodomite' – was seen in terms of 'a temporary aberration', the homosexual 'was now a species'. The homosexual had come into existence; he was now 'a personage, a past, a case history, and a childhood. … Nothing that went into his total composition was unaffected by his sexuality' (Foucault 1978: 43). What we have here is a crucial shift from behaviour to identity. Although this new homosexual identity naturally predisposed its owners to homosexual activity, men could now be classified as homosexual even if they had never been involved in homosexual acts.

For Foucault, homosexuality and homosexuals were *produced* by a nineteenth-century discourse that claimed new knowledge with regard to sexuality. This 'production' of homosexuality (and of other 'perversions' that were similarly tied to new identities) led to its codification (and condemnation) in legal, medical, psychological, and religious discourses. It led to the fixation of identities (homosexual, heterosexual) and the surveillance of the border between them. In other words, this production of homosexuality is intimately connected with power. Just like other sexual identities, homosexuality is 'a result and an instrument of power's designs'. We should not make the mistake of thinking that what Foucault has in mind is only how homosexuality allowed the various authorities – legal, medical, religious – to tighten the screws of social and cultural repression and to legitimate themselves further, although they certainly availed themselves of the opportunity. 'Power' often has a virtually autonomous status in Foucault's work. It works *through* us and imprisons us, even if occasionally it may also work to our advantage. In Foucault's view, the 'production' of homosexuality by the human sciences has led to a very general surveillance under whose regime we even regulate and police our own sexuality. As Jonathan Dollimore summarizes Foucault's argument: 'Perversion is the product and vehicle of power, a construction which enables it to gain a purchase within the realm of the psychosexual: authority legitimates itself by fastening upon discursively constructed, sexually perverse identities of its own making' (Dollimore 1991: 106).

QUEER THEORY

Queer theory's point of departure is that there is no 'natural' sexuality – a status traditionally accorded to heterosexuality – and that there is no stable relationship between biological sex (male or female, to mention the most frequent categories), gender, and sexual desire. Casting its net much wider than gay or lesbian criticism, it had from the beginning a strong interest in everything that contributes to the destabilization of standard sexual categories – including 'gay' and 'lesbian' – and used for instance trans identities to question existing categorizations and to expose them as constructions. Starting from what may be called a basis in LGBTQ+ studies, it expanded this in itself not inconsiderable territory to question all categorizations, all borders and lines of demarcation. As Donald E. Hall put it, 'it is broadly useful to think of the adjective "queer" in this way: it is to abrade the classifications, to sit athwart conventional categories or traverse several' (Hall 2003: 13). More recently, we find Judith Butler, one of queer theory's most important theorists, speaking of 'the word "queer," understood less as an identity than as a movement of thought and language contrary to accepted forms of authority, always deviating' (Butler 2016: 17). This deliberate contrariness does not condemn queer theory to the margins. To quote Hall again: 'In its emphasis on the disruptive, the constructed, the tactical, and performative, queer analysis reveals some of the ways in which many late-modern individuals experience the fractured and contingent nature of human existence in the twenty-first century' (5). But let us first look at the emergence of queer theory and its interest in the issue of power, which is one of queer theory's major themes.

For early queer theorists like the British critics Jonathan Dollimore and Alan Sinfield, the power that is at work in the field of sexuality can be contested. Queer theory questions traditional constructions of sexuality and sees non-heterosexual forms of sexuality as sites where hegemonic power can be undermined. In Sinfield's words, subcultures – in which he expressly includes sexual subcultures – 'may be power bases – points at which alternative or oppositional ideologies may achieve plausibility' (Sinfield 2005: xvii). British queer theory, whose political context is 'a general left-wing orientation' (73), takes the assumptions and the interests of cultural materialism into the contemporary debate on sexuality. For Sinfield, sexuality is a faultline (see Chapter 6), a point at which the hegemonic surface may crack and reveal the warring forces underneath: 'Sexuality is an unstable construct in our societies, and hence produces endless textual work. Such an awkward issue has continually to be revisited, disavowed, rediscovered, affirmed' (56). Sexual dissidence – the title of Dollimore's 1991 book – is therefore always at least potentially a political act. As queer theorists, Sinfield and his British colleagues apply the methods of cultural materialism. They read literary texts against the grain – 'cultural materialists read for incoherence' (Sinfield 2005: 38) – because faultline stories 'hinge upon a fundamental, unresolved ideological complication that finds its way, willy-nilly, into texts' (4). They examine the constructions that a culture has put upon sexually ambivalent texts in order to expose its ideological repressiveness (see Sinfield's *Cultural Politics: Queer Reading* from which I am quoting here for a discussion of the reception of Tennessee Williams's plays). At the institutional level they question 'literature' itself – in particular the ideologically motivated marginalization and exclusions that have played a crucial role in the creation of the idea of 'literature'. This is not to say that we should turn our backs to the literary tradition. We should, however, approach it from a faultline perspective. As Sinfield tells us: 'successful [texts] are usually risky; they flirt, at least, with the danger that prevailing values might not be satisfactory, or might not prevail' (56).

The queer theory that develops out of cultural materialism draws on Foucault and has strong affinities with British cultural studies. In the United States, however, queer theory has followed a different path. That theory develops out of feminism and more specifically out of the work of two prominent and highly influential theorists, Eve Kosofsky Sedgwick and Judith Butler, who in their turn draw on Foucault and Derrida and who, with the feminist critic Gayle Rubin, argued 'that feminism might be insufficient to attend to sexuality as object' (McBean 2020: 131).

Lesbian criticism had split off from feminist criticism because lesbian critics felt that mainstream feminism did not do justice to the lesbian presence in literature. Striking out on their own, they assumed that there was such a thing as a lesbian identity – a core identity that all lesbians shared – that expressed itself in certain ways in literary texts. However, in the course of the 1990s a number of influential lesbian critics began to reject such an essentialist identity and to suggest that sexual identities – not just lesbianism or homosexuality – were social constructions that needed to be deconstructed just like gender and race had been deconstructed to expose the binary oppositions at work within them. Like gender categories, traditional sexual categories now were assumed to be 'regulatory fictions' – instruments of a repressive discourse about sexuality. The obvious privileging of the heterosexual orientation of the majority at the expense of all other sexual orientations was the work of a centre that defined itself through that what it excluded. In other words, sexuality was added to the axes that for the theorists we have discussed have traditionally organized Western society.

For Eve Kosofsky Sedgwick the power structure working within the hetero/homo axis is central to the organization of Western culture. In her *Between Men* of 1985 she argues that in a society dominated by men women are basically instruments with the help of which men establish or confirm intermale relations. In a patriarchy the *real* relations exist between men so that women function primarily within male-male relationships – as 'symbolic property' that can even be exchanged. The structure of such a male-dominated society is therefore *homosocial* – a term that should not be confused with homosexual, especially not since homosocial societies usually see homosexuality in strongly negative terms. 'Homosocial' indicates the true nature of *social* relationships, not of sexual ones. Still, because sexuality is an important 'signifier of power relations' – a signifier which interacts with other 'power asymmetries' (Sedgwick 1985: 7) – sexual classification in fixed categories is central to a homosocially structured society. Sedgwick redefines, in Donald E. Hall's words, 'heterosexuality as a fear of male homosexuality that motivates men to route their desire for another through women' (Hall 2003: 198). For Sedgwick, the homosocial nature of the Victorian society that she focuses on inevitably informs its writing: its literature, too, reveals that the underlying relationships of the Victorian period were relationships between men. In Joseph Bristow's somewhat milder formulation, '[Sedgwick's] analysis focuses on how western cultures endorse a patriarchal imperative that often encourages men to work in the social interests of other men by subordinating women' (Bristow 2001: 225).

In a later book, Sedgwick proposes an equally wide-ranging thesis. *Epistemology of the Closet* (1990) begins with a Derridean deconstruction of the heterosexuality – homosexuality opposition that according to Foucault dates from the late nineteenth century, when the homosexual became a distinct 'species':

> The analytic move [this book] makes is to demonstrate that categories presented in a culture as symmetrical binary oppositions – heterosexual/homosexual, in this case – actually subsist in a more unsettled and dynamic tacit relation according to which, first, term B is not symmetrical with but subordinated to term A; but, second, the ontologically valorised term A actually depends for its meaning on the simultaneous subsumption and exclusion of term B; hence, third, the question of priority between the supposed central and the supposed marginal category of each dyad is irresolvable unstable, an instability caused by the fact that term B is constituted as at once internal and external to term A.
>
> (Sedgwick 1990: 9–10)

Sexualities, *Epistemology of the Closet* tells us, are less stable and more interwoven than the rigid heterosexual/homosexual opposition suggests. Yet, in spite of that, the

> homo/heterosexual definition has been a presiding master term of the past century, one that has the same, primary importance for all modern Western identity and social organization (and not merely for homosexual identity and culture) as do the more traditionally visible cruxes of gender, class, and race ...
>
> (Sedgwick 1990: 11)

The heterosexual/homosexual binary is central to modern Western culture because it has given a new, sexual dimension to the meaning of such oppositions as natural/unnatural, wholeness/decadence, public/private, knowledge/ignorance, secrecy/disclosure, and other binaries which evoke associations that they did not suggest before the appearance of the homosexual as 'species'. *Epistemology of the Closet* backs up these arguments with detailed analyses of late nineteenth and early twentieth century texts, including Herman Melville's *Billy Budd*, Oscar Wilde's *The Picture of Dorian Gray*, Henry James's 'The Beast in the Jungle' and Marcel Proust's *À la Recherche du temps perdu*.

In the same year that *Epistemology of the Closet* appeared, Judith Butler published her own analysis of the 'naturalness' attributed to heterosexuality. Her *Gender Trouble: Feminism and the Subversion of Identity* (1990) still stands as the most influential book within the field of queer theory. Butler radically denies the pretensions to 'naturalness' of heterosexuality. For her, heterosexuality is not only a 'melancholic' structure but also, in a sense, second-best. Sigmund Freud had argued that we end up with a melancholic ego because as infants we are forced to give up our sexual desire for our parents as a result of the incest taboo. For Butler there is an even more fundamental taboo, the taboo that rules out homosexuality. Butler argues that our sexual identities are founded on the fact that we are absolutely forbidden to realize a primary homosexual desire. Heterosexual identity, then, is not only 'melancholic' because it is the result of a deep sense of loss, it is also built upon the repression of homosexual desire. Heterosexuality, in other words, is unthinkable without homosexuality. As Sarah Salih puts it, in her discussion of Butler's work, a heterosexual identity

> is 'acquired' through the repudiation of homosexual attachments, and the abjected same-sex of desire is installed in the ego as a melancholic identification, so that I can only be a woman to the extent that I have desired a woman, and I can only be a man to the extent that I have desired a man.

(Salih 2002: 132)

Heterosexuality, then, is not the 'natural' state of affairs that it usually claims to be. (Neither is homosexuality, which no longer is the primary desire that we once experienced.) But if heterosexuality is not 'natural' behaviour, then how should we see it? Like all forms of sexuality, heterosexuality is *performative*. In fact, what I consider to be my identity is performative. My 'I', as Butler puts it in an article published the year after *Gender Trouble* had appeared, is 'the effect of a certain repetition, one which produces the semblance of a continuity or coherence' (Butler 1991: 18). My sexual orientation is likewise the effect of repetition, of the fact that I repeatedly *perform* certain sexual acts. In other words, a string of identical or similar performances takes the place of sexual identity (and of identity as such). As Butler herself tells us in *Gender Trouble*: 'There is no gender identity behind the expressions of gender; that identity is performatively constituted by the very "expressions" that are said to be its results' (Butler 1990: 25). Gender 'is always a doing, though not a doing by a subject who might be said to pre-exist the deed' (25). As these quotations make clear, Butler also reverses our common sense assumptions about our 'I': instead of an 'I' that exists prior to our actions – sexual or otherwise – we have an 'I' that is the result of repetition. It is the continuous repetition of a certain set of acts – which of course will differ from person to person – that creates what might be called an identity effect. But that effect cannot hide that we lack something and so we try to compensate for that lack, a move that does not necessarily make things better:

> In my view, the self only becomes a self on the condition that it has suffered a separation ... a loss which is suspended and provisionally resolved through a melancholic incorporation of some 'Other.' That 'Other' installed in the self thus establishes the permanent incapacity of the 'self' to achieve self-identity; it is as if it were always already disrupted by the Other; the disruption of the Other at the heart of the self is the very condition of the self's possibility.
>
> (Butler 1990: 27)

It is important to note that 'performativity' does not imply choice. There is no pre-discursive, ungendered subject prior to gender identification whose gender, by choice, originates within itself. Heterosexuality is a 'repetition that can only produce the *effect* of its own originality; in other words, compulsory heterosexual identities, those ... phantasms of "man" and "woman," are theatrically produced effects that posture as grounds, origins, the normative measure of the real' (21). Heterosexual activity can only try to pass itself off as the authentic form of sexuality by suggesting that other forms of sexuality like lesbianism and homosexuality are *in*authentic: by setting up oppositions in which it turns itself into the centre by relegating other sexualities to the margins. It needs non-heterosexual identities and activities to authenticate and validate itself.

Heterosexuality and others forms of sexuality are deeply implicated in each other and they are all equally inauthentic.

If what I take to be my 'self' is the effect of repetition of acts that do not originate within me, then what are the possibilities for agency, for the freedom necessary to effectuate change? In *Gender Trouble* Butler speaks of 'the performative possibilities for proliferating gender configurations outside the restricting frames of masculine domination' (Butler 1990: 141). We cannot help performing gender – which is 'a regulated process of repetition' – and repeating our gendered identity, but those repetitions will not always be completely identical and it is the slight variations from one performance to the next that create the necessary space for change, for 'something we might still call agency', as she calls it in *Excitable Speech* (Butler 1997: 38). More recently, Butler, using the term queer in a broad sense, has offered what seems a more optimistic reading of the possibility for agency: 'We do not precisely overcome our formations, but we do veer from the apparent aims at times, and this means that finding a queer way and becoming an agent are somehow linked' (Butler 2016: 18–19).

With her deconstruction of the difference between gender and sexuality Butler would seem to come close to lifting sexuality out of the biological sphere and to drawing it into the realm of culture. For the queer theory that emerged in the late 1980s and early 1990s the argument that, just like gender, sexuality was constructed rather than given was an important step forward. For some theorists, the constructed nature of both gender and sexuality became visible in the practice of cross-dressing, and in particular cross-dressing by males (in which Butler has also repeatedly shown her interest). Cross-dressing is of course perfect for destabilizing generally accepted views of gender and sexuality: a man in a long evening dress or pleated skirt will in most places draw a good deal of attention. Cross-dressing undermines the claim to naturalness of heterosexual identities and emphasizes a theatrical, performance-like dimension of gender and sexual orientation. But men in drag are even more interesting to queer theorists because they blur the boundary between gender and sexuality (which the feminists had fought so hard to establish with the argument that while sexuality is a biological given, gender is nothing but a social construct). The appropriation of gender characteristics normally associated with the other sex clearly has significance beyond gender and is simultaneously a *sexual* act. In drag, gender and sexuality become inseparable. From the perspective of queer theory cross-dressers effectively illustrate the constructed character of gender and sexuality. I should point out that not all critics were completely convinced. The prominent theorist Donna Haraway, whom we will meet later (and who has an advanced degree in biology), had her hesitations about denying the difference between sex and gender: 'to lose authoritative accounts of sex, which set up productive tensions with gender, seems to be to lose too much; it seems to be to lose not just analytic power within a particular Western tradition but also the body itself as anything but a blank page for social inscription' (Haraway 1988: 591). Haraway's objection may seem merely strategic, but Jay Prosser's doubts about Butler's 'performativity' in the case of the 'literality' involved in transsexuality (Prosser 1998: 58) were clearly fundamental. In any case, Butler's deconstruction of sexuality and of the 'self', of individual identity, was instrumental in the development of what Judith Halberstam called 'new sexual vocabularies that acknowledge sexualities and genders as styles rather than life-styles, as fictions rather than facts of life, and as potentialities rather than as fixed identities' (Halberstam 1998 [1994]: 759). But it was also instrumental in the emergence of a queer theory that casts its net much, much wider.

In her 'Queer and Now' of 1993, Eve Kosofsky Sedgwick noted:

> a lot of the most exciting recent work around "queer" spins the term outward along dimensions that can't be subsumed under gender and sexuality at all: the ways that race, ethnicity, postcolonial nationality criss-cross with these and *other* identity-fracturing discourses, for example. ... Thereby, the gravity (I mean the *gravitas*, the meaning, but also the *center* of gravity) of the term "queer" itself deepens and shifts.
> (Sedgwick 1993: 8–9)

We have already seen Donald E. Hall's description of 'queer' as the questioning of all classifications, of all 'conventional categories' and in a more recent discussion of queer narrative Ann Mulhall speaks of queer studies as 'a central project of exposing and challenging normativity' (Mulhall 2020: 142). There is, then, hardly a limit to the scope of queer studies. Still, for some critics even such attempts at definition are too restrictive, too normative, and acutely endanger the whole project. As the critic and writer Garth Greenwell recently said: 'queerness is allergic to definition … the minute we start trying to answer the question, "What do you mean by queer?" we have fallen into a kind of straight logic. We've given up the whole game if we start trying to say what is queer and what isn't' (Dinshaw and Greenwell 2022: 272). Judith Butler, too, has warned against an academic domestication of queer studies.

Queer literary criticism has played a significant role in exposing the hidden essentialism in the stable characters and fixed sexual identities that we see in many of the coming-out narratives that have been published in the last thirty-odd years. Perhaps more importantly, it has made a major contribution to the recognition of fictional and non-fictional expressions of sexualities that had so-far been neglected, as in Imogen Binnie's trans novel *Nevada* (2013) or Juliet Jacques's self-explanatory *Trans: A Memoir* (2016).

SUGGESTIONS FOR FURTHER READING

Eve Kosofsky Sedgwick's *Between Men* (1985) and *Epistemology of the Closet* (1991) are classics, but unfortunately do not make for easy reading. The opening chapters, however, should be accessible. Judith Butler's books – *Gender Trouble: Feminism and the Subversion of Identity* (1990), *Bodies that Matter* (1993) – also tend to be difficult, but her 'Imitation and Gender Insubordination' (1991) is a very accessible exception to the rule. Annamarie Jagose's *Queer Theory* (1997) is an early overview, while Alan Sinfield's *Cultural Politics: Queer Reading* (2nd edition 2005) offers a lively account of the major themes of cultural materialism and of the leftist-oriented queer theory that emerged in the United Kingdom. *Black Queer Studies: A Critical Anthology* (2005), edited by E. Patrick Johnson and Mae G. Henderson, is an early collection of essays at the interface of Black studies and queer studies *The Routledge Queer Studies Reader* (2012), edited by Donald Hall et al., collects an impressive number of major contributions to the debate on queer theory. *The Cambridge Companion to Queer Studies* (2020), edited by Siobhan B. Somerville, is a collection of recent essays. Hannah McCann and Whitney Monaghan's *Queer Theory Now: From Foundation to Futures* (2022) offers a good overview of the development of queer theory while

Will Stockton's very readable *An Introduction to Queer Literary Studies: Reading Queerly* (2022) focuses on queer literary-critical practice. Mimi Marinucci's *Feminism is Queer: The Intimate Connection between Queer and Feminist Theory* (2nd edition 2022) attempts to bridge the widening gulf between feminist and queer studies.

More traditional (and usually more accessible) forms of gay and lesbian criticism are to be found in for instance Mark Lilly's *Gay Men's Literature in the Twentieth Century* (1993), and Gregory Woods's excellent and thorough *A History of Gay Literature: The Male Tradition* (1998). Terry Castle's *The Apparitional Lesbian: Female Homosexuality and Modern Culture* (1993) is a good example of a more traditional, but sophisticated lesbian criticism (see for instance her interpretation of Sylvia Townsend Warner's *Summer Will Show*, 1936). Castle's *The Literature of Lesbianism* (2003) is an enormously comprehensive historical anthology of lesbian writing from the Renaissance onwards. The equally massive *Cambridge History of Gay and Lesbian Literature* (2015), edited by E.L. McCallum and Mikko Tuhkanen, has its starting point in antiquity and offers a global scope. Joseph Bristow's *Sexuality* (2nd edition 2011) is a good overview of a controversial subject.

DECENTRING THE HUMAN
POSTHUMANISM, ECOCRITICISM, NEW MATERIALISM, ANIMAL STUDIES

POSTHUMANISM

Humanism has been variously defined, but it usually includes the belief that our rationality, individual autonomy and agency make us superior to the rest of creation. 'Posthumanism' is shorthand for a fundamental questioning of that belief without abandoning humanism altogether. As the prominent American posthumanist theorist Cary Wolfe put it in his *What Is Posthumanism?* (2010), 'the point is not to reject humanism *tout court* – indeed, there are many values and aspirations to admire in humanism – but rather to show how those aspirations are undercut by the philosophical and ethical frameworks used to conceptualize them' (Wolfe 2010: xvi). If this reminds us of deconstructionist practices we are right on track. Wolfe problematizes humanism from within a Derridean framework and so does the British posthumanist Neil Badmington who like Wolfe seeks to modify humanism from within, if only because thinking 'outside' humanism is impossible:

> If the version of posthumanism I am trying to develop here repeats humanism, it does so *in a certain way* and with a view to the deconstruction of anthropocentric thought. If the pure outside is a myth, it is nonetheless possible to 'lodg[e] oneself within traditional conceptuality in order to destroy it' [quoting Derrida], to reveal the internal instabilities, the fatal contradictions, that expose how humanism is forever rewriting itself as posthumanism.
>
> (Badmington 2003: 14)

DOI: 10.4324/9781003373438-10

So how is posthumanism different from humanism while 'repeating' at least some its positions? Although there are different strands within posthuman thought, they pursue the same end. One might say, in Christopher Peterson's words, that they all 'embrace ... a conception of the human that refuses to define itself in violent opposition to the nonhuman' (Peterson 2011: 127). Or, in the somewhat stronger terms of Richard Grusin, 'the nonhuman turn ... is engaged in decentering the human in favor of a turn toward and concern for the nonhuman, understood variously in terms of animals, affectivity, bodies, organic and geophysical systems, materiality, or technologies' (Grusin 2015: vii). This wish to decentre brings out what posthumanists see as the central flaw in humanism: its so-called exceptionalism, its assertion of mankind's uniqueness and superiority vis-à-vis the world of nature – including the material world – from which it deliberately sets itself apart and which from a humanist perspective only acquires value in relation to human beings. Posthumanism questions that exceptionalism and its corollary, human superiority, and the assumption that value is uniquely tied to human judgment.

One of the seminal texts of posthumanism is Donna Haraway's polemical 1985 essay 'A Cyborg Manifesto: Science, Technology, and Socialist-Feminism in the Late Twentieth Century' (in spite of her later claim, in *When Species Meet* of 2007, that she is 'not a posthumanist'). In a cyborg – a combination of *cyb*ernetic and *org*anism – cybernetic and organic parts work together to create a being that is neither fully human nor completely machine-like but ends up somewhere in between. Interestingly, that is not how cyborgs are usually portrayed. In William Gibson's famous so-called cyberpunk novels of the 1980s – *Neuromancer* (1984), *Count Zero* (1986), and *Mona Lisa Overdrive* (1988) – the emphasis is strongly on the human qualities of its numerous cyborgs. In fact, having a human consciousness is enough to qualify as fully human, even with a body that is almost wholly prosthetic. And, if I may allow myself a brief digression, mind and matter are even kept firmly apart when the cyborg in question is in fact a machine (and therefore, strictly speaking, not a cyborg at all because it lacks organic matter). In the science fiction writer (and scientist) Isaac Asimov's story 'All the Troubles in the World' (1958) the megacomputer Multivac, which practically runs the whole world, has become so deadly tired that it thinks up a plan to have itself killed (for which, rather ironically, it needs human help). And in the novelist Richard Powers's *Galatea 2.2* (1995) a computer that because of brilliant programming has acquired consciousness does indeed effectively kill itself once it has fully understood the horrors that humans are capable of. In both cases the machines have minds so human that deep unhappiness leads to the autonomous decision to commit suicide. But these machines do not strike us as machines. There is nothing in their thinking that is alien. That is also true of the so-called 'replicants' in the movies *Blade Runner* (1982) and *Blade Runner 2049* (2017) who would appear to be wholly organic and who are practically undistinguishable from human beings. Representations of the cyborg tend to focus on its humane characteristics – its consciousness, its awareness of itself, and its very human emotions – or on their total absence. If the human-like individuality and autonomy that characterizes these machine-minds is absent, as in *Star Trek*'s human 'borgs', whose minds are fully controlled by an outside force, the cyborgs are presented as robotic, as machines. The cyborgs that we meet in fiction or in films have a fully human consciousness or no consciousness at all.

That is, however, not what Haraway has in mind. In 'A Cyborg Manifesto' she argues that the figure of the cyborg – and in either a literal or a figurative sense 'we are all … hybrids of machine and organism' – explicitly compromises the boundary between natural organism and machine, just like it undermines human/animal, male/female and physical/non-physical distinctions. It therefore questions the central position that humanism has traditionally accorded the human. We do no stand apart from the world, watching it from a superior distance, but are fully entangled with it and 'like any other component or subsystem, must be localized in a system architecture whose basic modes of operation are probabilistic' (Haraway 1990: 212). Because of this inevitable entanglement, what we need, Haraway tells us in an essay on feminist epistemology, is not 'the knowledges ruled by phallogocentrism (nostalgia for the presence of the one true Word) and disembodied vision' (Haraway 1988: 589), but less patriarchal, authoritarian, and anthropocentric '[s]ituated knowledges … that require the object of knowledge to be pictured as an actor and agent, not as a screen or ground or a resource' (592). We can come by such knowledges only through non-judgmental modesty, never through a master-slave relationship with the object of inquiry (592), and in later publications Haraway introduces the figure of the 'modest witness' who meets the object of research with full respect and empathy, in a relationship of response, even, or perhaps especially, if that object – Haraway was trained as a biologist – is a laboratory animal used in cancer research (as for instance the genetically modified 'oncomouse', the world's first patented animal, in her 1997 *Modest_Witness@Second_Millennium.FemaleMan$^©$Meets_OncoMouse^{TM}*). As we will see, the idea that we can see an 'object of knowledge' as 'an actor and agent' ties in with later developments in thinking about the agential qualities of the material world and about how human lives are affected by non-human forms of agency.

When Species Meet (2008), which belongs as much to the then new field of animal studies as to posthumanism, focuses on so-called companion animals, a category first of all represented by Haraway's own dog, but stretched to include other non-human 'companions' like the laboratory animals of her earlier work and even symbiotic bacteria. It is, in the words of one reviewer, 'a book about how to think about connections among species – about the importance of moving past myths of exceptionalism to recognize the ties that bind humans to other species as well as to other humans' (Mullin 2008: 374). Although Haraway sees the book as 'my effort to be in alliance and in tension with posthumanist projects' (Gane 2006: 140), the alliance clearly dominates. Like the cyborg, the companion species relates the human to the non-human, and through its feedback-loop interactions with humans tends to blur the distinction between them: 'I am who I become with companion species, who and which make a mess out of the categories in the making of kin and kind' (Haraway 2008: 19). In less Derridean phraseology (the book pays close attention to Derrida's influential essay 'The Animal That Therefore I Am' of 2002): 'We are in a knot of species coshaping one another in layers of reciprocating complexity' (Haraway 2008: 42). This is not a plea for seeing those other species as equal to our own, but for an acceptance of our situatedness within that knot and an acceptance of our reciprocal relations with the other species involved. If we accept that reciprocity as a defining feature of what it means to be human, then we have, in a sense, been posthuman ever since we became human –

that is, long before humanism came along and separated us from the non-human. 'We have never been human', as the first section of *When Species Meet* tells us, because animals have always contributed to human practices, because the human has always been shaped in its interrelationship with the hon-human.

The point that we have never been human is also be made by posthumanist theory, which positions itself in the poststructuralist tradition and tries to arrive at a posthumanist view of the subject on the basis of the work of Derrida and other theorists, such as the Italian philosopher Giorgio Agamben (see for instance *The Open: Man and Animal* of 2004). Cary Wolfe, whose above mentioned *What Is Posthumanism?* is a major contribution to the debate, argues, like Haraway, that posthumanism is nothing new: '"post-humanism" as I use the term ... returns us to our messy, material and embodied contingency – including (but not limited to) our evolutionary inheritance and symbiotic entanglements *as animals*, as fellow creatures' (Cole 2011: 102). Our status as fellow creatures is of course a basic assumption of Haraway's *When Species Meet* and it is also basic to the field of animal studies, which I have just mentioned and one of whose aims is, in the words of Greg Garrard, 'to undermine the moral and legal distinction between humans and animals' (Garrard 2004: 149). But that will have to wait.

Another important line of posthuman criticism focuses on the interface where we meet the world of digital information and intelligent machines, an interface which over the last thirty-odd years has been intensively explored by N. Katherine Hayles. In an article published in 2006, 'Unfinished Work: From Cyborg to Cognisphere', Hayles argues that Haraway's cyborg still operated within a humanist sphere, as an autonomous subject:

> Problems with the cyborg as a metaphor include the implication that the liberal humanist subject, however problematized by its hybridization with cybernetic mechanism, continues as a singular entity operating with localized agency. In other words, the cyborg is not *networked* enough to encompass the emergent possibilities associated with the internet and the world-wide web and other phenomena of the contemporary digital era.

> (Hayles 2006: 159)

Hayles's view of the posthuman is closer to the one she attributes to 'the American tradition in cybernetics' (Hayles 1997: 242), which downplays the importance of human consciousness and the uniqueness and integrity of the human body, which it is perfectly willing to improve upon with prostheses or through biological interventions (such as gene therapy), and which, most importantly, 'configures human being so that it can be seamlessly articulated with intelligent machines' (242).

Much of Hayles's work has addressed the ways in which we inevitably enter into processes of interaction when we are involved with 'intelligent machines' and how through such interaction our own intelligence is in a sense co-produced by the machines we work with, thus crossing the border into posthuman territory. In her discussion of Richard Powers's *Galatea 2.2*, in which researchers work to build an artificial intelligence that is complex enough to pass a master degree's examination in English – involving not just ordinary but literary language – Hayles, blurring the border between human and machine, emphasizes how the computer (called Helen) interacts with her tutor: 'As he is training her, the experience of working with her is also training him, denaturalizing his experience of language so that he becomes increasingly conscious of its tangled, recursive nature' (Hayles 1997: 249). Even more invasive is the active involvement of the machine when we read electronic hyper-texts. Because such texts 'are written and read in distributed cognitive environments, the reader is necessarily constructed as a cyborg, spliced into an integrated circuit with one or more intelligent machines. To be positioned as a cyborg is inevitably in some sense to become a cyborg, so electronic hypertexts, regardless of their content, tend toward cyborg subjectivity' (Hayles 2000: n.p.). In the heart of the computer, where everything is coded into strings of ones and zeros, the different ontological levels of character, writer, and reader, disappear and 'the subjectivity we attribute to characters, authors, and ourselves as readers' begins to 'mingl[e]' with 'the non-anthropomorphic actions of the computer program' (ibid.).

For Hayles the posthuman is bound up with of our use of a technology that has become an active component of our own intelligence, eroding the self-sufficiency and autonomy that humanist thinking traditionally attributes to the subject: 'As you gaze at the flickering signifiers rolling down the computer screens … you have already become posthuman' (Hayles 1999: xiv). Seeing posthumanism as the latest but decisive stage in 'technogenesis, the idea that humans and technology have evolved together' (Hayles 2012: 10), Hayles argues that 'the tension between the between the liberal humanist tradition and the posthuman' need no longer concern us now that the real issue is 'different versions of the posthuman as they evolve in conjunction with intelligent machines' (Hayles 2005: 2). Clearly, in all those versions the human will not be what it used to be. The various strands of posthumanism tell us that the human species does not stand apart from the natural world or from that of the machines that it has created, but is inextricably bound up with those worlds, so that its belief in its autonomy and superiority is an illusion.

REPRESENTATION AND THE WORLD OF NATURE

In *The Two Towers*, the second part of Peter Jackson's film version of J.R.R. Tolkien's epic narrative *The Lord of the Rings* (and the second book of the trilogy), we meet the Ents. The Ents are ancient, treelike creatures, gigantic of stature and with slow rumbling voices that call to mind gusts of wind in autumn trees. Although they have lived in Tolkien's Middle Earth since time immemorial, they have no interest in the business of humans – or elves, dwarves, and other non-human races – and keep to themselves in remote forests, with whose great trees they feel more kinship than with anything else alive. No wonder, then, that they refuse to take sides in the war that breaks out between the forces of evil and those who try to save Middle Earth from death and destruction. But their feeling that this is not their war changes completely when they see the bleak wasteland that the wizard Saruman, who has joined the evil side, has created in his preparations for war. As far as the eye can see, woods have been felled and burned and all that remains are charred stumps in a grey and black desert. Enraged by this wanton destruction of the natural world, the Ents attack, scattering Saruman's Orc forces before them and using their incredible strength to wreck the dam that Saruman has had built in order to harness and utilize a river's natural power. The river's pent-up waters, freed from their yoke, flood Saruman's plain, extinguishing the hellish fires that burn above and below the

ground, destroying foul armies, and returning the potential for life
to a place taken over by death.

The message is clear: there is a close link between the natural
and the good, just as there is a close link between unnatural
environments and evil. The lands of Sauron, who in Middle Earth
is the Evil One himself, are a barren volcanic wasteland, whereas
the Shire, where the peaceful, if somewhat simple-minded Hobbits
live, is a pastoral idyll of rolling hills and fertile valleys.

Such an intimate connection between landscape and moral framework is nothing new. In fact, the term 'pastoral' that I just used
standardly refers to a literary genre in which since classical times a
particular landscape and a certain harmonious moral order have
been associated with each other and have been juxtaposed with a
more urban and corrupted order. Literary academics have for a
long time been aware of that connection, not just in the pastoral,
but in every imaginable genre and every imaginable form. Sometimes the connection is rather obvious, as in *The Lord of the Rings*,
sometimes it is quite subtle, as in the novels of Jane Austen, where
upon closer inspection moral authority always turns out to be linked
to an attitude of respect and even reverence for nature, whereas a
lack of that respect is unfailingly indicative of moral fallibility or
worse (see Bate 2000). Nature would seem to be a self-evident
source of metaphors for our own moral concerns.

The role of nature is not limited to that of moral barometer.
Nature may appear in aesthetic terms, admired for its majesty, its – less
awesome – beauty, or even for a wholly unintimidating gentleness. It
may be praised for its authenticity and its pristine quality may be
favourably contrasted with the domesticated landscapes that we
humans have created. In more religious terms, its state of grace may
be held up in contrast to our own fallen state. It may be used to
convey a feeling of nostalgia, as in the eighteenth-century English
poet William Cowper's 'The Poplar-Field':

> The poplars are felled; farewell to the shade,
> And the whispering sound of the cool colonnade!

In its wilder states nature may function as a place of temptation
and trial (as in Nathaniel Hawthorne's short story 'Young Goodman
Brown'), but it may also serve as a place of freedom (as in the

Leatherstocking Tales of James Fenimore Cooper and countless other American writers) and even as a place of healing and redemption (as in the work of D.H. Lawrence and many nature writers). But nature may also be presented as wholly enigmatic, something upon which we project our own fears and desires. In Herman Melville's *Moby-Dick* the white whale that will in the end destroy the monomaniacal Captain Ahab and his crew (except for Ishmael, the novel's narrator) remains an inscrutable force of nature, presumably only goaded into action by Ahab's apparent resolve to kill him or die in the attempt.

The imaginative uses of nature are practically inexhaustible because nature is everywhere. After all, even today's weather is nature, as is the cat who comes up to me in the morning expecting another day of culinary delights. Or *is* he? Does a thoroughly domesticated animal still qualify as 'nature'? Is it still possible to speak of nature, in the sense of something truly itself, wholly authentic, completely untouched by human intervention? Or are even the places that seem to be untouched now affected by a process of global warming caused by our carbon dioxide emissions? But why would we define nature as untouched and authentic in the first place? Are the trees that we have planted in city parks somehow not authentic? What *is* nature? Is nature not another human construction?

DOMINION

While an interest in the ways that nature features in the products of our imagination has for a long time featured in literary criticism, the sort of questions I just asked are fairly new. This is not to say that there never was an interest in the way we intervened in natural processes or affected our natural environment. We have just seen how William Cowper lamented the felling of a 'colonnade' of poplars. But almost invariably such laments centred on *our* feelings, looked exclusively at things from our human point of view. In another poem we find Cowper very straightforwardly expressing such a human-centred view of the natural world:

> I am monarch of all I survey,
> My right there is none to dispute;
> From the centre all round to the sea,
> I am Lord of the fowl and the brute.

We may, to be fair to Cowper, not ascribe this view to Cowper himself. I have quoted here from his 'Verses Supposed to be Written by Alexander Selkirk' (1782), which purportedly gives us the sentiments of the sailor whose sojourn on an uninhabited island had much earlier provided Daniel Defoe with the material for his novel *Robinson Crusoe* (1719), in which the eponymous hero quickly turns the island on which he finds himself into a version of early eighteenth-century rural but already rather thoroughly cultivated England.

It does, however, not really matter what Cowper thought of the supremely self-confident and assertive outlook that he attributes to Selkirk in these lines. What is important that in Europe and its colonies that position was widely shared. Had not God Himself, in Genesis 1, verse 26 (King James version), ordained that we, human beings, would have a special place in His creation, and would have 'dominion over the fish of the sea, and over the fowl of the air, and over the cattle, and over all the earth, and over every creeping thing that creepeth upon the earth'? In Western culture our relationship with the natural world has, for a very long time, remained virtually unquestioned because our dominion over that world was anchored in God's word. The exact meaning of dominion in this particular context was indeed debated by theologians – after all, dominion may give rise to all sorts of practices ranging from responsible stewardship to exploitation – but the hierarchy it implies, with us as masters and the natural world in a position of servitude, seemed clear enough. It is only in more recent times that we find a critical awareness of the exploitation to which unchecked dominion may lead. In his 1854 *Walden* we find the American nature writer Henry David Thoreau complaining that 'the landscape is deformed' by 'avarice and selfishness' and that the farmer 'knows Nature but as a robber'. And contemporaries of Thoreau were outraged by the mass slaughter of bisons on the American Great Plains, resulting in the near extinction of the species by 1890. Clearly, 'dominion' was not supposed to include the reduction, within one single century, of herds totalling enormous numbers to a bare three hundred animals. In the United Kingdom, the consequences of the industrial revolution for a landscape that had remained essentially unchanged for centuries provoked similar protests. But the relationship of dominion, so central to Western culture's views of humans and the natural world, still remained largely unchallenged. Arguably, the Enlightenment, with its triumphant view of human reason as the high point of creation, deepened the gulf between humans and the world of nature. And for those who, embracing the scientific discoveries of the seventeenth and eighteenth centuries, regarded the universe as nothing but a vast machine, governed by eternal natural laws, there was no reason to look at nature with anything but indifference. The scientific revolution involuntarily facilitated a utilitarian, calculating view of the natural world that not much later would become the driving force behind its exploitation by the industrial revolution.

It is only in the last fifty years that the seemingly 'natural' hierarchical relationship between human beings and the natural world has begun to be thoroughly questioned, not in the least because we had reached the point, unimaginable until then, that with our nuclear arsenals we could practically – if not completely – wipe out ourselves and all other living things. Total destruction clearly stretches the idea of dominion beyond acceptable limits. Moreover, even if we succeeded in keeping our ballistic missiles under lock and key we *still* seemed on the point of creating damage to the natural world that was truly irreversible. In 1962 Rachel Carson told a startled public in her book *Silent Spring* that with the way things were going, with an uncontrolled use of agricultural pesticides, there would soon be no birds left to brighten our springs. Carson's book and other urgent warnings that we were taking irresponsible risks with our natural environment led to a broad environmental awareness which, in its turn, led to an activist ecological movement that in the early 1990s inspired the branches of literary and cultural studies that are now called ecocriticism.

ECOCRITICISM

Ecocriticism and its close ally animal studies do a great many widely different things. First of all, they examine representations of nature in literary texts, but also in non-literary texts and other modes of cultural productions such as nature and travel writing (Thoreau's *Walden*, Robert Macfarlane's *The Old Ways: A Journey on Foot* of 2012), government reports, developers' plans, ecological studies, philosophical treatises, wild-life documentaries (Richard

Attenborough comes to mind), films (such as the *Jurassic Park* film series, with *Jurassic World: Dominion* as its most recent instalment in 2022), computer games, and so on. Ecocriticism may look at the function of 'nature' in suburbia, at the uses of 'nature' in theme parks, at the way 'nature' is given a presence inside and outside shopping malls, at roof gardens, at fashions – as they come and go – in the florist business, at the landscaping of golf links. It analyses the way nature is constructed in the most diverse cultural productions and brings to light past and contemporary discourses regarding our natural environment, tracing historical changes in the meaning and value attributed to 'nature', 'wilderness', and natural phenomena in general. In so doing it reveals the hierarchies and power relations that pervade those discourses and that establish the value systems that they either explicitly or implicitly propagate.

The most obvious hierarchy privileges us humans at the expense of the natural world, but there are many more hierarchies at work in our representations of nature. To give a familiar example: a major discourse found in nature writing will extol the virtues of the wilderness and of the wild animals that inhabit it and present those in terms of a robust masculinity. Where traditional criticism was mostly content with simply noting that masculinity – if it had registered at all – ecocriticism will see it in terms of the masculine/feminine binary and connect it with other such binaries that involve relations of power. In for instance environmental crises caused by oil spills or the dumping of toxic waste – a major interest of social ecocritics – oppositions involving race, ethnicity, poverty (or combinations of these) are as often as not closely interwoven with the human/nature binary. Here 'human' stands for economic interests and 'nature' includes those, for instance indigenous people, who, like the natural environment, suffer the consequences of an exploitative mindset. Ecocritics, siding with posthumanists in the deconstruction of the human/nature binary, call for a reconsideration of the values that are based upon that binary and that underlie much of Western society. Climate change makes such a revaluation ever more urgent.

Ecocriticism clearly functions within the radically questioning intellectual climate of contemporary literary and cultural studies. But it does so with a difference because of its specifically 'green' agenda. 'Ecocriticism began', Jonathan Bate tells us, 'in consciousness-raising' (Bate 2000: 8), in alerting us to the way in which our activities posed an ever greater threat to our natural environment and in making us think about what it means to live *with* rather than simply *on* the earth. Its analyses of the discourses that govern our representations of nature focus therefore on the various ways in which these discourses have contributed, and still contribute, to our environmental problems. Rejecting the standard hierarchical relation in the human/nature opposition (in which economic interest prevails) it refuses to adopt a human-centred perspective. (It does of course realize that that refusal is in itself anthropocentric, in the sense that it is a unilateral decision that has not been taken after intense rounds of consultation with the representatives of nature, but that cannot be helped.) Ecocriticism takes an 'earth-centred approach to literary studies', as Cheryll Glotfelty put it in 1996 in the introduction to her and Harold Fromm's seminal *Ecocriticism Reader* (Glotfelty and Fromm 1996: xix). The interests of a natural world that is seriously under threat come first or are at least equal to other interests, such as the social injustices that usually come with environmental degradation. Like the other new modes of criticism discussed in this book, ecocriticism makes us ask new questions of canonical texts, often leading to reappraisals, and has called our attention to texts that for whatever reason had remained under the radar but that, seen in the light of ecocriticism, turn out to have an unexpected relevance.

Ecocriticism's moral and political agenda and the rejection of anthropocentrism are practically the only things that its various strands have in common. Within ecocritical studies we find the same variation of positions that we find in the ecological movement from which it took its original inspiration. Within that movement we find proponents of 'deep ecology', who find real authenticity and purity only in the virgin wilderness, who attribute intrinsic value to all life, and who believe that the interests of nonhuman life on this planet can be protected only by a drastic reduction of its human population. For deep ecologists nature takes precedence over us, human beings. As Rupert Birkin, in D.H. Lawrence's *Women in Love* (1920) puts it rather radically, 'Let mankind pass away — time it did' (Lawrence 1960: 65).

For ecofeminists, the historically unequal relationship — a relationship of domination — between us human beings and nature mirrors that between men and women and has, not accidentally, the same origins: our Judaeo-Christian heritage, which historically has privileged men, and the Enlightenment, which, building upon a long history of inequality, constructed men as responsible and rational and women as their more 'natural' – but less rational and therefore inferior – opposite. This has led some ecofeminists to identify rationality itself as primarily responsible for our environmental crisis and to adopt a wilfully anti-rational, mystical approach to the natural world. Queer ecocritics have examined the relationship to the environment of non-heterosexual actors, both in real life and in textual and visual culture, and have drawn attention to instances of 'heteronormativity' in zoology, with heterosexual prejudice leading to misinterpretations of animal behaviour. Marxist ecologists, in their turn, see the degraded state of our environment as the direct result of the unrestricted operations of international capital. The exploitation of the environment that is responsible for the environmental crisis follows the pattern of the capitalistic exploitation of labour and it is that exploitation that should have our attention in the first instance. (For deep ecologists, who would point to the environmental disasters in the former Soviet Union, this would leave the unequal relationship between humans and nature intact.) Marxist ecologists would also argue that the principle of the 'free' market contributes to environmental problems because the market will always try to meet demand, even if supply can be realized only at great cost to the environment.

Social ecologists will be interested in the social cost of environmental problems. Not surprisingly, that cost – the waste disposal site around the corner, the oil refinery across the canal, the new runway ending near your back yard – is usually borne by the socially and politically powerless and social ecologists target the power relations involved in the decision-making that leads to socio-environmental problems. Writings related to the enormous environmental problems created by the Western world's pollution and its staggering production of waste – and the discourses of pollution and waste themselves – have in recent years drawn ever-increasing ecocritical attention. Since especially members of ethnic minorities in the Western world and, with the outsourcing of much dirty and dangerous work, an increasing number of inhabitants of developing countries are confronted with socio-environmental problems not of their own making, critics have come to realize that social ecocriticism has a productive interface with postcolonial studies (for an early example of that interface see Graham Huggan's '"Greening" Postcolonialism: Ecocritical Perspectives' of 2004). Other topics that have the interest of both ecocriticism and postcolonial studies are the environmental impact of mining activities in developing countries, the cultural impact of large-scale (Western) tourism, and, most importantly, the effects of global warming, which is a global problem for which the industrialized Western world is largely responsible.

In the last ten or fifteen years a number of ecocritics have embraced the new materialism, a recent development in theorizing which claims that theory, with its focus on discourses and discursive constructs, has neglected the role that matter, the material world, plays in the constitution of our human worlds. Inspired by, or drawing on, the sociologist Bruno Latour's actor-network-theory, they argue that matter, although not an intentional agent in the sense that we can speak of conscious interventions, in countless ways influences our lives. From this perspective, anything that occasions a change in a certain situation is a (non-human) actor. There is the pollen that causes your hay fever, the flat tyre that makes you miss your train, the falling branch that lands you in hospital – to offer some examples. For new materialism the view of matter as completely passive and inert has contributed to our sense that we may freely exploit the natural world. Material ecocriticism follows this 'post-constructionist turn' – which does not deny the importance of discourses, but qualifies their monopolistic position – in ascribing some sort of agency to nature while simultaneously downplaying human control of things. In the words of two material ecocritics, 'the human species is being relocated within a natural environment whose material forces themselves manifest certain agentic capacities and in which the domain of unintended and unanticipated effects is considerably broadened' (Coole and Frost 2010: 10). The importance of 'material forces' does perhaps not come as a surprise – some years ago, near where I live, a quarter of a million people had to be evacuated because of dangerously rising rivers – but it is a welcome reminder that nature is not necessarily in step with us. However, material ecocriticism's interest in non-human agency also includes far more surprising phenomena such as the forms of communication that we now know exist in the world of plants and trees and other newly discovered natural phenomena that may give us occasion to rethink the world.

ECOCRITICAL REALISM

I have just said that ecocriticism is different from other modes of contemporary criticism in that it has a specifically 'green' agenda. But there is another, more fundamental difference. Ecocritics range in their views of nature from a deep ecological faith in nature's perfect – and stable – self-organization to the idea that nature is always changing, always in a state of process, with for instance certain species 'naturally' going toward extinction. And in their sense of how we should tackle ecological problems they range from radically anti-modern solutions (away from the modern, technological, and utilitarian centralized state and back to self-supporting carbon-neutral communes) to enlisting the help of advanced technology to undo the damage that other technologies have done.

But all ecocritics agree on a fundamental principle that has often been under attack in contemporary literary and cultural studies: they agree that we can roughly know the world as it is. There would, after all, be no reason to have ecological concerns if we did not really know for sure that our human activities caused real damage to the natural environment. Although ecocritics disagree on the extent to which we can know things and are, on the whole, not naïve in epistemological matters, they agree that we can know enough to be sure that we are on a destructive – and ultimately self-destructive – course. An environmental disaster – say, the meltdown in the nuclear power plant at Chernobyl, in 1986 – is not a linguistic or social construction, even if all reports on what happened will inevitably show the respective agendas of their creators. As a result of their epistemological realism – not shared, I should say, by those ecologists who see science exclusively as complicit with the forces of exploitation – the relations of ecocritics with the world of science differ markedly from, for instance, those of the poststructuralist critics who tend to see science first of all as a cluster of repressive discourses and reality as a linguistic construction. For many ecocritics, and certainly for the environmentalists, science is a source of truths with regard to the natural world. They are willing to accept scientific data and are prepared to take seriously solutions suggested by the scientific community – provided, of course, that these are 'earth'- rather than human-centred.

THE ANTHROPOCENE

In the year 2000 Paul Crutzen, a Nobel Prize-winning scientist, coined the term Anthropocene for a new geological epoch in which human activity has irreversibly altered the world. The term has since been enthusiastically adopted by ecocriticism although there is no consensus about the Anthropocene's onset. Crutzen saw James Watt's invention of the steam engine (1784) as its start date, others have pushed it back to the beginnings of agriculture in prehistoric times, again others have opted for the nuclear tests of the 1940s and 1950s which have left their evidence in rock strata all over the world. As Timothy Clark remarks, the Anthropocene 'is inherently uncertain, producing a great deal of pretentiousness, while drawing lines of conceptual demarcation that are both unsatisfactory and intellectually stimulating … its very ambiguity and contentiousness is part of its catalytic intellectual work' (Clark 2019: 28). In any case, whatever its beginnings, we may assume that the Anthropocene is here and its most alarming feature is the global warming that is the result of carbon dioxide and methane emissions and that climatologists tell us is responsible for unseasonable heat waves and tornadoes, severe droughts, devastating forest fires, flooding in seemingly safe areas, and other scary developments, including rising water levels that eventually will threaten large population centres. It is a scenario that has triggered numerous literary responses, varying from low-key realism in Barbara Kingsolver's *Flight Behavior* (2012) to the semi-apocalyptical mode of Megan Hunter's *The End We Start From* (2017), in which in London the waters keep rising, or Claire Vaye Watkins's *Gold, Fame, Citrus* (2015) in which practically all of California has disappeared under giant sand dunes. Such catastrophes could come to pass, if we may believe what climatologists tells us – and if we do not change our ways – but obviously not in the near future. This 'speculative fiction', as it is called by the writer Margaret Atwood, who herself has made significant contributions to the genre (see her *MaddAddam* trilogy, 2003–2013), has close affinities with science fiction and is because of our familiarity with that genre perhaps less effective as a warning shot than less spectacular but more recognizable scenarios. In *Flight Behavior* millions of migrating butterflies who should trek on to Mexico halt their journey in the Appalachians. The local, largely evangelical, population sees in the mass of orange butterflies nothing but the majesty of God's creation and is not interested in the scientists who tell them that the butterflies have been misled by the unusual temperatures that are the result of climate change and will not survive the Appalachian winter. As one of them says, shrugging off human responsibility, 'Weather is the Lord's business'. Kingsolver's small-scale, day-to-day Anthropocene effectively combines the realist novel's focus on character and interpersonal relations with the long term global vision implicit in climate and climate change. In Richard Powers's climate novel *The Overstory* (2018) one of its characters pessimistically says: 'the world is failing precisely because no novel can make the contest for the *world* as compelling as the struggles between a few lost people' (Powers 2018: 478), a deficiency that Amitav Ghosh in his *The Great Derangement: Climate Change and the Unthinkable* (2016) attributes to a short-sighted and mistaken preoccupation with individual identity and moral growth (or failure) on the part of contemporary novelists. But *Flight Behavior* suggests otherwise and so does *The Overstory* (although it cannot possibly be called low-key). In any case, the fictionalization of the climate crisis in so-called cli-fi (climate fiction) has led to an interesting discussion about the novel's narrative possibilities with regard to climate change.

A FINAL WORD: ANIMAL STUDIES

Animal studies, not so much a subdiscipline of ecocriticism as an intimately related development that got a major boost by one of Derrida's interventions, is another nail in the coffin of traditional humanism. It examines, and questions, representations of animals through the ages, including the various ways in which they have been anthropomorphized (with for instance Winnie the Pooh, Mickey Mouse, and Paddington Bear featuring at the cute end of the scale). It looks at representations of animal 'alterity' – forms of non-human subjectivity – and at the relations between humans and animals. Animal studies rejects the human–animal opposition and seeks 'to undermine the moral and legal distinction between humans and animals', to quote Greg Garrard (2004: 149) once again. That does not mean that animal studies critics claim the same rights for animals that we humans (at least ideally) enjoy – although some of them do, arguing that all sentient species are intrinsically equal. But they are certainly willing to grant animals, at least those that are sentient, far more rights than they have and condemn the current exploitation of the animal world. On what basis can we justify exploiting other sentient species? Both the Christian and the humanist tradition have pointed at our mental superiority, which supposedly puts us in a class all by ourselves and creates what seems to be a solid distinction between us and all other species (an idea called 'speciesism' by the philosopher Peter Singer). For critics working in animal studies that superiority is the illusory product of the construction of animals as inferior, a view that we find in too many literary texts and other means of representation.

SUGGESTIONS FOR FURTHER READING

The Cambridge Companion to Literature and the Posthuman (2017), edited by Bruce Clark and Manuela Rossini, traces the posthuman from the medieval period to our postmodern times in science fiction and autobiography, but also in film, comics and graphic novels. Sonia Baelo-Allué and Mónica Calvo-Pascual's *Transhumanism and Posthumanism in Twenty-first Century Narrative: Perspectives on the Non-Human in Literature and Culture* (2021) collects fifteen essays on fiction by Dave Eggers, William Gibson, Don DeLillo, Margaret Atwood and others.

Ecocriticism's late arrival is illustrated by the fact that the first introduction to the field, Greg Garrard's *Ecocriticism*, dates from 2004. But that introduction, now in its third edition (2022), is excellent. It describes the various strands within the ecocritical enterprise and includes a discussion of animal studies. Another good introduction is Timothy Clark's *The Value of Ecocriticism* (2019). *The Oxford Handbook of Ecocriticism* (2014), edited by Garrard, is a wide-ranging collection that gives us a good idea of ecocriticism in action, as does the more modest *Nature and Literary*

Studies (2022), edited by Peter Remien and Scott Slovic. Ken Hiltner's *Ecocriticism: The Essential Reader* (2015) collects many of the contributions that established the field. The founding text of ecofeminism is Louise Westling's *The Green Breast of the New World: Landscape, Gender, and American Fiction* (1996). Douglas A. Vakoch's *The Routledge Handbook of Ecofeminism and Literature* (2023) shows how ecofeminist literary criticism has since evolved. *Ecofeminism: Feminist Intersections with Other Animals and the Earth* (2nd edition 2022), edited by Carol J. Adams and Lori Gruen, connects ecofeminism with affect and with climate.

A spate of recent books is concerned with literary responses to climate change. *Climate and Literature* (2019) and *The Cambridge Companion to Literature and Climate* (2022), both edited by Adeline Johns-Putra, Pieter Vermeulen's *Literature and the Anthropocene* (2020), and *The Cambridge Companion to Literature and the Anthropocene* (2021), edited by John Parham, examine how the literary imagination deals with the menace posed by climate change. In *Climate Change, Literature, and Environmental Justice* (2022) Janet Fiskio 'examines the connections between climate disruption and white supremacy'. The essays collected in Serenella Iovino and Serpil Oppermann's *Material Ecocriticism* (2014) give a good idea of material ecocriticism in practice, while Frédéric Neyat's *Literature and Materialisms* (2020) is more theoretical in its rethinking of 'the material imbrication of theory and fiction'. Clark's *The Value of Ecocriticism*, mentioned above, offers a more down-to-earth and sceptical view. *Literature and Animal Studies* (2016) by Mario Ortiz Robles tracks the presence of animals in a wide range of texts, as do the essays collected in Lynn Turner's *Edinburgh Companion to Animal Studies* (2017). *Animals, Animality, and Literature* (2018) edited by Bruce Boehrer, Molly Hand and Brian Massumi, takes us through literary history in its survey of literary animal studies.

'THEORY', POST-THEORY, NEW CHALLENGES

LOOKING BACK ON 'THEORY': IDENTITARIAN CRITICISM

If we look back on the history of modern literary theory we will notice that the emergence and subsequent rise of poststructuralist theorizing inaugurated a number of fundamental developments. There is for instance the rise of theoretical approaches based on a presumed collective identity. The tacit assumption of the New Critics, of Leavis and his followers, of Formalism, Structuralism and other modes of theorizing that belonged to the old order, was that their observations and analyses were generally valid because they felt that they operated from a neutral position. Not neutral in the sense that they did not take sides in disagreements about theoretical positions or in interpretations and evaluations of literary texts, but neutral with respect to for instance gender, race, and ethnicity, which were considered extraneous to the business of literary theorizing. Theorists and critics were convinced that they dealt with literature from a position that transcended such differences. Their belief in the possibility of such an Olympian impartiality was not necessarily shared by for instance Black writers and critics, but it was widely accepted until in the 1970s and 1980s the notion that in particular gender and race could never be left out of the equation put an end to impartiality. Ever since, collective identities have played a major role in literary studies.

Feminist literary theory and criticism organized itself around a collective female identity and theorized how writing by female authors differed from that of their male colleagues. African-

DOI: 10.4324/9781003373438-11

American theory and criticism organized itself around a Black identity and offered analyses of Black writing. We find a similar development with respect to Mexican-American writing and other so-called ethnic literatures. However, although no longer all-encompassing, those collective identities were of course still pretty comprehensive and were soon felt to be unduly homogenizing by those who could not fully subscribe to their reigning assumptions. And so, in another round of identity-based theorizing, we got more narrowly defined identities and, with it, more fragmentation. Lesbian studies split off from feminist studies because feminist theory and criticism insufficiently and inadequately represented lesbian perspectives and was in its turn deserted by queer studies – which around the same time also split off from gay studies – which argued that lesbian (and gay) views of same-sex orientation were too traditional and did not do justice to queer experience.

But it is of course quite possible to belong to two or more groups that claim a collective identity. In fact, many of us will have double or multiple identities. Shouldn't that imply a double (or multiple) focus, leading to so-called intersectional theorizations? Is being Black and lesbian not fundamentally different from being white and lesbian? And so we got intersectional approaches to literature that recognized the undeniable fact that many of us straddle the boundaries between identities. We see that intersectionality in, for instance, disability studies, a body of identitarian theory and criticism that established itself in the 1990s (the first edition of Lennard J. Davis's *Disability Studies Reader* was published in 1997). Disability studies as a literary-critical discipline focuses on the cultural representation of disability and interrogates and deconstructs the meanings that over time have been attributed to disability and the values that have been, and still are, associated with it. Starting with a rather undifferentiated notion of identity, disability studies soon was supplemented with the subdiscipline of queer disability studies and, after the Black critic Christopher Bell's attack on what he saw as 'white disability studies', with another intersectional subfield.

THE SUBJECT

Another striking feature of post-1960s literary theory is its view of us human beings, of the subject. Whereas the theorists and critics that dominated English and American literary until well into the 1970s saw the subject as capable of self-knowledge, as autonomous, and as a fundamentally free agent, the generations of theorists that succeeded them took the opposite view. From that perspective we first of all have no knowledge of who we really are. While much of Sigmund Freud's psychoanalytic theorizing has not survived the advance of medical science, many literary theorists still accept his hypothesis that we have an unconscious that stores whatever we repress and to which we have no access so that we will never have a coherent self and will never really know ourselves. For Lacan, whose view of the subject owed much to Freud, what we believe to be our identity is based on misrecognition and the same holds for Althusser whose interpellations, when responded to, give us a false sense of who we are. For Foucault and for the poststructuralist critics who followed his lead we are the product of discourses over which we have no control so that we can never have a stable centre while the centre that we believe we have is not authentic. The identity-based theorizing that I have just discussed offers some consolation in the sense that the collective identity around which it organizes itself is more or less a known quantity but it does not really solve the problem. The subject itself remains decentred.

From the perspective of having, or wanting to have, true knowledge of things, this is an unfortunate state of affairs, but that does not really bother post-1960s theory. In the introduction to their *Theory after 'Theory'* (2011), a wide-ranging collection of essays on literary theory, Jane Elliott and Derek Attridge reviewed the main characteristics and aims of what they simply call 'Theory', that is, the Anglo-American literary theorizing that takes its intellectual inspiration from poststructuralism. To the 'recurring gestures' of Theory — I'll drop the quotation marks — belong the 'foregrounding of culture over nature' (as in the blurring of the line between gender and sexuality) and 'the conviction that epistemological closure is necessarily a form of domination' — in other words, the belief that claims to knowledge always involve an unwarranted and undesirable exertion of power (Elliott and Attridge 2011: 2). Seeing resistance to the establishment of uncontestable facts – of undisputed knowledge – as an act of political resistance, Theory embraced 'temporal disruption, epistemological uncertainty and logical paradox' (3), and invested much effort in 'the attempt to locate a form of thought or experience that might escape current systems without immediately becoming a system itself' (6) since that would merely substitute one form of domination for another. In such an intellectual climate knowledge of whatever form cannot have a high priority. Apart from that, Theory rejected the 'ideals of Liberal selfhood' – which include self-knowledge and the freedom to act upon that knowledge – because those ideals were 'usually seen to require the production of Others who were necessarily designated incapable of achieving these ideals of rationality and self-definition' (6). Liberal humanism, seemingly on the barricades to defend self-knowledge, individual freedom and personal growth, stood accused of constructing itself through the denigration of those who were denied rationality and self-determination.

This summing up makes clear that, while it sought to undermine everything that common sense and tradition had told us, Theory did not suggest new certainties, new truths. On the contrary, in its struggle against systematization, unity, permanence, knowledge, sameness, purity, and other instantiations of what it saw as repression, Theory brought into the field indeterminacy, undecidability, fluidity, fragmentation, hybridity, alterity, and similar intellectual weapons. Its default position was one of deep suspicion, as in these observations on the rights of the individual by the Italian philosopher Giorgio Agamben, who in the 1990s and early 2000s regularly figured in the debate:

> It is almost as if, starting from a certain point, decisive political events were double-sided: the spaces, the liberties, and the rights won by individuals in their conflicts with central powers always simultaneously prepared a tacit but increasing inscription of individuals' lives within the state order, thus offering a new and more dreadful foundation for the very sovereign power from which they wanted to liberate themselves.

> (Agamben 1998: 121)

This deeply suspicious attitude did not only characterize Theory's philosophical and political analyses, it also pervaded its critical practice. Its readings of texts, from the Classics to contemporary literature, invariably exposed moral and political failings that earlier interpretations had overlooked or simply refused to see. Subjected to the most rigorous close readings, texts were made to reveal their unconscious prejudices and hidden agendas – an outcome that at times, in the case of 'reading against the grain' or of so-called 'productive reading', reminded one of forced confessions. Discrimination and maltreatment of women, Blacks, people of colour, lesbians, gays, trans people, Jews, the working class, the elderly, the disabled, were found virtually everywhere. Since such discrimination and maltreatment are a historical reality their ubiquity in literary representations should not surprise us. But Theory did not see much else. And so, what increasingly was seen as Theory's monopolizing of the moral high ground and its knee-jerk condemnations of practically all of Western literature began to grate. As the English critic Valentine Cunningham (who in no way denied Theory's important contribution to literary studies) memorably put it:

> The text is a criminal occasion; it criminalizes; it abets and affirms the reader's own criminality. Of necessity Theory accuses the text of crime, arraigns it before the dock of righteous criticism, affirms its guilt. The text arises as a result of oppression; it's in the pay of malign institutions, wicked state apparatuses, false consciousness; it's the agent of oppressions, repressions, subjugations. It needs careful policing and, naturally, psychoanalytic treatment.
>
> (Cunningham 2002: 61)

Eve Kosofsky Sedgwick had voiced a similar concern when she argued that 'the methodological centrality of suspicion to current critical practice has involved a concomitant privileging of the concept of paranoia (Sedgwick 1997: 5). Instead of 'paranoid reading' she proposed a 'reparative reading' that aimed 'to assemble and confer plenitude on an object that will then have resources to offer to an inchoate self' (149), in other words, to arrive at a positive exchange with the text in question. This call for a less single-mindedly suspicious and negative critical practice, reinforced by the influential sociologist Bruno Latour's argument that 'critique' – his term for Theory-based criticism – had 'run out of steam' (Latour 2004), has led to various attempts to develop a criticism that did justice to a text's more overt intentions and its apparently positive qualities.

Stephen Best and Sharon Marcus proposed what they call 'surface reading', a mode of reading that with its focus on what a text most clearly presents to its readers aims to take it 'at face value' and does not brush the obvious aside in search for deeply hidden counter-signals. As they themselves put it: 'The purpose of criticism is thus a relatively modest one: to indicate what the text says about itself' (Best and Marcus 2009: 11). Others suggested a 'descriptive turn' whose reading practice can be captured in Heather Love's phrase 'close but not deep' in which the 'depth' of 'depth hermeneutics' (Kosofsky Sedgwick's 'paranoid' mode of reading) is replaced by a different sort of depth that is found 'by attributing life, richness, warmth, and voice to texts' (Love 2010: 388). Rita Felski, one the most prominent advocates of a 'post-critique' that must replace a criticism based on fundamental suspicion, has claimed that paranoid reading effectively destroys the reading experience, which ideally should include a combination of recognition, enchantment, shock and wonder (see Felski 2008), in short, the reasons why most readers read in the first place. In her *The Limits of Critique* of 2015 Felski argues that – when reading with an open mind – 'we can be aroused, disturbed, surprised' by literary texts, or even 'brought to act in ways that we did not expect and may find it hard to explain' (Felski 2015: 167). In this scenario the text may function as an actor as understood in Bruno Latour's actor-network-theory, which, as we have seen, grants agency to non-human actors.

AGENCY

This brings me to again another major issue in post-1960s theory: the matter of agency – conscious, intentional, deliberate, and reasoned agency – and, with it, the possibility of political intervention, of resistance to the established order. For all traditional theorists and critics, except those with Marxist leanings, agency was not a point of discussion. Liberal humanism assumes that we ourselves are in the driving seat, in that we are in control of our actions which we ideally base on our knowledge of who we are and on the reasoning of which we are capable. Our actions have their origin in our authentic self. Given our capacity for self-knowledge and for action on the basis of rational considerations the possibility of political intervention never was an issue. Theory, however, tells us that what we think of as the 'self' that is in that driving seat and that makes our decisions for us, is not an authentic, coherent, and whole self at all.

What we see in most attempts to go beyond Theory's paranoid mode of reading is that they do not reinstate the humanist subject but still lean towards Theory's view of the self. In Felski's case, readers who are affected by a text to the point that they start to take action are prompted to do so by that text, not by the outcome of a process of intentional deliberation. They act in response to an unintended emotion in a possibly unexpected way that they themselves may find 'hard to explain'. In such cases agency is shared with the text and heavily qualified. Still, Felski would seem to allow us marginally more agency than those theorists who claim that it is the clashes between conflicting discourses, performative modes, or other power structures, or else the misinterpretations of interpellations, that make it possible for us to act because such clashes and misinterpretations may cause temporary power vacuums that briefly offer us a modicum of freedom. Such a freedom is crucial for Theory's emancipatory political ends which would have no chance whatever of being realized if purposeful action would not be possible. And so we usually find the tacit assumption that somehow some sort of agency on the part of the subject — of you and me — will enable political intervention, even if the exact margins of our freedom are never spelled out. But that should not surprise us. The problem of free will is one the thorniest problems in philosophy and has in over 2,000 years of philosophical debate not been resolved (for an excellent and very lucid discussion, see Robert Kane's *A Contemporary Introduction to Free Will*).

TRAUMA STUDIES AND AFFECT THEORY

Often enough, Theory does not explicitly deal with issues of intentional agency and conscious control. There are, however, exceptions to this rule. Agency and control play an important, if not crucial, role in trauma studies and so-called affect theory, two fields of theoretical inquiry that emerged in the 1990s. Trauma studies focuses on the literary representation of trauma, its consequences and its aftermath, in which a trauma is understood as an individually or collectively experienced event that is so disturbing and so overwhelming that the mind is incapable of processing and assimilating it. As a result, the memory of trauma, with everything connected to it, is forced underground, so to speak, but may, if triggered by an ostensibly innocuous incident, erupt at any given moment. But even when not actively remembered, trauma severely affects its victim's identity. In its extremity, trauma also exceeds or at least severely tests language's expressive possibilities so that the narrative representation that allows us to deal with less destructive events and memories is not, or at the very least not easily, available. For reasons that do not have to be spelled out, trauma studies has after its emergence in the 1990s through the work of Cathy Caruth (see Caruth 1996) shown itself highly relevant for Holocaust studies, postcolonial criticism, Black studies and, most recently, climate fiction.

Affect theory is concerned with the ways how what we see, read, feel, hear, smell – more in general, what we experience – affects us. There is no consensus, though, on how 'affect' must be defined. For Brian Massumi, one of affect theory's pioneers, who borrows his view of affect from Deleuze and Guattari, affect 'is embodied in purely autonomic reactions' (Massumi 2002: 25) to external stimuli. An affect is in first instance limited to the body. Our affective response to an external stimulus is pre-conscious and therefore non-intentional and it does not involve language and our cognitive apparatus. Massumi makes a sharp distinction between a response based on affect and emotion, which he sees as based on conscious awareness. That distinction, however, is questioned by other theorists. The neurologist Antonio Damasio and critics following his lead claim that some cognitive processes operate at a pre-conscious level so that an approach that sees pre-consciousness as excluding cognition and intentionality does not do justice to our mental procedures. Again others, casting their net considerably wider than Massumi, make no hard and fast distinction between affect and emotion. The prominent affect critic Ruth Leys explicitly rejects the idea that 'affects … are nonsignifying, automatic processes that take place below the threshold of conscious awareness and meaning' (Leys 2017: 4–5), while for the humanist philosopher Martha Nussbaum affect theory must include the study of how literary texts influence us through their deliberate eliciting, and subsequent manipulation, of emotions such as sympathy, pity, disgust, or loathing. Clearly the rousing of such emotions involves cognition on the part of the reader, an understanding that may, for instance, sharpen moral awareness. In any case, in fields of critical inquiry such as trauma studies and affect theory the problem of intentional agency and the moral responsibility that comes with the exertion of free will are never far away.

BEYOND THEORY?

Although still a powerful presence in literary studies, Theory and its subdisciplines have since the turn of the millennium lost a good deal of their appeal. But going beyond Theory – or critique, as it is often called – into a new territory of postcritique while holding on to Theory's undeniable achievements is not easy, as it made clear by Elizabeth Anker and Rita Felski's *Critique and Postcritique* (2017), whose introductory chapter very usefully spells out all of Theory's shortcomings. That does not mean that critics who feel uncomfortable with Theory's basic assumptions with regard to for instance language, knowledge or the self have nowhere to go. The last twenty-odd years have witnessed a number of developments that are obviously familiar with Theory but that respectfully keep their distance. There is a renewed philosophical interest in the notion that we can come to know, at least partly, a reality that is independent of our linguistic practices and conceptual resources, and theorists are exploring the potential of such 'speculative realism' for theoretical projects, while seeking to maintain the critical and emancipatory function that for many critics is criticism's true mission. There is clearly common ground with mainstream ecocriticism, although ecocritics would probably balk at the 'speculative' aspect of speculative realism. We also find a renewed interest in what Theory dismissed as 'liberal humanism'. In a spirited contribution to the *Theory after 'Theory'* collection that I mentioned above, Amanda Anderson defends the 'liberal aesthetic' and, more importantly, liberalism itself:

The liberal tradition is characterized by devotion to the examined life in its many dimensions, including the rigorous scrutiny of principles, assumptions and belief systems; the questioning of authority and tradition; the dedication to argument, debate and deliberative processes of legitimation and justification; and the commitment to openness and transparency. ... Acknowledging the philosophical complexities and existential predicaments attending liberal thought allows us to begin to conceptualize, and to disclose, a richer tradition of liberal aesthetics.

(Anderson 2011: 251)

Implicit in Anderson's appraisal of liberalism is the suggestion that a modest liberalism, aware of its limitations, is at least in actual critical practice much closer to Theory than either party had thought possible.

COGNITIVE LITERARY STUDIES AND WORLD LITERATURE

Two approaches that largely ignore Theory are cognitive literary studies and what is called 'world literature'. Cognitive literary studies, which established itself in the last fifteen years, investigates, in the words of one of its most prominent advocates, 'the role of universally shared features of human cognition in historically specific forms of cultural production' (Zunshine 2010: 3). A good example is Patrick Colm Hogan's early essay 'Literary Universals', which presents as universals such 'basic techniques' as symbolism and imagery, assonance, alliteration, and verbal parallelism (Hogan 1997: 43). To forestall any notion that cognitive literary studies is a rather simplistic undertaking, let me quote from a later Hogan essay that discusses the 'synthesizing' of affective science and literary study:

Literary works help us to give us a sense of precisely what systems are involved in any given emotion, how those systems interact, how the excitations or inhibitions of these systems fluctuate, what consequences these fluctuations have, and so on.

(Hogan 2015: 280)

Cognitive literary studies, with its focus on the mental processes involved in knowing – Zunshine's 'universally shared features of human cognition' – and on how these shape literary practice is after big game.

The same can be said of the concept of 'world literature', vigorously promoted by David Damrosch's *What Is World Literature?* of 2003 and since then picked up by other critics. In what amounts to a reconfiguration of the field of comparative literature studies, Damrosch proposes that we read works of world literature – 'all literary works that circulate beyond their culture of origin, either in translation or in their original language' (Damrosch 2003: 4) – with an awareness of their original cultural context, but also of the new life they have acquired after moving into a new context. As Damrosch argues, '[a] culture's norms and needs profoundly shape the selection of works that enter into it as world literature, influencing the ways they are translated, marketed and read' (26). Works of world literature will be 'multiply refracted in the process of transculturation' (24) and it is the critic's business to pay close attention to that process. Damrosch and other critics who champion world literature steer clear of the anti-humanist premises of Theory, but their refusal to read a text only in its original cultural context and their giving equal weight to the text's transformations in new contexts – historical, geographical, linguistic – make them, too, attentive to 'hybridity, creolization, and métissage' (84). In fact, the power of such a text 'comes from our doubled experience of both registers together' (164). Arguably, 'world literature' is a way of reading rather than a corpus of literary texts that have successfully and permanently crossed linguistic and cultural borders. It is based on the willingness to see texts in wholly new contexts in order to enrich their meaning.

Next to world literature we have in recent years seen the emergence of another internationally oriented approach to literature, 'transnational literature', defined by one of its promotors as 'a *kind* of literature, emergent at a specific historical moment, linked by a shared set of identifiable subjects, and composed of texts connected by the use of similar literary devices particularly well fitted to explore them' (Jay 2021: 2). The obvious example is the recent literature that deals with transnational experience, that is, with 'migration, displacement, exile, border crossings, cosmopolitanism, globalization, and the forms of personal and cultural hybridity these forces have produced' (3). Transnational literature, then, is not rival to world literature but a welcome internationalization of certain literary modes.

DIGITAL HUMANITIES

I have earlier in this chapter mentioned 'surface reading' which, like almost all approaches that have been discussed in this book, relies on 'close reading', on the detailed analysis of texts. In the last twenty-odd years we have seen the rise of a diametrically opposed mode of reading, appropriately called 'distant reading' by Franco Moretti, one of its prominent practitioners – and sometimes called 'not reading' by critics who abhor the practice. Strictly speaking, those critics have a point. The reading in 'distant reading' is done by computers, and does therefore perhaps not qualify as reading. 'Distant reading' and comparable practices like 'distant viewing' belong to what is called 'digital humanities', an increasingly important field of research that makes use of computational and statistical methods to tackle problems and to answer questions that are simply too big for individual researchers. But let me, before I go on to discuss digital humanities (or, to be more precise, digital humanities for literary studies) admit that the inclusion of digital humanities in a book that focuses on literary theory may rise eyebrows. A good many critics would argue that digital humanities is not based on theoretical assumptions but is merely a modus operandi, a cluster of methods (not all of which are relevant for literary studies, with its focus upon texts; paintings, chamber music, or films have their own computational approaches). Those critics, too, have a point. Digital approaches to the study of literature are indeed methods, not theorizations. They do not offer theories about literature and may, in principle, serve diametrically opposed theories. Still, one cannot very well ignore them in a world in which digitization – the so-called 'remediation' in digital form, that is, in discrete binary code, of information stored in a traditional medium (printed book, painting, long-playing record) – has become ubiquitous. It is, in fact, that wholesale digitization, including the digitization of literary texts – past and present, ephemeral and canonical – as in Project Gutenberg or in Google Books, that has made computational approaches to the study of literature not only possible but also almost inevitable. Although texts digitized by optical character recognition (OCR) are rarely wholly without mistakes – and tend to have more mistakes the older they get – they can be used for most computational methods.

So what can such digital approaches to literature do? Fortunately, texts are an easy target for quantitative and statistical purposes. They easily lend themselves to counting and comparable operations because they consist of words, that is, discrete units separated by an identifiable element (a space). Computational methods can compare two or more versions of the same text. They can search for words or truncated words (the string 'post' would find both 'postmodern' and 'poststructuralist' – and of course 'posterity' and 'postman'). They can do proximity searches that find words that are relatively close to each other in a text – say within ten words of each other – and they can similarly find clusters of words. Such searches may be prompted by a research question, or they may be inspired by simple curiosity, with the outcome a surprise that may then be interpreted. Computational methods can, with varying margins of error, and if there is enough material to make statistical operations possible, identify the authors of anonymous texts or texts that have perhaps been wrongly attributed, taking into account punctuation, vocabulary, grammatical idiosyncrasies, the length of sentences, and so on. The assumption here is that authors have an individual style that they themselves may not be aware of and that has enough quantifiable aspects to make identification possible. Computational methods can confirm our readerly intuitions and for instance show that the frequency of words implying doubt and uncertainty in Joseph Conrad's *Heart of Darkness* differs in a statistically significant way from that in a large corpus of standard English (Stubbs 2005).

But computational and statistical methods are also useful, or perhaps even more useful, if applied on a much larger scale. Franco Moretti has argued that literary history as it has been constructed by literary historians is seriously flawed because it is based on a very small, and not representative, selection of canonized texts. To illustrate his point, of all the novels that were published in English in the nineteenth century – probably around 30,000 – less than one per cent has made it into the canon and therefore into literary history. Reading the other 29,700 probably not very interesting novels is not a serious option, not even for large teams of literary historians, no matter how dedicated, but a computer, if properly instructed, will gladly do it. Such a 'data mining' approach will tell us nothing about the relative merits of the novels in question, but, as Johanna Drucker tells us,

> Patterns of changes in vocabulary, nomenclature, terminology, moods, themes, and a nearly inexhaustible number of other topics can be detected using distant reading techniques, and larger social and cultural questions can be asked about what has been included in and left out of traditional studies of literary and historical materials.
>
> (Drucker 2021: 113)

It is worth pointing out that the work of Moretti and others on literary genres usefully illustrates how computational approaches and conventional methods interact. If you want to sort a large number of novels by genre using a computational method you have to make sure that your software can do so. In other words, you have to tell it, so to speak, what to look for. It needs to know what characterizes the genres in question. It needs generic markers that will enable it to classify the novels it 'reads'. But those generic markers – machine-readable units such as textual features – must be selected by way of a careful reading of a number of the texts involved. At the beginning of the cycle we find decisions made on the basis of close reading.

Actual reading is hard to avoid. Ted Underwood relied on bibliographies of science fiction novels to develop a program that in nine out of ten cases correctly identified a novel as science fiction. Here much of the preparatory reading had been done by those science fiction scholars whose bibliographies he had used. Underwood's major purpose, by the way, was to answer certain questions on the history of the genre. A similar computational approach to the history of detective fiction led him to conclude that 'the textual differences that distinguish twentieth-century stories of detection from other genres can be traced back very clearly as far as [Edgar Allan Poe's] "The Murders in the Rue Morgue" – and not much farther ... Poe's stories already display many of the same features that distinguish twentieth-century crime fiction from other genres' (Underwood 2016). Computational methods can not only distinguish one genre from another, they can also distinguish fiction from non-fiction (a distinction questioned by many post-structuralist critics). Andrew Piper has shown that in the case of nineteenth-century novels a computational approach that bases itself exclusively on internal evidence – and therefore not on possible references to the real world – can with ninety-five per cent accuracy make a distinction between non-fiction and fiction. What is more, those differences are consistent over time: 'not only are the differences between fiction and nonfiction robust across time and languages, but we can use models built in one time period to strongly predict those of another' (Piper 2018: 105).

Computational methods have been accused of being at best apolitical and critics have pointed at the danger of computation incorporating social, racial, and gender-related prejudices in its algorithms. Safiya Umoja Noble's *Algorithms of Oppression: How Search Engines Reinforce Racism* (2018) shows this danger with regard to the search machines that we use on a daily – if not hourly – basis. Her call to develop a 'Critical Black Digital Humanities' (Noble 2019) is echoed by the work of others, such as Roopika Risam, whose *New Digital Worlds: Postcolonial Digital Humanities in Theory, Praxis, and Pedagogy* (2018) looks from another angle but with a similarly critical attitude at the digital humanities project. This is not to say that race or gender have been completely ignored by researchers using digital methods, as is illustrated by Richard Jean So's computational study of racial inequality in post-war fiction (So 2020), or the work on gender and authorship, and gender and characterization, by Underwood, David Bamman and Sabrina Lee (Underwood et al. 2018). A computational method is just that – it is a method, an instrument, and not a theory. Still, like theories, methods may be biased and their biases, better hidden than those of theories, must be carefully examined.

PRINT CULTURE STUDIES

As I have suggested, for those critics who 'do' Theory, a computational approach to literary studies is not theoretical enough, or not theoretical at all (while for most humanist critics, for whom the individual literary text is of prime importance, it is positively wrong-headed). Another field of research that does not easily get a theoretical stamp of approval is what is usually called print culture studies, although it also goes by other names. Print culture studies has over the last twenty-odd years attracted a growing interest, not least from those scholars who had become tired of what seemed to them Theory's ever more dazzling pirouettes: astonishing spins, involving great skill, but very little progress. So what exactly is print culture? It is a field that is so vast that a succinct and precise definition is hard to give. Print culture scholars are interested in everything that has been printed – its production, its circulation, and its reception – and in everything in which printed material has played or plays a role. 'Printed material' is not limited to books, to the 'codex' form that we are familiar with – individual sheets bound within covers – but includes scrolls, such as the famous Dead Sea scrolls, the calligraphic Bibles and theological tracts produced in medieval monasteries, newspapers, magazines, and even ebooks and audiobooks, which are not printed but are directly based on printed material. Print culture studies is interested in the material aspects of what is printed, in the history of printing, in the social impact of printing – from the rise of silent reading, after the invention of the printing press had made books widely available, to the role of books in the diffusion of Enlightenment thinking. It is interested in the economic aspects of publishing and selling books, in the roles that authorities play in either hindering (through censorship) or facilitating (via public libraries) the reading of books, in how printed sources are used in films or in computer games, and in the reverse process in which books are based on for instance a sequence of films such as the *Star Trek* saga – are such books commissioned, are they the result of private initiatives on the part of hopeful writers, do they emerge from so-called 'fan fiction'? The list of subjects for research and questions that could be asked is almost endless. What they have in common, though, is that they do not focus on content. Clearly content plays a crucial role in the social impact that a book or an inflammatory magazine piece may have, but in print culture studies content is definitely secondary.

As the random listing above illustrates, print culture studies is an umbrella term under which wildly dissimilar scholarly practices are brought together. In her excellent introduction to the field Simone Murray very usefully distinguishes four 'key' subfields: 'medium theory; book history; political economy; and cultural policy'

(Murray 2021: 10). As she points out, these subfields have their origins in media studies, cultural history, economics, and politics, a combination of disciplines that in themselves combine diverse approaches and fields of interest. I will here follow Murray in her exemplary disentangling of this knot. Medium theory – not to be confused with media studies – examines the specific features that characterize the book in its capacity as means of communication. It asks how these features are different from those of other means of communication and what it means to get your information in printed form – does the medium affect the message, as the communication theorist Marshall McLuhan argued long ago? It also wants to know how the book, in its various historical manifestations, affected the worlds in which it made its appearance. It has been argued that the book created 'readerly interiority' – an until then unprecedented intimate relationship between writer and reader. And it is clear that the printed book, which made its European debut around 1440, transformed European culture, its religious landscape – by way of the translation and dissemination of the Bible into various vernaculars – and European history. Would for instance the Enlightenment and the French Revolution have been possible without the mass circulation of new and revolutionary ideas through printed materials such as pamphlets and books (like the *Encyclopédie*)? From our vantage point in a world saturated with books it is practically impossible to imagine how people thought and felt in a bookless world, just as it is now practically impossible to imagine what a world without the internet and mobile phones was like or to grasp how the digitization of the world has changed us.

Fortunately, print culture studies is also concerned with less sweeping questions and with issues that are more manageable. Let us follow the completed manuscript of a novel to its ultimate destination: the reader. First of all, its author has to interest a literary agent – not an absolute condition, but a sensible move because many publishers reject unsolicited manuscripts out of hand. Then the agent finds a publisher, either a subsidiary of one of the few gigantic international publishing conglomerates or a so-called independent publisher. An editor will go through the manuscript and discuss recommendations with the author. The finalized manuscript will then go to a copy-editor who will scrutinize the text to eliminate all typos and infelicities that have escaped the author's attention. After the copy-editing it goes to the typesetter, which is the first time it is paginated in its final form. It then goes to a proofreader, which is a last chance to catch errors (some of which may have been introduced by the typesetter). Finally, the novel is published.

But how does it reach the reader? Publicity — good reviews are perfect — is essential. After all, bookshops must be persuaded to stock the book and to give it a prominent place on the shelves or, even better, in a window. Quite often, the bookshop, either belonging to a chain of bookshops or an independent one, will expect the publisher to pay for that visibility ('pay-for-display'). If the author is lucky, the novel will be ordered by public libraries, picked up by a book club, or selected for a special offer (three novels for the price of two, for instance). And then there is of course online retailing, which by now controls a large part of the market, and we have the ever-increasing role of social media. Not surprisingly, many novels sink without a trace. No reviews, no interest on the part of bookshops, or, if there is some interest, no prominent display and a return of the book to sender (the publisher) after the agreed waiting period is over (the rather curious but common sale or return practice that offers bookshops some protection). Every step in this cycle is of interest to print culture scholars, not least because the manuscript goes through a protracted process of selection. For example, it may be rejected by an agent, by publishers, or, once it has been published, by the editors who commission reviews, by bookshops, librarians, and, finally, readers, who do not really reject the book but simply may not know that it exists. In that selection process commercial interests will be paramount, or at least important — I will return to that nuancing below — but the culture factor is ever present. Feminist and Black scholars have argued that gender and racial prejudice have seriously hampered publishing efforts by women writers and Black writers (while reminding us that access to print culture has long been denied to women and much longer to a large part of the Black population). And let us not forget reader prejudice. The Brontë sisters and Mary Anne Evans (better known as George Eliot) used male pseudonyms, and J.K. Rowling, of *Harry Potter* fame, deliberately left her gender in the dark by using her initials.

Publishing books is a business. But there is more to it. Many independent publishers cross-subsidize: they use the money they make on best-selling books to publish books that they believe should be out there, but that will quite probably never earn their way. Their reasons may be primarily aesthetic, or primarily ideological (the novel in question may champion gay rights or promote indigenous culture), or may be of academic interest. Cultural and political concerns are never far away in the case of books, leading to censorship and other forms of book repression – and occasionally to book burning – but also to an impressive number of annual awards and prizes for the best books in various categories, handed out by private parties and national, regional, and even local authorities. Those authorities often also subsidize translations into other languages of books they think worth promoting, and they may offer writing grants to promising young authors. All of these actors have their reasons for what they do and those actors and their reasons are of great interest to the print culture scholars who focus on cultural policy, of which the municipal, regional, or national library itself is a prime example. Why do authorities invest in public libraries and what are those libraries' policies – what books do they exclude and on what grounds (in many European countries public libraries will not stock Adolf Hitler's *Mein Kampf*). And what drives such costly digital library projects as Project Gutenberg and Google Books? In short, what do all these actors expect from books – or at least from the books of their choice, if they practice censorship (which raises the question what they fear from the books they censor).

Print culture has so many cultural, commercial, legal, and political aspects, all of which have their own histories, with again other traditions, practices, and laws applying across the border with the neighbouring country, that these paragraphs cannot possibly do it justice. Hopefully, what has come across is that its study is an exciting and dynamic field of inquiry in which various disciplines interact and complement each other.

MEDIA STUDIES

Another territory into which literary critics – and, in this case theorists – are increasingly interested is that of media studies. We all know more or less what is meant by 'the media'. We know that media are means of communication and we would not be surprised to hear that Media Studies has its origin in the study of communication. But the telephone is a means of communication, and so is semaphoring − the now probably rare use of flags and light signals to convey a message − and we don't think of telephony or the waving of flags when we think of the media and neither does media studies. Wide-ranging though it is, media studies does not cover all means of communication. It focuses on means of *mass* communication, that is, communication that can simultaneously reach a large number of people in different and distant locations (which excludes not only the telephone, flags and light signals, but also the live performance of a rock band playing to an audience of 100,000 − although not the streaming of that concert). For obvious reasons media studies does not cover books, a field in which literary studies has cornered the market, but it also, and perhaps more surprisingly, largely leaves film to film studies, a sort of sister discipline with which it has a good deal in common. But even without such mass media as books and films media studies is a vast and complex field that in the last ten of fifteen years has seen great changes, with ever more means of communication going digital and sharing integrated platforms that allow us to watch content wherever we are and whatever we are doing.

With media studies we return to theory, including its various poststructuralist or poststructuralist-inflected versions. As Julian McDougall and Claire Pollard point out in their introduction to the field, 'the analytical skills to critically interpret media texts' that are essential for media students 'makes Media Studies a kind of extension of English' (McDougall and Pollard 2019: 8). We see this in its use of concepts like genre and narrative, in its practice of 'close reading' − including the 'reading' of images − and in its analyses of, for instance, practices of representation and of the influence of ideology in which we meet the same names and the same theories that we have met in literary studies and in cultural studies. Media studies is also like the study of literature in that it 'is like a matrix where any theory can be applied to any text' (145). As in literary studies, a media 'text' can be analysed from an impressive range of different perspectives: poststructuralist, feminist, postcolonial, ecological, queer, and so on. In media studies content is as important as it is in the study of literature. But media studies also shares many concerns with the study of print culture. Like print culture studies, Media studies is interested in questions of gatekeeping – who controls media content and how is that power used, or, as the case may be, abused? Who regulates the media, who finances them and why (apart from the profit motive)? Who has access to the media and who is denied access (as in some authoritarian regimes)? What cultural, religious, or ethnic identities do the media distinguish and support (or disparage)?

And then there are the demographics of the media's audiences. Gender, age, class, and other factors will play a role in the reception of media productions while productions may in their turn target specific demographic groups. Media studies combines the study of content with the study of how that content is created, packaged, promoted, distributed, received (or censored), appropriated, remediated – in short, the study of how media content makes its way into the world and how it affects that world. Media studies has much in common with literary studies in its study of content and with cultural studies in its interest in the socio–cultural effects of that content. What does the omnipresence of the media mean for our social life and for the society we live in? Finally, there is a third aspect to media studies that we do not find in literary studies or in the study of print culture: the actual production of a 'media text', involving camera work, sound, editing, and other activities that at every point demand creative thinking.

How do we 'read' a media 'text'? Clearly the 'language' of the media is more complicated than that of literary texts. It may indeed include language, written or spoken (or both), but it will usually also include images, either still or moving (or both). Whereas language is linear, an image is spatial and involves a different cognitive process in which the various elements making up the image ask to be 'read' simultaneously. And there is a fundamental difference between a linguistic sign and a visual sign. The word tree, encountered in a novel, allows readers a good deal of leeway in their realization of its meaning. A picture of a tree will leave far less to the imagination. Interpretative leeway will need to be created through a sequence of images. But to return to the question of how to read a media text. We know how to analyse what is said or printed, but what about visual meaning? Analysing visual meaning involves an understanding of how it is created. We must, for instance, pay attention to the position and movement of the camera. Do we have a long shot or a point of view shot drawing us into the scene? Does the camera move and what is the effect of its movement? What is the role of sound – much of which is added later – in what we are viewing? Where do we see signs of editing and how do those editing decisions affect the narrative?

In discussing narrative we return to literary studies. Much of what can be said about literary narrative can also be used in media studies. The terminology needn't be exactly the same, but the conceptual apparatus of for instance Proppian formalism or structuralist narratology lends itself to the analysis of media narratives (including the way news is presented). And like literature, the media has its genres, often closely resembling those of literature, and constructed in a similar way with the help of a limited set of conventions that hardly change over time. Equally important in both fields is the notion of representation. Everything is mediated or re-presented, and with re-presentation comes distortion. That leads us, as in literary studies, to ideology. Representations will be ideologically laden. Althusser's notion of interpellations that coercively invite us to take up certain subject positions, Gramsci's notion of hegemony, of manufactured consent, but also the cultural studies perspective that allows the subject at least a modicum of agency all have a place in media studies theorizing. If we conceive of ideology in broader terms, we see leftist media theorists looking for political biases, feminists looking for biases that reflect and thereby reinforce patriarchal relations, queer theorists looking for unfavourable representations of so-called deviant behaviour – all of them engaged in detecting and deconstructing representations that do not attempt to reflect reality but instead create their own reality.

A representation that creates rather than reflects reality – in its simplest form a lie, in a complex form a subtle distortion – carries power. Since the media are omnipresent the question of their power features prominently on the agenda of media critics. At the time of writing, almost one-third of the American electorate believe that Donald Trump won the 2020 presidential elections, an unfounded belief that was strongly encouraged by a number of influential media outlets. If the media can be so influential, we must know how it succeeds in being so persuasive and analyse the ways it can successfully communicate a false reality. Such an analysis will of course benefit from a thorough knowledge of the production side of things. But that does not really have a place in a book on literary theory.

FINAL AND INCONCLUSIVE WORDS

There is no telling which way literary theory will go. It is not impossible that in the first decades of the new millennium we have witnessed a parting of the ways between those theorists who continue to be inspired by the poststructuralist and related perspectives that have their source in Continental philosophy and those who pursue a line that is closer to philosophical realism and to a liberal humanist perspective. But that should put nobody off. Ever since, long ago, the idea was abandoned that a literary text can have only one single meaning, major texts have been examined from countless different perspectives and submitted to countless critical strategies. The resulting interpretations may reinforce, complement, or contradict one another, but they always give us a fuller sense of the potential of those texts. We should not be afraid of critical pluralism or eclecticism. Contemporary critical practice could do worse than echo the nineteenth-century American poet Walt Whitman in one of his more exuberant moods:

> Do I contradict myself?
> Very well then I contradict myself,
> (I am large, I contain multitudes.)
> (Walt Whitman, 'Song of
> Myself', 1855)

SUGGESTIONS FOR FURTHER READING

The introductions to Jane Elliott and Derek Attridge's *Theory after 'Theory'* (2011) and Elizabeth Anker and Rita Felski's *Critique and Postcritique* (2017) give a good idea of the growing unease and frustration with poststructuralist criticism (or 'critique'). Trauma studies is expertly and even-handedly discussed in Roger Luckhurst's *The Trauma Question* (2008) and, more recently, by Lucy Bond and Stef Craps in *Trauma* (2020). Alex Houen's *Affect and Literature* (2020) is an excellent introduction to affect studies. *Introduction to Cognitive Cultural Studies* (2010), edited by Lisa Zunshine, collects important contributions to cognitive literary studies, while Terence Cave's *Thinking with Literature: Towards a Cognitive Criticism* (2016), seeing the literary work as 'the unique product of human cognition', uses insights from the cognitive sciences in close readings of literary texts from Shakespeare to Jonathan Franzen. Good and very readable introductions to 'world literature' are Mads Rosendahl Thomsen's *Mapping World Literature* (2008) and Theo D'haen's *The Routledge Concise History of World Literature* (2nd edition 2024). *The Cambridge Companion to World Literature* (2018), edited by Ben Etherington and Jarad Zimbler, is a wide-ranging collection of essays on different aspects of world literature. *The Routledge Companion to World Literature* (2nd edition 2023), edited by Theo D'haen, David Damrosch, and Djelal Kadir, thoroughly covers 'world literature' in practically all its aspects. In *Transnational Literature: The Basics* (2021) Paul Jay gives us a good introduction to a young discipline.

Martin Paul Eve's *The Digital Humanities and Literary Study* (2022) is an eminently readable overview that focuses on those questions in literary studies that can be addressed with the help of computational methods and technological analyses. Johanna Drucker's *The Digital Humanities Coursebook: An Introduction to Digital Methods for Research and Scholarship* (2021) covers all digital humanities and is, as its title tells us, both introductory and structured as a course. Kathryn C. Wymer's *Introduction to Digital Humanities: Enhancing Scholarship with the Use of Technology* (2021) is another accessible introduction that demonstrates the promise of its title. *The Bloomsbury Handbook to the Digital Humanities* (2023), edited by James O'Sullivan, is a wide-ranging and comprehensive collection that includes essays on race and digital humanities and on postcolonial, queer, feminist, and multilingual digital humanities. An excellent, comprehensive, and very readable overview of print culture studies is Simone Murray's *Introduction to Contemporary Print Culture: Books as Media* (2021). *Agent of Change: Print Culture Studies after Elizabeth L. Eisenstein* (2007), edited by Sabrina Alcorn Baron et al., collects twenty essays that give a good idea of the range of print culture studies. Amaranth Borsuk's *The Book* (2018) is a lively introduction to the history of the book and book art that emphasizes the continuity between print media and digital media.

Julian McDougall and Claire Pollard, *Media Studies: The Basics* (2nd edition 2019) and Brian L. Ott and Robert L. Mack, *Critical Media Studies: An Introduction* (3rd edition 2020) offer good introductions to Media Studies, as does Sarah Casey Benyahia et al.'s *Media Studies: The Essential Resource* (2014). *Keywords for Media Studies* (2017), edited by Laurie Ouellette and Jonathan Gray, collects over sixty brief essays that comprehensively cover the field.

BIBLIOGRAPHY

Abu-Mannen, B. (ed.) (2019) *After Said: Postcolonial Literary Studies in the Twenty-first Century*, Cambridge: Cambridge University Press.

Achebe, C. (1976 [1958]) *Things Fall Apart*. London: Heinemann.

Achebe, C. (1995 [1974]) 'Colonialist Criticism', in B. Ashcroft, G. Griffith, and H. Tiffin (eds), *The Postcolonial Studies Reader*, London: Routledge.

Adams, C.J. and L. Gruen (eds) (2022) *Ecofeminism: Feminist Intersections with Other Animals and the Earth*, 2nd edition, London: Bloomsbury.

Ahmad, A. (1992) *In Theory: Classes, Nations, Literatures*, London: Verso.

Agamben, G. (1998) *Homo Sacer: Sovereign Power and Bare Life*, Stanford, CA: Stanford University Press.

Althusser, L. (2001) *Lenin and Philosophy and Other Essays*, New York: Monthly Review Press.

Anderson, A. (2011) 'The Liberal Aesthetic', in J. Elliott, and D. Attridge (eds), *Theory after 'Theory'*, 249–262, New York: Routledge.

Anker, E.S. and R. Felski (eds) (2017) *Critique and Postcritique*, Durham, NC: Duke University Press, 2017.

Arnold, M. (1970) *Matthew Arnold: Selected Prose*, ed. P.J. Keating, Harmondsworth: Penguin.

Arnold, M. (1971 [1869]) *Culture and Anarchy*, ed. J. Dover Wilson, Cambridge: Cambridge University Press.

Ashcroft, B., G. Griffith, and H. Tiffin (eds) (1995) *The Postcolonial Studies Reader*, London: Routledge.

Ashcroft, B., G. Griffith, and H. Tiffin (2013) *Key Concepts in Post-Colonial Studies*, 3rd edition, London: Routledge.

Ashcroft, B., G. Griffith, and H. Tiffin (eds) (2005) *The Postcolonial Studies Reader*, 2nd edition, London: Routledge.

Attridge, D. (2018) 'Derrida as Reader', in J.-M. Rabaté (ed.), *After Derrida: Literature, Theory and Criticism in the Twenty-First Century*, Cambridge: Cambridge University Press.

Badmington, N. (ed.) (2000) *Posthumanism*, Basingstoke: Palgrave Macmillan.

Badmington, N. (2003) 'Theorizing Posthumanism', *Cultural Critique* 53: 10–27.

Baelo-Allué, S. and M. Calvo-Pascual (eds) (2021) *Transhumanism and Post-humanism in Twenty-First Century Narrative: Perspectives on the Non-Human in Literature and Culture*, New York: Routledge.

Baker, H.A. Jr (1972) *Long Black Song: Essays in Black-American Culture*, Charlottesville, VA: University Press of Virginia.

Baker, H.A. Jr (1984) *Blues, Ideology, and Afro-American Literature: A Vernacular Theory*, Chicago, IL: University of Chicago Press.

Bakhtin, M. (1981) *The Dialogic Imagination: Four Essays*, ed. M. Holquist, Austin, TX: University of Texas Press.

Baldick, C. (1983) *The Social Mission of English Criticism, 1848–1932*, Oxford: Clarendon Press.

Baldick, C. (1996) *Criticism and Literary Theory 1890 to the Present*, London: Longman.

Barker, C. and E.A. Jane (2016), *Cultural Studies: Theory and Practice*, 5th edition, London: Sage.

Baron, S.A.*et al.* (eds) (2007) *Agent of Change: Print Culture Studies after Elisabeth L. Eisenstein*, Amherst, MA: University of Massachusetts Press.

Barthes, R. (1990) *The Fashion System*, Berkeley, CA: University of California Press [1967].

Barthes, R. (1972 [1957]) *Mythologies*, London: Jonathan Cape.

Barthes, R. (1975 [1970]) *S/Z*, New York: Hill and Wang.

Barthes, R. (1977) *Image–Music–Text*, London: Fontana.

Barthes, R. (1986) *The Rustle of Language*, New York: Farrar, Strauss and Giroux.

Barthes, R. (2000 [1968]) 'The Death of the Author', in D. Lodge and N. Wood (eds), *Modern Criticism and Theory: A Reader*, 2nd edition, Harlow: Longman.

Bate, J. (2000) *The Song of the Earth*, London: Picador.

Belsey, C. (1980) *Critical Practice*, London: Methuen (2nd edition: Routledge, 2002).

Belsey, C. (1985) *The Subject of Tragedy: Identity and Difference in Renaissance Drama*, London: Methuen.

Belsey, C. (2002) *Poststructuralism: A Very Short Introduction*, Oxford: Oxford University Press.

Belsey, C. (2005) *Culture and the Real*, London: Routledge.

Bennett, T. (2003) *Formalism and Marxism*, London: Routledge.

Benyahia, S.C.*et al.* (2014) *Media Studies: The Essential Resource*, London: Routledge.

Bertens, H. (1995) *The Idea of the Postmodern: A History*, London: Routledge.

Bertens, H. and D.W. Fokkema (eds) (1997) *International Postmodernism: Theory and Literary Practice*, Amsterdam: Benjamins.

Best, S. and D. Kellner (1991) *Postmodern Theory: Critical Interrogations*, New York: Guilford.

Best, S. and S. Marcus (2009) 'Surface Reading: An Introduction', *Representations* 108(1): 1–21.

Bhabha, H.K. (ed.) (1990) *Nation and Narration*, London: Routledge.

Bhabha, H.K. (1992) 'Postcolonial Criticism', in S. Greenblatt and G. Gunn (eds), *Redrawing the Boundaries: The Transformation of English and American Studies*, New York: MLA.

Bhabha, H.K. (1994) *The Location of Culture*, London: Routledge.

Bobo, J. (ed.) (2001) *Black Feminist Cultural Criticism*, Malden, MA: Blackwell.

Boehrer, B.*et al.* (eds) (2018) *Animals, Animality, and Literature*, Cambridge: Cambridge University Press.

Boehmer, E. (2005) *Colonial & Postcolonial Literature: Migrant Metaphors*, 2nd edition, Oxford: Oxford University Press.

Bond, L. and S. Craps (2020) *Trauma*, New York: Routledge.

Booth, W. (1961) *The Rhetoric of Fiction*, Chicago, IL: University of Chicago Press.

Borlik, T.A. (2012) *Ecocriticism and Early Modern English Literature*, New York: Routledge.

Borsuk, A. (2018) *The Book*, Cambridge, MA: MIT Press.

Bowie, M. (1991) *Lacan*, London: Fontana.

Brannigan, J. (1998) *New Historicism and Cultural Materialism*, Basingstoke: Macmillan.

Brathwaite, E. (1974) *Contradicting Omens: Cultural Diversity and Integration in the Caribbean*, Mona: Sacavou Publications.

Bremond, C. (1966) 'La logique des possibles narratifs', *Communications* 8.

Brennan, T. (ed.) (1990) *Between Feminism and Psychoanalysis*, London: Routledge.

Bristow, J. (2001) 'Gay, Lesbian, Bisexual, Queer and Transgender Criticism', in C. Knellwolf and C. Norris (eds), *The Cambridge History of Literary Criticism, vol. 9: Twentieth-Century Historical, Philosophical and Psychological Perspectives*, Cambridge: Cambridge University Press.

Bristow, J. (2011) *Sexuality*, 2nd edition, London: Routledge.

Brooks, C. (1942) *The Well-Wrought Urn: Studies in the Structure of Poetry*, London: Harcourt.

Brooks, C. (1972 [1942]) 'The Language of Paradox', in D. Lodge (ed.), *20th Century Literary Criticism*, London: Longman.

Brooks, C. and R. P. Warren (1976 [1939]) *Understanding Poetry*, 4th edition, New York: Holt.

Brooks, P. (1984) *Reading for the Plot*, Cambridge, MA: Harvard University Press.

Butler, C. (2002) *Postmodernism: A Very Short Introduction*, Oxford: Oxford University Press.

Butler, J. (1990) *Gender Trouble: Feminism and the Subversion of Identity*, London: Routledge.

Butler, J. (1991) 'Imitation and Gender Subordination', in D. Fuss (ed.), *Inside/Out: Lesbian Theories, Gay Theories*, London: Routledge.

Butler, J. (1997) *Excitable Speech: A Politics of the Performative*, London: Routledge.

Butler, J. (2016) 'Rethinking Vulnerability and Resistance', in J. Butler, Z. Gambetti, and L. Sabsay (eds), *Vulnerability in Resistance*, Durham, NC: Duke University Press.

Camden, V. (2022) *The Cambridge Companion to Literature and Psychoanalysis*, Cambridge: Cambridge University Press.

Carby, H. (1987) *Reconstructing Womanhood: The Emergence of the Afro-American Woman Novelist*, New York: Oxford University Press.

Carmichael, D.A. (ed.) (2006) *The Landscape of Hollywood Westerns: Ecocriticism in an American Film Genre*, Salt Lake City, UT: University of Utah Press.

Caruth, C. (1996) *Unclaimed Experience: Trauma, Narrative and History*, Baltimore, MD: Johns Hopkins University Press.

Castle, T. (1993) *The Apparitional Lesbian: Female Homosexuality and Modern Culture*, New York: Columbia University Press.

Castle, T. (ed.) (2003) *The Literature of Lesbianism: A Historical Anthology from Ariosto to Stonewall*, New York: Columbia University Press.

Cave, T. (2016) *Thinking with Literature: Towards a Cognitive Criticism*, Oxford: Oxford University Press.

Césaire, A. (1997 [1955]) 'From Discourse on Colonialism', in B. Moore-Gilbert, G. Stanton, and W. Maley (eds), *Postcolonial Criticism*, London: Routledge.

Chew, S. and D. Richards (eds) (2014) *A Concise Companion to Postcolonial Literature*, Hoboken, NJ: Wiley Blackwell.

Choudhury, B. (ed.) (2016) *Reading Postcolonial Theory: Key Texts in Context*. New Delhi.

Christian, B. (1985) *Black Feminist Criticism: Perspectives on Black Women Writers*, New York: Pergamon.

Christian, B. (2007) *New Black Feminist Criticism, 1985–2000*, ed. G. Bowles, M.G. Fabi, and A. Keizer, Urbana, IL: University of Illinois Press.

Cixous, H. (1981 [1975]) 'The Laugh of the Medusa', in E. Marks and I. de Courvitron (eds), *New French Feminism: An Anthology*, Hemel Hempstead: Harvester Wheatsheaf.

Cixous, H. (2000 [1975]) 'Sorties', in D. Lodge and N. Wood (eds), *Modern Criticism and Theory: A Reader*, 2nd edition, Harlow: Longman.

Clark, T. (2019) *The Value of Ecocriticism*, Cambridge: Cambridge University Press.

Clark, B. and M. Rossini (eds) (2016) *The Cambridge Companion to Literature and the Posthuman*, Cambridge: Cambridge University Press.

Cole, L.*et al.* (2011) 'Speciesism, Identity Politics, and Ecocriticism: A Conversation with Humanists and Posthumanists', *The Eighteenth Century* 52(1): 87–106.

Collier, P. and H. Geyer-Ryan (eds) (1990) *Literary Theory Today*, Cambridge: Polity.

Collins, P.H. (2000) *Black Feminist Thought: Knowledge, Consciousness and the Politics of Empowerment.* 2nd edition, New York: Routledge.

Cooke, J. (ed.) (2020) *The New Feminist Literary Studies*, Cambridge: Cambridge University Press.

Coole, D. and S. Frost (eds) (2010) *New Materialism: Ontology, Agency, and Politics*, Durham, NC: Duke University Press.

Crosby, A.W. (1986) *Ecological Imperialism: The Biological Expansion of Europe, 900–1900*, Cambridge: Cambridge University Press.

Culler, J. (1975) *Structuralist Poetics: Structuralism, Linguistics and the Study of Literature*, Ithaca, NY: Cornell University Press.

Culler, J. (1982) *On Deconstruction: Theory and Criticism after Structuralism*, Ithaca, NY: Cornell University Press.

Culler, J. (ed.) (2006) *Structuralism*, London: Routledge.

Cunningham, V. (2002) *Reading After Theory*, Oxford: Blackwell.

Currie, M. (1998) *Postmodern Narrative Theory*, Basingstoke: Palgrave.

Cusset, F. (2008) *French Theory: How Foucault, Derrida, Deleuze, and Co. Transformed the Intellectual Life of the United States*, trans. J. Fort, Minneapolis, MN: University of Minnesota Press.

Damrosch, D. (2003) *What Is World Literature?*Princeton, NJ: Princeton University Press.

Davis, G. (ed.) (2008) *Praising It New: The Best of the New Criticism*, Athens, OH: Swallow Press/Ohio University Press.

Davis, L.J. (ed.) (1997) *The Disabilities Studies Reader*, London: Routledge.

Davis, R. C. (ed.) (1983) *Lacan and Narration: The Psychoanalytic Difference in Narrative Theory*, Baltimore, MD: Johns Hopkins University Press.

Dawson, P. and M. Mäkelä (eds) (2022) *The Routledge Companion to Narrative*, New York: Routledge.

Deleuze, G. and F. Guattari (1986 [1975]) *Kafka: Towards a Minor Literature*, Minneapolis, MN: University of Minnesota Press.

DeMello, M. (2012) *Animals and Society: An Introduction to Human-Animal Studies*, New York: Columbia University Press.

Derrida, J. (1971 [1971]) 'Signature Event Context', *Glyph: Textual Studies* 1: 172–197.

Derrida, J. (1976 [1967]) *Of Grammatology*, transl. G. Chakravorty Spivak, Baltimore, MD: Johns Hopkins University Press.

Derrida, J. (1984) *Margins of Philosophy*, Chicago, IL: University of Chicago Press.

Derrida, J. (1987) 'Devant la Loi', in A. Udoff (ed.), *Kafka and the Contemporary Critical Performance: Centenary Readings*, Bloomington, IN: Indiana University Press.

Derrida, J. (1988 [1977]) 'Limited Inc a b c', in J. Derrida, *Limited Inc.*, trans. S. Weber, ed. G. Graff, Evanston, IL: Northwestern University Press.

Derrida, J. (1996 [1982]) 'From Différance', in K. Ryan (ed.), *New Historicism and Cultural Materialism: A Reader*, London: Arnold.

Derrida, J. (2000 [1970]) 'Structure, Sign, and Play', in D. Lodge and N. Wood (eds), *Modern Criticism and Theory: A Reader*, 2nd edition, Harlow: Longman.

D'haen, T. (2024) *The Routledge Concise History of World Literature*, 2nd edition, New York: Routledge.

D'haen, T., D. Damrosch, and D. Kadir (eds) (2023) *The Routledge Companion to World Literature*, 2nd edition, New York: Routledge.

Dinshaw, C. and G. Greenwell (2022) 'Creative Writing and Critical Thought I: Queer Theory/Queer Fiction', *New Literary History* 53(2): 265–283.

Dollimore, J. (1984) *Radical Tragedy: Religion, Ideology and Power in the Drama of Shakespeare and his Contemporaries*, Hemel Hempstead: Harvester Wheatsheaf.

Dollimore, J. (1991) *Sexual Dissidence: Augustine to Wilde, Freud to Foucault*, Oxford: Oxford University Press.

Dollimore, J. and A. Sinfield (eds) (1985) *Political Shakespeare: New Essays in Cultural Materialism*, Manchester: Manchester University Press.

Donnell, A. (2006) *Twentieth-Century Caribbean Literature: Critical Moments in Anglophone Literary History*, London: Routledge.

Downing, L. (2008) *The Cambridge Introduction to Michel Foucault*, Cambridge: Cambridge University Press.

Drakakis, J. (1985) *Alternative Shakespeares*, London: Methuen.

Drolet, M. (ed.) (2003) *The Postmodernism Reader: Foundational Texts*, New York: Routledge.

Drucker, J. (2021) *The Digital Humanities Coursebook: An Introduction to Digital Methods for Research and Scholarship*, New York: Routledge.

During, S. (2005) *Cultural Studies: A Critical Introduction*, New York: Routledge.

During, S. (ed.) (2007) *The Cultural Studies Reader*, 3rd edition, New York: Routledge.

During, S. (2012) 'Empire's Present', *New Literary History* 43(2): 331–340.

Eagleton, T. (1976) *Criticism and Ideology*, London: Verso.

Eagleton, T. (1991) *Ideology: An Introduction*, London: Verso.

Eagleton, M. (ed.) (2011) *Feminist Literary Theory: A Reader*, 3rd edition, Oxford: Blackwell.

Eichenbaum, B. (1965 [1926]) 'The Theory of the "Formal Method"', in B. Eichenbaum, *Russian Formalist Criticism: Four Essays*, trans. L.T. Leemon and M.J. Reis, Lincoln, NE: University of Nebraska Press, 1965.

Eichenbaum, B. (1998 [1926]) 'Introduction to the Formal Method', in J. Rivkin and M. Ryan (eds), *Literary Theory: An Anthology*, Oxford: Blackwell.

Elliott, J. and D. Attridge (eds) (2011) *Theory after 'Theory'*, New York: Routledge.

Eliot, T.S. (1969) *Selected Essays*, London: Faber and Faber.

Eliot, T.S. (1972 [1919]) 'Tradition and the Individual Talent', in D. Lodge (ed.), *20th Century Literary Criticism*, London: Longman.

Erlich, V. (1981) *Russian Formalism: History-Doctrine*, 3rd edition, New Haven, CT: Yale University Press.

Ervin, H.A. (ed.) (1999) *African American Literary Criticism, 1773–2000*, New York: Twayne.

Ervin, H.A. (2004) *The Handbook of African American Literature*, Gainesville, FL: University Press of Florida.

Etherington, B. and J. Zimbler (eds) (2018) *The Cambridge Companion to World Literature*, Cambridge: Cambridge University Press.

Eve, M.P. (2022) *The Digital Humanities and Literary Study*, Oxford: Oxford University Press.

Faderman, L. (1981) *Surpassing the Love of Men: Romantic Friendship and Love Between Women from the Renaissance to the Present*, New York: Morrow.

Fanon, F. (1963 [1961]) *The Wretched of the Earth*. New York: Grove.

Fanon, F. (1997 [1955]) 'On National Culture', in B. Moore-Gilbert, G. Stanton, and W. Maley (eds), *Postcolonial Criticism*, London: Routledge.

Felman, S. (1982) 'Turning the Screw of Interpretation', in S. Felman (ed.), *Literature and Psychoanalysis: The Question of Reading: Otherwise*, Baltimore, MD: Johns Hopkins University Press.

Felski, R. (2008) *Uses of Literature*, Malden, MA: Blackwell.

Felski, R. (2015) *The Limits of Critique*, Chicago, IL: University of Chicago Press.

Fink, B. (1996) 'Reading Hamlet with Lacan', in W. Apollon and R. Feinstein (eds), *Lacan, Politics, Aesthetics*, Albany, NY: SUNY Press.

Fiskio, J. (2022) *Climate Change, Literature, and Environmental Justice*, Cambridge: Cambridge University Press.

Foley, B. (2019) *Marxist Literary Criticism Today*, London: Pluto.

Foster, J. H. (1985 [1956]) *Sex Variant Women in Literature: A Historical and Quantitative Survey*, 3rd edition, Tallahassee, FL: Naiad Press.

Foucault, M. (1972 [1969]) *The Archaeology of Knowledge*, London: Tavistock.

Foucault, M. (1977 [1975]) *Discipline and Punish*, London: Allan Lane.

Foucault, M. (1978) *An Introduction: The History of Sexuality, Vol. 1*, trans. R. Hurley, New York: Pantheon Books.

Foucault, M. (1980) *Power/Knowledge: Selected Interviews and Other Writings*, C. Gordon (ed.) London: Harvester Wheatsheaf.

Foucault, M. (1985) *The Use of Pleasure: The History of Sexuality, Vol. 2*, trans. R. Hurley, New York: Random House.

Foucault, M. (2000 [1969]) 'What Is an Author?' in D. Lodge and N. Wood (eds), *Modern Criticism and Theory: A Reader*, 2nd edition, Harlow: Longman.

Freund, E. (1987) *The Return of the Reader: Reader-Response Criticism*, London: Methuen.

Frow, J. (1986) *Marxism and Literary History*, New Haven, CT: Yale University Press.

Gallagher, C. (1989) 'Marxism and the New Historicism', in H.A. Veeser (ed.), *The New Historicism*, London: Routledge.

Gallagher, C. and S. Greenblatt (2000) *Practicing New Historicism*, Chicago, IL: University of Chicago Press.

Gandhi, L. (2019) *Postcolonial Theory: A Critical Introduction*, 2nd edition, New York: Columbia University Press.

Gane, N. (2006) 'When We Have Never Been Human, What Is to Be Done?: Interview with Donna Haraway', *Theory, Culture, & Society* 23(7–8): 135–158.

Garrard, G. (2004) *Ecocriticism*, New York: Routledge (3rd edition 2022).

Garrard, G. (ed.) (2014) *The Oxford Handbook of Ecocriticism*, Oxford: Oxford University Press.

Garrett, M. (2018) *The Cambridge Companion to Narrative Theory*, Cambridge: Cambridge University Press.

Garvin, P. (ed.) (1964) *A Prague School Reader on Esthetics, Literary Structuralism and Style*, Washington, DC: Georgetown University Press.

Gates, H.L. Jr (1987) *Figures in Black: Words, Signs and the 'Racial' Self*, Oxford: Oxford University Press.

Gates, H.L. Jr (1988) *The Signifying Monkey: A Theory of African-American Literary Criticism*, Oxford: Oxford University Press (republished with a new foreword in 2014).

Gates, H.L. Jr (ed.) (1990) *Reading Black, Reading Feminist*, New York: NAL.

Gates, H.L. Jr (1992) 'African American Criticism', in S. Greenblatt and G. Gunn (eds), *Redrawing the Boundaries: The Transformation of English and American Studies*, New York: MLA.

Gates, H.L. Jr (1998 [1989]) 'The Blackness of Blackness: A Critique on the Sign and the Signifyin' Monkey', in J. Rivkin and M. Ryan (eds), *Literary Theory: An Anthology*, Oxford: Blackwell.

Genette, G. (1980 [1972]) *Narrative Discourse*, Oxford: Blackwell.

Gikandi, S. (2011) 'Theory after Postcolonial Theory: Rethinking the Work of Mimesis', in J. Elliott and D. Attridge (eds), *Theory after 'Theory'*, New York: Routledge.

Gilbert, S.M. and S. Gubar (1979) *The Madwoman in the Attic: The Woman Writer and the Nineteenth-Century Literary Imagination*, New Haven, CT: Yale University Press.

Gilbert, S.M. and S. Gubar (eds) (2007 [1979]) *Feminist Literary Theory and Criticism: A Norton Reader*, New York: Norton.

Gilroy, P. (1987) *There Ain't No Black in the Union Jack: The Cultural Politics of Race and Nation*, London: Hutchinson.

Glotfelty, C., and H. Fromm (eds) (1996) *The Ecocriticism Reader: Landmarks in Literary Ecology*, Athens, GA: University of Georgia Press.

Goldberg, D. T. and A. Quayson (eds) (2002) *Relocating Postcolonialism*, Oxford: Blackwell.

Goodman, R.T. (ed.) (2015) *Literature and the Development of Feminist Theory*, Cambridge: Cambridge University Press.

Goodman, R.T. (ed.) (2019) *The Bloomsbury Handbook of 21st-Century Feminist Theory*, London: Bloomsbury.

Gordon, C. (ed.) (1980) *Power/Knowledge: Selected Interviews and Other Writings*, London: Harvester Wheatsheaf.

Gosh, A. (2017) *The Great Derangement: Climate Change and the Unthinkable*, Chicago, IL: University of Chicago Press.

Graff, G. (1987) *Professing Literature: An Institutional History*, Chicago, IL: University of Chicago Press.

Graham, M. (2004) *The Cambridge Companion to the African American Novel*, New York: Cambridge University Press.

Gramsci, A. (1998 [1971]) '"Hegemony" (from "The Formation of Intellectuals")', in J. Rivkin and M. Ryan (eds), *Literary Theory: An Anthology*, Oxford: Blackwell.

Greenblatt, S. (1980) *Renaissance Self-Fashioning: From More to Shakespeare*, Chicago, IL: University of Chicago Press.

Greenblatt, S. (1981) 'Invisible Bullets: Renaissance Authority and its Subversion', *Glyph* 8.

Greenblatt, S. (1989) 'Towards a Poetics of Culture', in H. A. Veeser (ed.), *The New Historicism*, London: Routledge.

Greenblatt, S. (1990) 'Resonance and Wonder', in P. Collier and H. Geyer-Ryan (eds), *Literary Theory Today*, Cambridge: Polity

Greenblatt, S. (1991) *Marvellous Possessions: The Wonder of the New World*, Oxford: Oxford University Press.

Greenblatt, S. (2004) *The Greenblatt Reader*, ed. M. Payne, Malden, MA: Blackwell.

Greenblatt, S. and G. Gunn (eds) (1992) *Redrawing the Boundaries: The Transformation of English and American Studies*, New York: MLA.

Greenham, D. (2018) *Close Reading: The Basics*, New York: Routledge.

Gregg, M. and G.J. Seigworth (eds) (2010) *The Affect Theory Reader*, Durham, NC: Duke University Press.

Gregson, I. (2004) *Postmodern Literature*, London: Hodder Arnold.

Greimas, A.J. (1983 [1966]) *Structural Semantics*, Lincoln, NE: Nebraska University Press.

Gross, A. and A. Vallely (eds) (2012) *Animals and the Human Imagination: A Companion to Animal Studies*, New York: Columbia University Press.

Grusin, R. (2015) *The Nonhuman Turn*, Minneapolis, MN: University of Minnesota Press.

Gunkel, D.J. (2021) *Deconstruction*, Cambridge, MA: MIT Press.

Halberstam, J. (1998 [1994]) 'F2M: The Making of Female Masculinity', in J. Rivkin and M. Ryan (eds), *Literary Theory: An Anthology*, Oxford: Blackwell.

Hall, D. E. (2003) *Queer Theories*, Basingstoke: Palgrave Macmillan.

Hall, D.E.*et al.* (eds) (2012) *The Routledge Queer Studies Reader*, New York: Routledge.

Hall, S. and P. Whannel (2018 [1964]) *The Popular Arts: A Critical Guide to the Mass Media*, Durham, NC: Duke University Press.

Haraway, D. (1988) 'Situated Knowledges: The Science Question in Feminism and the Privilege of Partial Perspective', *Feminist Studies* 14(3): 575–599.

Haraway, D. (1990 [1985]) 'A Manifesto for Cyborgs: Science, Technology, and Socialist Feminism in the 1980s', in L. Nicholson (ed.), *Feminism/ Postmodernism*, London: Routledge.

Haraway, D. (1997) *Modest_Witness@Second_Millennium.FemaleMan$^©$_Meets_Onco-mouse^{TM}*, London: Routledge.

Haraway, D. (2008) *When Species Meet*, Minneapolis, MN: University of Minnesota Press.

Harrison, N. (2003) *Postcolonial Criticism: History, Theory and the World of Fiction*, Cambridge: Polity.

Hartley, L.P. (1953) *The Go-Between*, London: Hamish Hamilton.

Haslett, M. (1999) *Marxist Literary and Cultural Theory*, Basingstoke: Macmillan.

Hawkes, T. (2003) *Structuralism and Semiotics*, 2nd edition, London: Methuen.

Hawthorn, J. (1998) *A Concise Glossary of Contemporary Literary Terms*, 3rd edition, London: Arnold.

Hayles, N.K. (1997) 'The Posthuman Body: Inscription and Incorporation in *Galatea 2.2* and *Snow Crash*', *Configurations* 5(2): 241–266.

Hayles, N.K. (1999) *How We Became Posthuman: Virtual Bodies in Cybernetics, Literature and Informatics*, Chicago, IL: University of Chicago Press.

Hayles, N.K. (2000) 'Flickering Connectivities in Shelley Jackson's *Patchwork Girl*: The Importance of Media-Specific Analysis', *Postmodern Culture* 10(2).

Hayles, N.K. (2005) *My Mother Was a Computer: Digital Subjects and Literary Texts*, Chicago, IL: University of Chicago Press.

Hayles, N.K. (2006) 'Unfinished Work: From Cyborg to Cognisphere', *Theory, Culture & Society* 23(7–8). (doi:10.1177/0263276406069229)

Hayles, N.K. (2012) *How We Think: Digital Media and Contemporary Technogenesis*, Chicago, IL: University of Chicago Press.

Hill, L. (2007) *The Cambridge Introduction to Jacques Derrida*, Cambridge: Cambridge University Press.

Hiltner, K. (2015) *Ecocriticism: The Essential Reader*, Abingdon: Routledge.

Hoban, R. (1982) *Riddley Walker*, London: Picador.

Hogan, P.C. (1997) 'Literary Universals', *Poetics Today* 18(2): 223–249.

Hogan, P.C. (2011) *Affective Narratology: The Emotional Structure of Stories*, Lincoln, NE: University of Nebraska Press.

Hogan, P.C. (2015) 'What Literature Teaches Us about Emotion: Synthesizing Affective Science and Literary Study', in L. Zunshine, (ed.), *The Oxford Handbook of Cognitive Literary Studies*, Oxford: Oxford University Press.

Hoggart, R. (1971 [1957]) *The Uses of Literacy: Aspects of Working-Class Life with Special Reference to Publications and Entertainments*, London: Penguin.

Holden, P., and R. J. Ruppel (eds) (2003) *Imperial Desire: Dissident Sexualities and Colonial Literature*, Minneapolis, MN: University of Minnesota Press.

Holland, N. M. (1975), *5 Readers Reading*, New York: Oxford University Press.

Homer, S. (2005) *Jacques Lacan*, New York: Routledge.

hooks, b. (1982) *Ain't I a Woman: Black Women and Feminism*, London: Pluto.

hooks, b. (1997 [1992]) 'Revolutionary Black Women: Making Ourselves Subject', in B. Moore-Gilbert, G. Stanton, and W. Maley (eds), *Postcolonial Criticism*, London: Routledge.

hooks, b. (2014 [1984]) *Feminist Theory: From Margin to Center*, New York: Routledge.

Houen, A. (ed.) (2020) *Affect and Literature*, Cambridge: Cambridge University Press.

Huggan, G. (2004) '"Greening" Postcolonialism: Ecological Perspectives', *Modern Fiction Studies* 50(3): 701–733.

Huggan, G. (2013) *The Oxford Handbook of Postcolonial Studies*, Oxford: Oxford University Press.

Huggan, G. and H. Tiffin (2010) *Postcolonial Ecocriticism: Literature, Animals, Environment*, London: Routledge.

Humm, M. (1995) *Practicing Feminist Criticism: An Introduction*, London: Prentice Hall.

Hutcheon, L. (1988) *A Poetics of Postmodernism: History, Theory, Fiction*, London: Routledge.

Innes, C.L. (2007) *The Cambridge Introduction to Postcolonial Literatures in English*, Cambridge: Cambridge University Press.

Iovino, S. and S. Oppermann (eds) (2014) *Material Ecocriticism*, Bloomington, IN: Indiana University Press.

Jagose, A. (1997) *Queer Theory: An Introduction*, New York: New York University Press.

Jakobson, R. (1960) 'Concluding Statement: Linguistics and Poetics', in T.A. Sebeok (ed.), *Style in Language*, Cambridge, MA: MIT Press.

Jakobson, R. (1987 [1934]) 'What Is Poetry', in K. Pomorska and R. Rudy (eds), *Language and Literature*, Cambridge, MA: Belknap Press.

Jameson, F. (1984) 'Postmodernism, or the Cultural Logic of Late Capitalism', *New Left Review* 146.

Jameson, F. (1991) *Postmodernism, or, The Cultural Logic of Late Capitalism*, Durham, NC: Duke University Press.

Jancovich, M. (1993) *The Cultural Politics of the New Criticism*, Cambridge: Cambridge University Press.

Jay, P. (2021) *Transnational Literature: The Basics*, New York: Routledge.

Johnson, B. (1980) *The Critical Difference*, Baltimore, MD: Johns Hopkins University Press.

Johnson, E.P. and M.G. Henderson (eds) (2005) *Black Queer Studies: A Critical Anthology*, Durham, NC: Duke University Press.

Johns-Putra, A. (2019) *Climate and Literature*, Cambridge: Cambridge University Press.

Johns-Putra, A. (2022) *The Cambridge Companion to Literature and Climate*, Cambridge: Cambridge University Press.

Kane, R. (2005) *A Contemporary Introduction to Free Will*, New York: Oxford University Press.

Kermode, F. (1988) *History and Value*, Oxford: Clarendon.

Kovalova, K. (ed.) (2016) *Black Feminist Criticism: Past and Present*, New York: Peter Lang.

Kristeva, J. (1984) *Revolution in Poetic Language*, New York: Columbia University Press [1974].

Lacan, J. (1977) 'Desire and the Interpretation of Desire in Hamlet', *Yale French Studies* 55–56: 11–52.

Lanser, S.S. (1981) *The Narrative Act: Point of View in Prose Fiction*, Princeton, NJ: Princeton University Press.

Lanser, S.S. (1997) *Fictions of Authority: Women Writers and the Narrative Voice*, Ithaca, NY: Cornell University Press.

Latour, B. (2004) 'Why Has Critique Run Out of Steam? From Matters of Fact to Matters of Concern', *Critical Inquiry* 30(2): 225–248.

Lawrence, D.H. (1960 [1920]) *Women, in Love*, Harmondsworth: Penguin.

Lawrence, D.H. (1972a [1925]) 'Morality and the Novel', in D. Lodge (ed.), *20th Century Literary Criticism*, London: Longman.

Lawrence, D.H. (1972b [1936]) 'Why the Novel Matters', in D. Lodge (ed.), *20th Century Literary Criticism*, London: Longman.

Lawrence, D.H. (1972c [1924]) 'The Spirit of Place', in D. Lodge (ed.), *20th Century Literary Criticism*, London: Longman.

Lazarus, N. (ed.) (2004) *The Cambridge Companion to Postcolonial Literary Studies*, Cambridge: Cambridge University Press.

Leader-Picone, C. (2019) *Black and More than Black: African-American Fiction in the Post Era*, Jackson, MS: University Press of Mississippi.

Leavis, F.R. (1932) *New Bearings in English Poetry*, London: Chatto and Windus.

Leavis, F.R. (1936) *Revaluation: Tradition and Development in English Poetry*, London: Chatto and Windus.

Leavis, F.R. (1962 [1948]) *The Great Tradition*, Harmondsworth: Penguin.

Leavis, F.R. (1967) *English Literature in Our Time and the University*, London: Chatto and Windus.

Leavis, F.R. (1975) *The Living Principle: 'English' as Discipline of Thought*, London: Chatto and Windus.

Leavis, F.R. and D. Thompson (1977 [1921]) *Culture and Environment: The Training of Critical Awareness*, New York: Praeger.

Lee, T.L. and M.J. Reis, (trans.) (2012 [1965]) *Russian Formalist Criticism: Four Essays*, 2nd edition, Lincoln, NE: University of Nebraska Press.

Lee, V. (ed.) (2006) *The Prentice Hall Anthology of African American Women's Literature*, Upper Saddle River, NJ: Pearson Prentice Hall.

Lévi-Strauss, C. (1982) *The Way of Masks*, Seattle, WA: University of Washington Press.

Leys, R. (2017) *The Ascent of Affect: Genealogy and Critique*, Chicago, IL: University of Chicago Press.

Lilly, M. (1993) *Gay Men's Literature in the Twentieth Century*, New York: New York University Press.

Lips, H. (2018) *Gender: The Basics*, London: Routledge.

Liveley, G. (2019) *Narratology*, Oxford: Oxford University Press.

Lodge, D. (ed.) (1972) *20th Century Literary Criticism*, London: Longman.

Lodge, D. (ed.) (1988) *Modern Criticism and Theory: A Reader*, London: Longman.

Lodge, D. and N. Wood (eds) (2000) *Modern Criticism and Theory: A Reader*, 2nd edition, Harlow: Longman.

Longhurst, B.*et al.* (eds) (2017) *Introducing Cultural Studies*, 3rd edition, London: Routledge.

Loomba, A. (2005) *Colonialism/Postcolonialism*, 2nd edition, London: Routledge.

Loomba, A., S. Kaul, M. Bunzl, A. Burton, and J. Esty (eds) (2005) *Postcolonial Studies and Beyond*, Durham, NC: Duke University Press.

Lorde, A. (1984) *Sister Outsider: Essays and Speeches*, Freedom, CA: Crossing Press.

Lorde, A. (1998 [1984]) 'Age, Race, Class, and Sex: Women Redefining Difference', in J. Rivkin and M. Ryan (eds), *Literary Theory: An Anthology*, Oxford: Blackwell.

Love, H. (2010) 'Close but not Deep: Literary Ethics and the Descriptive Turn', *New Literary History* 41(2): 371–391.

Luckhurst, R. (2008) *The Trauma Question*, London: Routledge.

Lukács, G. (1970 [1954]) 'Art and Objective Truth', in A. Kahn (ed.), *Writer, Critic and Other Essays*, London: Merlin.

Lukács, G. (1972 [1957]) 'The Ideology of Modernism', in D. Lodge (ed.), *20th Century Literary Criticism*, London: Longman.

Lyotard, J.-F. (1984 [1979]) *The Postmodern Condition: A Report on Knowledge*, Minneapolis, MN: University of Minnesota Press.

McBean, S. (2020) 'Queer Feminism', in J. Cooke (ed.), *The New Feminist Literary Studies*, Cambridge: Cambridge University Press.

McCallum, E.L. and M. Tuhkanen (eds) (2011) *Queer Times, Queer Becomings*, Albany, NY: SUNY Press.

McCallum, E.L. and M. Tuhkanen (eds) (2015) *The Cambridge History of Gay and Lesbian Literature*, Cambridge: Cambridge University Press.

McCann, H. and W. Monaghan (2022) *Queer Theory Now: From Foundation to Futures*, London: Bloomsbury.

McDougall, J. and C. Pollard (2019) *Media Studies: The Basics*, 2nd edition, New York: Routledge.

McHale, B. (1987) *Postmodernist Fiction*, London: Methuen.

Macherey, P. (1978 [1966]) *A Theory of Literary Production*, London: Routledge.

McMillan, G. (ed.) (2022) *The Routledge Companion to Literature and Class*, New York: Routledge.

Makdisi, S. (2019) 'Orientalism Today', in B. Abu-Mannen (ed.), *After Said: Postcolonial Literary Studies in the Twenty-First Century*, Cambridge: Cambridge University Press.

Malpas, S. (2005) *The Postmodern*, New York: Routledge.

Marinucci, M. (2022) *Feminism in Queer: The Intimate Connection between Queer and Feminist Theory*, 2nd edition, New York: Bloomsbury.

Marlow, C. (2017) *Shakespeare and Cultural Materialist Theory*. London: Bloomsbury.

Martin, M.M. (2023) *Psychoanalysis and Literary Theory: An Introduction*, New York: Routledge.

Marx, K. (1970 [1859]) *A Contribution to the Critique of Political Economy*, Moscow: Progress Publishers.

Massumi, B (2002) 'The Autonomy of Affect', in B. Massumi, *Parables for the Virtual: Movement, Affect, Sensation*, Durham, NC: Duke University Press.

Matejka, L. and K. Pomorska (eds) (2002 [1978]) *Readings in Russian Poetics: Formalist and Structuralist Views*, Champaign, IL: Dalkey Archive Press.

Merrill, J. (2022) *The Origins of Russian Literary Theory: Folklore, Philosophy, Form*, Evanston, IL: Northwestern University Press.

Miall, D.S. (2006) *Literary Reading: Empirical and Theoretical Studies*, New York: Peter Lang.

Miller, J.H. (1976) 'Stevens' Rock and Criticism as Cure, II', *Georgia Review* 30.

Miller, J. (2022) *The Origins of Russian Literary Theory: Folklore, Philology, Form*, Evanston, IL: Northwestern University Press.

Millet, K. (1970) *Sexual Politics*, Garden City, NY: Doubleday.

Milner, A. J. (2002) *Re-imagining Cultural Studies: The Promise of Cultural Materialism*, London: Sage.

Mills, S., L. Pearce, S. Spaull and E. Millard (1989) *Feminist Readings, Feminists Reading*, Hemel Hempstead: Harvester Wheatsheaf.

Montrose, L. (1983) '"Shaping Fantasies": Figuration of Gender and Power in Elizabethan Culture', *Representations*, 1(2): 61–94.

Montrose, L. (1989) 'The Poetics and Politics of Culture', in H. A. Veeser (ed.), *The New Historicism*, London: Routledge.

Montrose, L. (1992) 'New Historicisms', in S. Greenblatt and G. Gunn (eds), *Redrawing the Boundaries: The Transformation of English and American Studies*, New York: MLA.

Montrose, L. (1994 [1980]) '"Eliza, Queene of Shepeardes," and the Pastoral of Power', in H. A. Veeser (ed.), *The New Historicism Reader*, London: Routledge.

Moore-Gilbert, B. (1997) *Postcolonial Theory: Contexts, Practices, Politics*, London: Verso.

Mugratski, M., S. Schadahat, and I. Wutsdorff (eds) (2023) *Central and Eastern European Literary Theory and the West*, Berlin: De Gruyter.

Mulhall, A (2020) 'Queer Narrative', in S.B. Somerville (ed.), *The Cambridge Companion to Queer Studies*, Cambridge: Cambridge University Press.

Mullin, M. (2008) 'Book Review: *When Species Meet* by Donna Haraway', *Theory, Culture & Society* 25(7–8): 373–376.

Murray, S. (2021) *Introduction to Contemporary Print Culture: Books as Media*, New York: Routledge.

Napier, W. (ed.) (2000) *African American Literary Theory: A Reader*, New York: New York University Press.

Nayar, P.K. (ed.) (2015) *Postcolonial Studies: An Anthology*, Oxford: Wiley Blackwell.

Newbolt Report (1921) *Report to the Board of Education on the Teaching of English in England*, London: HMSO.

Newby, E. (1974 [1958]) *A Short Walk in the Hindu Kush*, London: Picador.

Neyat, F. (2020) *Literature and Materialisms*, New York: Routledge.

Noble, S.U. (2018) *Algorithms of Oppression: How Search Engines Reinforce Racism*, New York: New York University Press.

Noble, S.U. (2019) 'Toward a Critical Black Digital Humanities', in M.K. Gold and L.F. Klein (eds), *Debates in the Digital Humanities 2019*, Minneapolis, MN: University of Minnesota Press.

Norris, C. (2002) *Deconstruction: Theory and Practice*, 3rd edition, London: Routledge.

Norris, C. (2003) 'Fiction, Philosophy, Possible Worlds', *Textual Practice* 17(2): 225–251.

Oliver, K. (ed.) (2000) *The French Feminism Reader*, Lanham, MD: Rowman and Littlefield.

Oswell, D. (2006) *Culture and Society: An Introduction to Cultural Studies*, Thousand Oaks, CA: Sage.

O'Sullivan, J. (ed.) (2023) *The Bloomsbury Handbook to Digital Humanities*, London: Bloomsbury.

Ott, B.L. and R.L. Mack (2020) *Critical Media Studies*, 3rd edition, Hoboken, NJ: Wiley.

Ouellette, L. and J. Gray (eds) (2017) *Keywords for Media Studies*, New York: New York University Press.

Parham, J. (ed.) (2021) *The Cambridge Companion to Literature and the Anthropocene*, Cambridge: Cambridge University Press.

Parry, B. (2002) 'Directions and Dead Ends in Postcolonial Studies', in D.T. Goldberg and A. Quayson (eds), *Relocating Postcolonialism*, Oxford: Blackwell.

Parry, B. (2004) *Postcolonial Studies: A Materialist Critique*, London: Routledge.

Parry, B. (2012) 'What Is Left in Postcolonial Studies?', *New Literary History* 43 (2): 341–358.

Parvini, N. (2012) *Shakespeare and Contemporary Theory: New Historicism and Cultural Materialism*, London: Bloomsbury.

Peterson, C. (2011) 'The Posthumanism to Come', *Angelaki* 16(2): 127–142.

Piper, A. (2018) *Enumerations: Data and Literary Study*, Chicago, IL: University of Chicago Press.

Plain, G. and S. Sellers (eds) (2007) *A History of Feminist Literary Criticism*, Cambridge: Cambridge University Press.

Powers. R. (2018) *The Overstory*, New York: Norton.

Pratt, M. L. (1992) *Imperial Eyes: Studies in Travel Writing and Transculturation*, London: Routledge.

Propp, V. (1968) *The Morphology of the Folk Tale*, 2nd edition, Austin, TX: University of Texas Press [1928]

Prosser, J. (1998) *Second Skin: The Body Narratives of Transsexuality*, New York: Columbia University Press.

Puckett, K. (2016) *Narrative Theory: A Critical Introduction*, Cambridge: Cambridge University Press.

Quayson, A. (ed.) (2012) *The Cambridge History of Postcolonial Literature*, Cambridge: Cambridge University Press.

Quayson, A. (ed.) (2015) *The Cambridge Companion to the Postcolonial Novel*, Cambridge: Cambridge University Press.

Rabinow, D. (ed.) (1984) *The Foucault Reader*, New York: Random House.

Rajamannar, S. (2012) *Reading the Animal in the Literature of the British Raj*, New York: Palgrave Macmillan.

Rajeev, S. P. (2006) *Postcolonial Poetry in English*, New York: Oxford University Press.

Ransom, J. C. (1938) *The World's Body*, New York: Scribner.

Ransom, J. C. (1972 [1937]) 'Criticism, Inc.', in D. Lodge (ed.), *20th Century Literary Criticism*, London: Longman.

Remien, P. and S. Slovic (2022) *Nature and Literary Studies*, Cambridge: Cambridge University Press.

Richards, I.A. (1926) *Science and Poetry*, London: Kegan Paul, Trench, Trubner.

Richards, I.A. (1929) *Practical Criticism*, London: Kegan Paul, Trench, Trubner.

Richards, I.A. (1934) *Coleridge on Imagination*, London: Kegan Paul, Trench, Trubner.

Richards, I.A. (1938) *Principles of Literary Criticism*, 2nd edition, New York: Harcourt Brace.

Richards, I.A. (1972a [1924]) 'Communication and the Artist', in D. Lodge (ed.), *20th Century Literary Criticism*, London: Longman.

Richards, I.A. (1972b [1929]) 'The Four Kinds of Meaning', in D. Lodge (ed.), *20th Century Literary Criticism*, London: Longman.

Richardson, B. (2019) *A Poetics of Plot for the Twenty-first Century*, Columbus, OH: Ohio State University Press.

Risam, R. (2018) *New Digital Worlds: Postcolonial Digital Humanities in Theory, Praxis, and Pedagogy*, Evanston, IL: Northwestern University Press.

Rivkin, J. and M. Ryan (eds) (1998) *Literary Theory: An Anthology*, Oxford: Blackwell.

Rivkin, J. and M. Ryan (eds) (2004) *Literary Theory: An Anthology*, 2nd edition, Oxford: Blackwell.

Robbins, R. (2000) *Literary Feminisms*, Basingstoke: Macmillan.

Robles, M.O. (2016) *Literature and Animal Studies*, New York: Routledge.

Rooney, E. (ed.) (2006) *The Cambridge Companion to Feminist Literary Theory*, Cambridge: Cambridge University Press.

Rosendahl Thomsen, M. (2008) *Mapping World Literature: International Canonization and Transnational Literatures*, London: Continuum.

Rule, J. (1975) *Lesbian Images*, Trumansberg, NY: Crossings Press.

Ryan, K. (ed.) (1996) *New Historicism and Cultural Materialism: A Reader*, London: Arnold.

Ryan, M. (2010) *Cultural Studies: A Practical Introduction*, Hoboken, NJ: Wiley Blackwell.

Said, E. (1991 [1978]) *Orientalism*, Harmondsworth: Penguin.

Salih, S. (2002) *Judith Butler*, New York: Routledge.

Saussure, F. de (1959 [1915]) *Course in General Linguistics*, New York: McGraw-Hill.

Scholes, R. (1974) *Structuralism in Literature: An Introduction*, New Haven, CT: Yale University Press.

Sebeok, T. (ed.) (1960) *Style in Language*, Cambridge, MA: Technology Press.

Sedgwick, E.K. (1985) *Between Men: English Literature and Male Homosocial Desire*, New York: Columbia University Press.

Sedgwick, E.K. (1990) *Epistemology of the Closet*, Berkeley, CA: University of California Press.

Sedgwick, E.K. (1993) 'Queer and Now', in E.K. Sedgwick, *Tendencies*, Durham, NC: Duke University Press.

Sedgwick, E.K. (1997) 'Paranoid Reading and Reparative Reading: or, You're So Paranoid, You Probably Think This Essay is About You', in E. K. Sedgwick (ed.), *Novel Gazing: Queer Readings in Fiction*, Durham, NC: Duke University Press.

Selden, R. (ed.) (1995) *The Cambridge History of Literary Criticism, Vol. 8 From Formalism to Poststructuralism*, Cambridge: Cambridge University Press.

Shklovsky, V. (1998 [1917]) 'Art as Technique', in J. Rivkin and M. Ryan (eds), *Literary Theory: An Anthology*, Oxford: Blackwell.

Showalter, E. (1985 [1979]) 'Towards a Feminist Poetics', in E. Showalter (ed.), *The New Feminist Criticism*, New York: Pantheon.

Sinfield, A. (1986) *Alfred Tennyson*, Oxford: Blackwell.

Sinfield, A. (1992) *Faultlines: Cultural Materialism and the Politics of Dissident Reading*, Oxford: Oxford University Press.

Sinfield, A. (1994) *The Wilde Century: Effeminacy, Oscar Wilde and the Queer Moment*, London: Cassell.

Sinfield, A. (2005) *Cultural Politics: Queer Reading*, 2nd edition, New York: Routledge.

Sinfield, A. (2006) *Shakespeare, Authority, Sexuality: Unfinished Business in Cultural Materialism*, New York: Routledge.

Smith, B. (1985 [1977]) 'Towards a Black Feminist Criticism', in E. Showalter (ed.), *The New Feminist Criticism*, New York: Pantheon.

So, R.J. (2020) *Redlining Culture: A Data History of Racial Inequality and Postwar Fiction*, New York: Columbia University Press.

Somerville, S.B. (ed.) (2020) *The Cambridge Companion to Queer Studies*, Cambridge: Cambridge University Press.

Spivak, G.C. (1995a [1985]) 'Three Women's Texts and a Critique of Imperialism', in B. Ashcroft, G. Griffith, and H. Tiffin (eds), *The Postcolonial Studies Reader*, London: Routledge.

Spivak, G.C. (1995b [1988]) 'Can the Subaltern Speak?', in B. Ashcroft, G. Griffith, and H. Tiffin (eds), *The Postcolonial Studies Reader*, London: Routledge.

Spivak, G.C. (1999) *A Critique of Postcolonial Reason: Toward a History of the Vanishing Present*, Cambridge, MA: Harvard University Press.

Spivak, G.C. (2000) 'Discussion: An Afterword on the New Subaltern', in P. Chatterjee and P. Jeganathan (eds), *Community, Gender and Violence*, London: Hurst.

Stam, R. and E. Shohat (2012) 'Whence and Whither Postcolonial Theory?', *New Literary History* 43(2): 371–390.

Steiner, P. (1995 [1984]) *Russian Formalism: A Metapoetics*, Ithaca, NY: Cornell University Press.

Stepto, R. (1979) *From Behind the Veil*, Urbana, IL: University of Illinois Press (2nd revised edition 1991).

Stewart, R. (2004) *The Places in Between*, London: Picador.

Stockton, W. (2022) *An Introduction to Queer Literary Studies*, New York: Routledge.

Storer, R. (2009) *F.R. Leavis*, New York: Routledge.

Streidter, J. (1989) *Literary Structure, Evolution, and Value: Russian Formalism and Czech Structuralism Reconsidered*, Cambridge, MA: Harvard University Press.

Stryker, S. and D. M. Blackston (eds) (2023) *The Transgender Studies Reader Remix*, New York: Routledge.

Stubbs, M. (2005) 'Conrad in the Computer: Examples of Quantitative Stylistic Methods', *Language and Literature*, 14(1): 5–24.

Sturrock, J. (2003) *Structuralism*, 2nd edition, with a new introduction by J.-M. Rabaté, Malden, MA: Blackwell.

Taylor, D. (ed.) (2011) *Michel Foucault: Key Concepts*, London: Routledge.

Thomas, B. (2015) *Narrative: The Basics*, New York: Routledge.

Thompson, M.C. (2022) *Phenomenal Blackness: Black Power, Philosophy, and Theory*, Chicago, IL: University of Chicago Press.

Todorov, T. (1969) *Grammaire du Decameron*, The Hague: Mouton.

Todorov, T. (1975 [1970]) *The Fantastic: A Structural Approach to a Literary Genre*, Ithaca, NY: Cornell University Press.

Todorov, T. (1977 [1971]) *The Poetics of Prose*, Oxford: Oxford University Press.

Tompkins, J.P. (ed.) (1980) *Reader-Response Criticism: From Formalism to Post-Structuralism*, Baltimore, MD: Johns Hopkins University Press.

Turner, L (ed.) (2017) *The Edinburgh Companion to Animal Studies*, Edinburgh: Edinburgh University Press.

Underwood, T. (2016) 'The Life Cycle of Genres', *Journal of Cultural Analytics* 1(1). (doi:10.22148/16.005)

Underwood, T., D. Bannam, and S. Lee (2018) 'The Transformation of Gender in English-Language Fiction', *Journal of Cultural Analytics* 3(1). (doi:10.22148/16.019)

Vakoch, A. (2012) *Feminist Ecocriticsm: Environment, Women, and Literature*, Lanham, MD: Lexington Books.

Vakoch, A. (ed.) (2023) *The Routledge Handbook of Ecofeminism and Literature*, New York: Routledge.

Vakoch, A. and S. Mickey (eds) (2018) *Literature and Ecofeminism: Intersectional and International Voices*, New York: Routledge.

Vermeulen, P. (2020) *Literature and the Anthropocene*, London: Routledge.

Veeser, H. A. (ed.) (1989) *The New Historicism*, London: Routledge.

Veeser, H. A. (ed.) (1994) *The New Historicism Reader*, London: Routledge.

Viswanathan, G. (1989) *Masks of Conquest: Literary Study and British Rule in India*, New York: Columbia University Press.

Waldan, P. (2013) *Animal Studies: An Introduction*, Oxford: Oxford University Press.

Wall, C. (ed.) (1989) *Changing Our Own Words*, New Brunswick, NJ: Rutgers University Press.

Warhol-Down, R. and D. Price Herndl (eds) (2009) *Feminisms Redux: An Anthology of Literary Criticism and Theory*, 3rd edition, New Brunswick, NJ: Rutgers University Press.

Warhol, R.R. and S.S. Lanser (eds) (2017) *Narrative Theory Unbound: Queer and Feminist Interventions*, Athens, OH: Ohio State University Press.

Wehrs, D.R. and T. Blake (eds) (2017) *The Palgrave Handbook of Affect Studies and Textual Criticism*, London: Palgrave Macmillan.

Westling, L.H. (1996) *The Green Breast of the New World: Landscape, Gender, and American Fiction*, Athens, GA: University of Georgia Press.

Williams, J. (2005) *Understanding Poststructuralism*, London: Routledge.

Williams, L.R. (1995) *Critical Desire: Psychoanalysis and the Literary Subject*, London: Arnold.

Williams, R. (1961 [1958]) *Culture and Society, 1780–1950*, Harmondsworth: Penguin.

Williams, R. (1965 [1961]) *The Long Revolution*, Harmondsworth: Penguin.

Williams, R. (1977) *Marxism and Literature*, Oxford: Oxford University Press.

Williams, R. (1996 [1980]) 'Base and Superstructure in Marxist Cultural Theory', in K. Ryan (ed.), *New Historicism and Cultural Materialism: A Reader*, London: Arnold.

Williams Page, Y. (ed.) (2011) *Icons of African-American Literature: The Black Literary World*, Santa Barbara, CA: Greenwood.

Willis, I. (2018) *Reception*, New York: Routledge.

Willis, S. (1987) *Specifying: Black Women Writing the American Experience*, Madison, WI: University of Wisconsin Press.

Wimsatt, W.K. (1965) *Hateful Contraries: Studies in Literature and Criticism*, Lexington, KY: University of Kentucky Press.

Wolfe, C. (2010) *What Is Posthumanism?*, Minneapolis, MN: University of Minnesota Press.

Woods, G. (1998) *A History of Gay Literature: The Male Tradition*, New Haven, CT: Yale University Press.

Wright, W. (1975) *Sixguns and Society: A Structural Study of the Western*, Berkeley: CA: University of California Press.

Wymer, K.C. (2021) *Introduction to Digital Humanities: Enhancing Scholarship with the Use of Technology*, New York: Routledge.

Young, R.J.C. (2001) *Postcolonialism: An Historical Introduction*, Oxford: Blackwell.

Young, R.J.C. (2012) 'Postcolonial Remains', *New Literary History*, 43(1): 19–42.

Young, R.J.C. (2022) *Postcolonialism: A Very Short Introduction*, 2nd edition, Oxford: Oxford University Press.

Young, T. (ed.) (2021) *Queer and Feminist Theories of Narrative*, New York: Routledge.

Zhang, D. (2021) *Literary Criticism, Culture and the Subject of English: F.R. Leavis and T.S. Eliot*, New York: Routledge.

Zimmerman, B. (1992) 'Lesbians Like This and That: Some Notes on Lesbian Criticism for the Nineties', in S. Munt (ed.), *New Lesbian Criticism: Literary and Cultural Readings*, Hemel Hempstead: Harvester Wheatsheaf.

Zunshine, L. (2010) *Introduction to Cognitive Cultural Studies*, Baltimore, MD: Johns Hopkins University Press.

Zunshine, L. (ed.) (2015) *The Oxford Handbook of Cognitive Literary Studies*, Oxford: Oxford University Press.

INDEX

Printed in the United States
by Baker & Taylor Publisher Services